The
Origins
of
Literary
Studies
in
America

The Origins of Literary Studies in America

A Documentary Anthology

GERALD GRAFF
MICHAEL WARNER

Editors

Routledge • New York • London

Published in 1989 by

Routledge
an imprint of Routledge, Chapman and Hall, Inc.
29 West 35th Street
New York, NY 10001

Published in Great Britain by

Routledge
11 New Fetter Lane
London EC4P 4EE

Copyright © 1989 by Routledge, Chapman and Hall, Inc.

Printed in the United States of America

Library of Congress Cataloging-in-Publication Data

The Origins of literary studies in America.

  Bibliography: p.
  1. English literature — Study and teaching (Higher) — United States — History.
  2. Universities and colleges — United States — Departments — History.
  I. Graff, Gerald.   II. Warner, Michael, 1958–
  PR51.U507   1988   807'.1173   88–18407
  ISBN 0–415–90024–7
  ISBN 0–415–90025–5 (pbk.)

British Library Cataloguing in Publication Data

The origins of literary studies in America:
  a documentary anthology
  1. United States. Higher education
  institutions. Curriculum subjects:
  Literature - to 1965.
  I. Graff, Gerald   II. Warner, Michael,
  1958–
  807'.1173

  ISBN 0–415–90024–7
  ISBN 0–415–90025–5 (pbk)

Contents

Prefatory Note
and Acknowledgments

Section I of the Introduction contains material adapted from two essays by Michael Warner, "Professionalization and the Rewards of Literature, 1875–1900," *Criticism*, 27 (Winter, 1985): pp. 1–28, and "Literary Studies and the History of the Book," *The Book: Newsletter of the Program in the History of the Book in American Culture*, Publication of the American Antiquarian Society, Worcester, Mass. (12 July, 1987): 3–9.

We have limited editorial notes to translations of unfamiliar foreign expressions and identifications of important references. Otherwise annotation has been kept to a minimum.

The editors wish to thank D. G. Myers of Northwestern University for research assistance and Professors Joseph Loewenstein and George Pepe of Washington University for help with the Latin translations.

Grateful acknowledgement is made to the Kent State University Press for permission to reprint material from *The Making of a Feminist: Early Journals and Letters of M. Carey Thomas* (1979), edited by Marjorie Housepian Dobkin; also to the Johns Hopkins University, The Milton S. Eisenhower Library, Special Collections Division, for permission to quote from a letter by William Hand Browne (Daniel C. Gilman Papers MS.1).

Introduction:
The Origins of Literary Studies in America

Gerald Graff and Michael Warner

This anthology attempts to bring together in one volume materials not otherwise easily available on the early history of the profession of academic literary studies in the United States. Our purpose, however, is more than antiquarian. It is our view that histories of literary studies are crucial in the rethinking of the discipline currently under way.

Interpretations of history already play a polemical role in the current public debate over humanities education, as the widespread demand for a "return" to traditional humanistic fundamentals in education legitimates itself by promoting a myth of history. According to this myth, the academic humanities up to recently were based on a coherent consensus on fundamental goals. Allegedly, it was not till the 1960s that this shared sense of the aims of the humanities gave way, under the combined assaults of campus radicals, permissive teachers, narrow vocationalists, selfish research specialists, and student consumers.

Education Secretary William Bennett set the pattern for this diagnosis in his influential *To Reclaim a Legacy* Report of 1984 (when Bennett was Chairman of the National Endowment for the Humanities). Bennett blamed the problems of the humanities on "a collective loss of nerve and faith on the part of both faculty and administrators during the late 1960s and 1970s."* This historical myth has subsequently been restated in best-selling books like Allan Bloom's *The Closing of the American Mind: How Higher Education has Failed Democracy and Impoverished the Souls of Today's Students* (New York, 1987) and E. D. Hirsch's *Cultural Literacy: What Every American Needs to Know* (New York, 1987), where educational fundamentalist proposals similar to that advanced by Bennett are again justified by the characterization of the 1960s as the turning point at which a heretofore intact humanistic consensus was lost. Because these defenders of the past know little about the actual past, they are

* William Bennett, "To Reclaim a Legacy," Report of the National Endowment for the Humanities, *Chronicle of Higher Education* 29, no. 11 (November 28, 1984): 16.

1

unaware that the diagnoses they offer were already clichés a hundred years ago, and that the cures they recommend have repeatedly been tried and have always led to futility.

The material we have gathered in this anthology suggests a very different interpretation of history from the one presented by these educational fundamentalists. Not that we would dispute that there was a greater degree of consensus in the past on the content and purposes of literary and humanistic education. How could this not have been the case in an institution which excluded most of those social groups in American culture which could have challenged the established consensus? It is only as previously excluded groups have entered the university that this earlier consensus has broken down. A good deal of the hysteria and outrage that has recently been expressed in reaction to the revision of the literary canon and the rise of radical new literary theories reflects the fact that ideas about literature that used to be unquestioned givens are now contested. That is, those who used to be able to assume that their views of what "literature" meant and of what books should be taught and why are now only one group among many and have to *argue* for their values rather than having them taken for granted. But our materials suggest that even at the dawn of professional literary studies, educational consensus was already profoundly shaky.

From their beginnings, academic literary studies were held together not by any shared definition of literature or of the discipline, but by tacit social agreements that enabled incompatible principles to coexist in an uneasy truce. That these conflicts have now become less easy to ignore makes it possible to see that the fault-lines have been present all along. But it is only in an atmosphere like the present one of institutional division, which generates curiosity about original principles and aims, that an anthology of this kind would have become thinkable at all. Documents from the founding period of any enterprise are a peculiarly revealing source of information about that enterprise's original purposes and motives. They speak with an unabashed clarity of intention which tends to become muted or covered over once the enterprise has achieved success and its representations of itself have become more sophisticatd and guarded. This is not surprising, for in the period when an enterprise is fighting to establish itself—in this case, to achieve the status of a "profession"—it has no choice but to recognize the considerations of strategy, politics, and public relations on which its success will largely depend. At a later stage, this political dimension of institutional struggle tends to be forgotten or viewed as a mere prelude to loftier accomplishments. One service an anthology such as this can perform is to illuminate those realities of institutional politics which tend over time to be obscured by abstract debates about ideals of "humanism" and the higher ends of literature and criticism.

Part of what it meant for literary studies to become established as a profession was that concerns such as the profession's own history and the effect of its modes of inquiry on classroom pedagogy became defined as incidental to its proper subject matter. The history of its own development as an institution has up to now had no serious status as a field within literary studies. And pedagogy has been defined as extrinsic to the "serious" work of the discipline, the systematic analysis of language and literature.

One consequence of this neglect of history is that prospective historians of literary studies inherit neither an agreed-upon canon of founding texts nor a consensus on the shape of the institutional story, though up to recently that story has often been thought of—not completely without justification—as a progression toward ever more sophisticated methods and an ever-expanding range of interests. Institutional historians of literary studies must construct their own canon with less help than usual—though also less constraint—from prior agreements, and they must treat earlier stories as understandings and assumptions to be analyzed rather than as foundations to be built upon. The present selection reflects the editors' particular sense of the central issues at stake in the early history of literary studies, but another set of texts from the same period could be chosen to illustrate the same issues—while still another set of texts could be chosen (or ours could be arranged differently) to point up entirely different themes from those highlighted here. We will take it as one measure of the success of this anthology if readers interrogate its materials in ways very different from our own.

Both in the selections and the present introduction, we have not hesitated to offer an interpretation of professional history, one which puts the emphasis on institutional controversies rather than agreements. Once we look past expressions of official rationale, an institution's founding impulses have a way of appearing less like a set of consistently worked out principles than a welter of conflicts, debates, and contradictions.

Part I, "Professionalization," illustrates the attitudes of the early advocates of modern language study, who were the advance guard in the professionalization of literary studies. Part II, "Counter-Statements and Reassessments," builds on and deepens the interpretations of professionalization presented in Part I. Many of the selections in this part represent the belletristic counterattack which arose virtually contemporaneously with the establishment of literary studies on scientific philological lines. Part III, "Memoirs and Personal Accounts," brings home the degree to which the stakes in the conflicts illustrated in Parts I and II were personal as well as institutional. Beliefs about literature and how it should be studied, like beliefs about any other organization of knowledge, imply structures of career and personality. Part III contains a variety of personal accounts from people whose relation to academic literary studies ranged from immersion to bitter alienation, but more typically reflected an anxious and frustrated internalization of conflicting allegiances.

I

When English departments were founded in American colleges and universities in the last quarter of the nineteenth century, they were really departments of English language and literature. Before then, colleges had had somebody, usually the professor of rhetoric and oratory, but sometimes a professor of history, or even biology, whose job included the task of introducing boys to the golden passages in Shakespeare and the poets. This task was less often entrusted to the professor of Greek and Latin, who had more important things to do in a college curriculum overwhelmingly dominated by those classical subjects. Literary studies had not been conducted in any systematic way, and "criticism" meant being able to tell the good bits from the bad bits. One did it as part of being a gentleman—just as one did not trouble oneself too much over textual interpretation because a gentleman could be depended on to undertand intuitively what a literary work meant.

The founding of English, however, and other departments of national languages and literatures, brought about quite a different business, and earned a hostile reaction both from the teachers of rhetoric and oratory and of the Greek and Roman classics. The most aggressive of the new English scholars were philologists, or what would nowadays be called linguists. Their training was in the historical and comparative study of languages, though they also developed for the first time a systematic bibliographic criticism. Their really innovative character, however, apart from the languages they worked on, lay in the fact that they were trained at all. It was the influx of philology that marked the professionalization of literary studies and its establishment in "departments" conceived, like others in the university, as independent entities that exercised autonomy over their curriculum and the selection of their faculty.

To be a rhetoric-and-oratory professor, one had had only to know the classics, have a pretty way of talking, and what some at the time referred to as "a general society-knowledge of literature." The paragons for this role were the men who succeeded each other in the Boylston chair at Harvard: Ticknor, Longfellow, Lowell. To be a philologist, on the other hand, one had to go to graduate school, something that at first existed only in Germany. In the 1870s and 1880s, Americans went to Germany and came back as philologists, and when they returned home they helped to set up new graduate programs in American universities.

These graduate programs, not only in old institutions like Harvard but also in new ones like Johns Hopkins, Cornell, and Chicago, were of course graduate programs in philology. They were where one went to learn about the Great Vowel Shift and Verner's Law. But the way one illustrated the Great Vowel Shift or Verner's Law in one's publications and courses was by reading the texts that gave evidence of them. This is where literature came in. In other words, the profession of "literary studies" was established before it began to consider literature its subject. But around the mid-1880s, some of the professionalizing philologists began to realize that their laboratory experiments had a larger appeal than their science.

To understand this larger appeal of literary study, one has to understand that while it was the scientific model of research that justified philological studies of literature to other professionals inside the university, it was the civic and humanistic claims of literature that justified those studies to outsiders. After the Civil War, educators and custodians of culture began to feel that the study of English literature had much to offer to a society whose sense of national unity seemed increasingly threatened by such divisive forces as industrial capitalism, European immigration, labor agitation and other forms of class conflict, and the increasing concentration of Americans in cities at the same time as they became dispersed across the continent. The teaching of English literature in schools and colleges promised to serve as a binding principle for Americans who had less in common than they had had in the small-town America before the Civil War. Some educators spoke frankly about using literary education as "an instrument of political education" (see the selection in Chapter 8 from John Churton Collins), or, even more frankly, as a means of keeping the lower orders in check. Others saw literary education as a potentially democratizing influence. But it is unlikely that "English" could have achieved its great institutional success if it had not promised large-scale benefits to the whole culture.

Philologists appealed to this nationalistic conception of English in repeating the argument, which derived from European romanticism, that nothing could better advance the cause of social unity than sowing the knowledge among the masses of the roots of the national language. As one professor argued, philological study was primary because "grammar is the key by which we unlock the treasures of literature." This project of research had an ambiguous relation to the more traditional tasks of literary evaluation and appreciation. For philologists, an enormous groundwork of historical, biographical, and linguistic information was preliminary to the study of literature, and they looked down on the criticism of the belletristic kind which had been the staple of journalism since the eighteenth century. In fact many of these philologists conceived linguistic study as an autonomous discipline, not only having no necessary relation to literature, but ideally having nothing to do with it.

In the 1880s, however, some philologists began to recognize that they could make an even more ambitious claim for their subject if they broadened its conception to include literary criticism. The enormous range of the texts they were busily editing, reprinting, and studying etymologically and grammatically put them in a position to lay claim to the systematic study of literature. Instead of standing above and apart from traditional criticism, philology would transform and replace traditional criticism—extending the systematic study of language into a historical study of literature. It is from this period that we can date the project of specialized historical criticism in which professors disputed not whether Robert Browning was a major poet, but questions like: in what situations does Milton use Latinate syntax? and, what were the sources of *A Winter's Tale*?

Another group, however, the heirs of Longfellow and Lowell, remained loyal to the belletristic idea of criticism. To this group, the scientific methods of the philologists seemed so alien to the values of appreciation and culture that they were not even an appropriate preliminary to literary study. The result of these tensions was a rift that came to be dramatized in the opposing labels of "critic" and "scholar." The ultimate backlash of criticism against philology—and with it against history—would come in the 1940s in the movement known as New Criticism. But in the early years of newly founded literature departments, it was the belletristic critics who led the resistance.

These belletristic critics defined the academic type that Stanley Fish has tellingly described as the "anti-professional"—though some of them would have said that it was not professionalism as such that they were objecting to but only certain narrow forms of professionalism. These anti-professionals looked back for inspiration to Victorians like Matthew Arnold and John Ruskin, seeing literature as a moral and spiritual force and a repository of "general ideas" which could be applied directly to the conduct of life and the improvement of the national culture. When they published criticism, which usually appeared in popular periodicals rather than specialized professional journals, it was usually to teach appreciation, or to recommend certain authors, or to suggest how literature contributed to the national character. From their point of view, the philologists' monopoly over English not only lamentably reduced criticism to a narrow and pedantic method; it also sacrificed national cultural ideals to the selfish interests of a professional group. When today's critics of American education blame professional self-interest for undermining the unity of the curriculum, they unwittingly repeat the complaints of a century ago.

The present anthology illustrates many of the issues at stake in this early conflict between philologists and belletrists. For it can be argued that it was this conflict, not the triumph of philology, that was formative for the discipline of literary studies. The more the academic profession took literature rather than language as its subject, the more this conflict became a dispute not just between professors and armchair men of letters, but between competing professional models—a dispute internal to the new profession itself. What had begun as a conflict of journalists and gentleman amateurs *against* professionalism became increasingly a conflict *within* professionalism, a conflict for the right to define what "professionalism" in literary studies would mean. This conflict continues today.

To put our point another way, the "discipline" of literary studies originated not in a unified, systematic body of goals and methods, but in a bitter and still unresolved conflict of political and literary allegiances. To see what this observation entails, considers how the standard typifications of each group has corresponded to conflicting models of social relations. The belletrist's ideal type is the popular teacher with no grasp of research—a proof not of incompetence (except to research scholars), but of superiority to pedestrian considerations of fact. In the classroom this teacher is pictured as a spellbinder, setting afire the imaginations of undergraduates, whom he arouses from their congenital apathy very much as New England ministers (frequently his ancestors) lifted their congregations from spiritual torpor. Or he is seen warming the students' hearts in private conversations in his cozy, book-lined study, or pausing to speak to the elderly ladies of the town while on his daily stroll. He is present, personable, sometimes given to eccentric crotchets—but in a lovable way that will provoke affectionate recollections in the memoirs of former students.

The professional's ideal type, on the other hand, is the (male) researcher. He is Ethan Brand or Roger Chillingworth to the non-professional's Mr. Chips. As a teacher and mentor he is a dismal failure—a proof not of his inadequacy (except to belletrists), but of his superiority to the dilletantism of classroom spellbinders and petty cultivators of taste. His setting is a solitary office, legendary for its mess because he has more important things on his mind than minor kinds of order. He is conspicuously absent from the circles in which his opposite number is so warmly present, forming his strongest associations not with local colleagues or townsfolk but with others in his field around the world. His associates communicate with him by writing—especially through offprints of published articles. In time, his very absence from the classroom will come to be a measure of his success, as full-time research with virtually no teaching becomes a realistic goal.

Of course in thus reducing the conflict of teacher and investigator to polemical ideal types, we recognize that no person then or since was simply one or the other. In fact, as Irving Babbitt pointed out in *Literature and the American College* (see Chapter 13), the professional and the dilettante often combined in the same person, who exhibited the one tendency in research and the other in teaching, or the one in professional publications and meetings and the other in public addresses and newspaper reviews. One source of interest of the selections in this anthology is the frequency with which they illustrate these self-divisions.

What is even more interesting, however, is the way the contrasts we have just drawn in professional typology suggest the transformation which was operating in industrial society at the time these contrasts were forming. The triumph of the research scholar over the belletrist was part of the shift from *Gemeinschaft* to *Gesellschaft*, in Ferdinand Tönnies's classic terms—though one should avoid sentimentalizing the pre-professional period as one of idyllic "community." The opposition of scholar and belletrist corresponded with larger oppositions such as capitalistic production vs. leisure, urban vs. pastoral, fact vs. value, functional rationality vs. traditional community, research vs. teaching, specialized major and graduate program vs. general education. The iconography of the college catalogue—with its stereotypical depiction of the small group of students, poetry volumes in hand, sprawled on the campus grass at the feet of a dedicated instructor—testifies to a sentimental image of teaching as pastoral romance, whose function is to redeem or compensate for the anti-values of industrialized research and vocational practicality. This pastoral conception of the humanities as an overlay of "values" which is to humanize the otherwise fallen realm of work and practical affairs remains central to the concept of general education. It conveniently masks the fact that the humanities have always been a site of conflict and have never been immune to the incursions of industrialism.

II

The implicit contest over models of social relations which we have been describing is responsible for much of the passion and intractability of debates over literary study. At issue in these debates are still unanswered questions about the impact of academic professionalization of literary studies on literature, criticism, and cultural dissemination. To what extent has the increasing monopoly of literature by universities altered our conception of the nature of literature and criticism? To what extend is the dissemination of literary tradition compatible with the scientific and revisionary impulses of professionalism? Such large questions can have no simple answer, but it may be useful to isolate some of their aspects here.

One can start by asking whether academization is responsible for the fact that we now tend to take it for granted that locating the "meaning" or meanings of literary works is the bottom-line activity of any literary criticism which aspires to more than journalistic status. That problems of textual meaning are not necessarily the natural and obvious object of criticism is recognized by students, who often anxiously wonder why their teachers expect them to look for "hidden meaning" in classroom texts. The systematic preoccupation with "hidden meaning" has a long history in theological and legal hermeneutics, but its entry into literary criticism comes relatively late. At the beginning of the period under review here, neither the philologists nor the belletrists took what we now think of as literary meaning to be worth comment. One looks in vain in either group's writings for anything resembling the kind of textual explication that would later occupy the center of literary study.

Like the classical instructors who had taught Greek and Latin literary texts as exemplifications of grammatical problems, modern language philologists initially assumed that the main obstacle to understanding literary works was inadequate information about the language or historical background of the text. For the belletristic critics, on the other hand (as we have already seen), the right kind of aesthetic and moral sensibility proved itself by an intuitive apprehension of meaning. To belabor interpretive questions implied an admission of vulgarity, for supposedly mere exposure to the products of literary genius was sufficient to arouse enthusiasm in the well-bred. The most effective way to teach great literature, then, was to let it simply teach itself. If the touchstone of a work's greatness was its ability to transcend the contexts of its time of creation and reception, it followed that the best way to teach that work was to disencumber it from both its contexts and from elaborate critical and pedagogical methods.

This way of thinking helps us understand the perennial appeal, much in evidence still today, of Woodrow Wilson's argument (in Chapter 9) that literature "has a quality to move you, and you can never mistake it, if you have any blood in you. And it has also a power to instruct you which is as effective as it is subtle, and which no research or systematic method can ever rival." An extension of these assumptions underlay Hiram Corson's theory (see Chapter 10), which he carried out in classroom practice, that the soundest method of teaching literature was not to analyze it at all but to read it aloud, to declaim it in such a way as to let its spiritual content speak for itself. To a greater or lesser degree, Wilson and Corson's views echoed the Protestant belief that the divine Word ignited the soul of the willing believer without the need for elaborate ecclesiastical and theological intervention.

Wilson and Corson, however, represented what was already a rearguard position in their time. As several of our selections show, the application of linguistic study to literature increasingly involved an interpretive conception of criticism. The clearest example here is the extraordinary essay by Richard Moulton on the possibility of "inductive criticism" (Chapter 7), but we can also see the critical conception taking form in the selections by Martin Wright Sampson and Charles Mills Gayley (in Chapter 6). For these scholars, the troubling thing about literary study as practiced in colleges and universities is the disparity between technical analysis and aesthetic and moral evaluation. The need to legitimate the new profession by contrasting its rigor with the discredited amateurism of mere appreciation is a continuous thread in these selections from the 1880s and 1890s.

As Moulton argues, the problem is that, historically, the tasks of aesthetic and moral evaluation had never been formalized into a body of knowledge which could be confirmed and replicated by a community over time. Perhaps there had been no need for such formalization in earlier cultures, but the vicissitudes of tastes and mores, which tend to be ever more unpredictable in a changing democratic society, now seem to require a rigorous attempt to define the principles of literary value. Moulton's solution is what he calls a "foundation axiom" for scholarly literary criticism: "Interpretation in literature is of the nature of a scientific hypothesis, the truth of which is tested by the degree of completeness with which it explains the details of the literary work as they actually stand." Although a counterreaction has recently set in against the empiricist assumptions of Moulton's axiom, it states with brilliant clarity a conception of criticism that would later be developed, in different directions, by figures such as I. A. Richards, Northrop Frye, and Roman Jakobson, and would eventually be tacitly presupposed by critics of all stripes. The conception was that interpretation could serve as the new basis for the discourse of a research community.

Such a discourse, however, would give interpretations the status of hypotheses rather than of moral assertions. Academic criticism thus effected a kind of desacralization of literature in the very process of elevating the subject to a status in higher education it had never occupied before. Moreover, to the extent that interpretation presupposed the self-correcting discourse of a research community rather than a pedagogical or public activity, academic criticism came to be alienated from its nominal constituency. The fissure between public and academic criticism, for which deconstructionists and theorists today have been made the scapegoats, goes back to the beginnings of academic criticism. Though academic criticism continued to justify its prestige in the university by claiming that it spoke for and to a general culture, the main object of interpretive discourse was to justify itself as knowledge, a fact which assumed that the main audience for criticism was other professional critics.

This was the complaint of the early belletristic critics, who set the pattern for all the subsequent attacks which have repetitively blamed academic criticism for taking literature away from its rightful audience and turning it into a private enclave for specialists. Typically, the professionals are accused of betraying their responsibility to students and public by surrounding literature with a mystifying jargon and exploiting it for selfish careerist interests or private political causes. Yet this familiar attack on "special interests" in the name of a supposedly "universal" community and its traditions simply begs the question, ignoring as it does that appreciation of these traditions has been used to distinguish the elite from the vulgarity of the masses. Which group is to have the right to say whose interests are merely "special" has always been the unacknowledged issue.

The tension between the claim of criticism to represent professional knowledge and its claim to represent public, normative needs is best dramatized by the material in Part II below. There the philologists repeatedly come under attack from the right for subverting the creation of a unifying national culture. This attack on academic criticism from the right for defaulting on its public responsibilities continues to be made in our day—but it is now joined by the left. What makes matters confusing is that the right blames academic criticism for having abandoned its national and humanistic traditions, whereas the left blames that criticism for remaining all too closely tied to those national and humanistic traditions. At the very moment critics on the right charge humanists with "a loss of nerve and faith," the left charges the same humanists with papering over the repressively hegemonic domination of humanistic values. Whereas the right denounces professionalism for obscuring the unity of the cultural heritage, the left denounces it for shoring up that heritage and reinforcing nationalist, bourgeois, imperialist, racist, masculinist, heterosexist, and ethnocentric biases.

To understand the political role of professional criticism in America, it is necessary to consider that the professionalization of literary studies appeared in the same period as the professionalization of law, medicine, and the social sciences. It was part of a broader social transformation—one which has been the subject of a number of distinguished recent studies, including Thomas L. Haskell's The *Emergence of Professional Social Science* (University of Illinois Press, 1977) and Burton J. Bledstein's The *Culture of Professionalism* (Norton, 1976). A methodological framework of great subtlety has been elaborated by Magali Sarfatti Larson in The *Rise of Professionalism* (University of California Press, 1977). Taken together, these standard studies suggest the possibility of structural homologies between the purposes and organizational patterns of English and those of, say, the nursing profession.

Both the left and the right view such homologies as ominous, but for different reasons. The right sees in them the encroachment of scientific and technological organization into the citadel of humane values; the left sees in them the complicity of high culture with the ideology of industrial and post-industrial capitalism. Much of the attack on professional literary studies, in sum, is really an attack on the nature of modern society as much as on any given program for criticism.

What then is the relation between professionalism and cultural tradition? Has professionalism served as an instrument for enforcing a coherent cultural tradition, or has it tended in some ways to fracture that tradition and rob it of its accessibility and power, for better or worse? The conflicting answers to these questions of the left and right reflect an ambiguity in the relations between professions and traditions.

Built into professional discourse is what we might call a critical principle: anything said professionally is presumably a hypothesis to be tested against the criticism of qualified insiders. It follows that no judgment is axiomatic and that all assertions are potentially corrigible. Built into literary culture, on the other hand, is a value of tradition that is presumably universal, normative, and above controversy. Because the authority of tradition lies in its being inherited rather than assembled through debate, its defining values are axiomatic.

Historically, professional literary criticism has found itself between the opposing needs of constructing debatable hypotheses, on one hand, and preserving a normative heritage, on the other.

The situation is further complicated in modern democratic societies, where the transmission of tradition is expected to exercise democratizing as well as preservative functions. In the United States, the project of transmitting high culture to the masses has always contained inherent ambiguities which have made it dangerous to generalize about its political effects apart from specific contexts. From a democratic point of view, the project can be praised as reparation to the masses of a culture which was extracted from their labor and then used to exclude them, or it can be condemned as an attempt to control the masses by indoctrinating them with ruling-class ideology. In such a society, however, the value of revision appears as a challenge to the value of tradition. The debatability and corrigibility of professional discourse amplifies the challenge to tradition already implicit in democracy.

Professional literary studies have internalized these tensions, initially in the conflict between scholarship and criticism and now today, increasingly, between both activities and "theory." In fact, "theory" could be workably defined as a kind of discourse that is generated when basic assumptions cease to be taken for granted and become open to debate. Theory calls attention to these tensions and conflicts, which otherwise tend to be mystified or hidden. The situation has made literary studies a peculiarly vital nexus of cultural forces, but it has also left them vulnerable on many sides.

In the twentieth century, the competition from mass culture has intensified this vulnerability. Early literary scholars could treat the constitution of literature and its tradition as empirical givens because they restricted the scope of their work to remoter historical periods. As literature departments have come to treat more recent literature (as well as American literature), they have increasingly found themselves in the position of arbiters of contemporary taste. But the same social transformation which brought literary studies into being separated them from upstart institutions which also claimed the right to make cultural evaluations, define traditions, and set the terms of cultural transmission. Agencies such as the film industry and television not only exercised autonomy in the way they defined and reproduced the cultural heritage, they redefined the meaning of culture itself.

Mass culture is only the most obvious and powerful of the agencies of culture that compete with the university in providing explanations of contemporary life. Primary and secondary education could be viewed in this light as well. To the extent that literary study took on itself the evaluative and appreciative tasks of criticism, it was likely to remain alienated from institutions which were shaping American values in other directions. Here lay the source of the angry tone of universal condemnation in which early professional scholars often referred to contemporary culture (an anger that has recently been raised to a hysterical pitch by those who believe that the classic texts have been driven out by pop culture on college reading lists). A characteristic instance of this denunciation of the contemporary is Charles Hall Grandgent's (see Chapter 14), whose title, "The Dark Ages," does not refer to antiquity.

In our own time, indications are that these tensions have reached a breaking point. Our culture's traditions and values have become so diverse and conflicting that only the blandest normative claims can be defended to a diverse audience. What is more, the entry of women and other heretofore excluded groups into the higher levels of the profession has introduced conflicts over heritage and value into the very core of literary studies. As a result, the determination of what books to teach and how to teach them has in many places ceased to be in the control of a narrow elite and been opened to voices whose heterogeneity approximates that of American culture itself.

What makes the current fulminations against the recent direction of literary studies so useless is that they are finally complaints about the presence of disagreement. Much of the present anger derives from reluctance to accept a situation in which contexts, procedures, definitions, distinctions, and categories which used to be the unquestioned province of privileged groups have suddenly become open to negotiation and debate. Again, what traditionalists cannot tolerate is a situation in which, having called the turn for so long, they suddenly have to *fight* for their viewpoint like everybody else. Those who still insist that the role of professional criticism and pedagogy must be to transmit a universally normative heritage have little choice but to despair over the loss of a unitary heritage or try to impose some arbitrary version of such a heritage by force. But our analysis suggests that though the transmission of such a heritage has certainly been the project of important factions, it has never been a possible role for the literary studies as a whole.

A different possible future for professional literary studies can be glimpsed in the pages of this book. Conflicts over value and tradition within the profession, especially those introduced by feminists and other movements of opposition, have in effect made the normative power of the cultural heritage a target of criticism. Instead of being seen as the ideal *result* of criticism, an unshakable and undebatable end-point, value and heritage have been redescribed as objects of its inquiry, perpetually under negotiation by competing groups. The result has been a new critical comparativism, which reinstates with a difference the interests of the old philologists in language, origins, and the comprehensive history of culture. These developments make it possible to imagine a redefinition of literary studies—one whose goal would be not to establish a tradition or a consensus so much as to clarify differences and conflicts.

Such a critical project might free itself from the contradictions we have seen to have plagued the profession of literary studies from the start. First, the critical and revisionist nature of professional discourse would no longer conflict with the object of study. The cultural traditions being studied would themselves be seen in their critical relation to competing traditions, with no one of them taken as *the* tradition. The axiomatic value would be not tradition as such, but the critical comparativism which alone is appropriate to the socially conflictual nature of traditions. Second, by taking a comparative stance that recognized the existence of multiple traditions, professional literary studies would no longer be undermining its own claims by its separation from other cultural institutions such as the mass media. This recognition that critical hermeneutics differs in kind from the reception of a heritage would be an enabling condition. A new coherence would emerge, but it would be a coherence based on the recognition of conflict rather than on a traditional consensus.

Such speculations go beyond the scope of the present anthology and will require more detailed elaboration elsewhere. Our hope, however, is that this anthology will contribute to the effort of institutional transformation that is now under way. A rereading of the profession's history can help revise its understanding of itself for the future and for the better.

Part I
PROFESSIONALIZATION

1

From *German Universities:*
A Narrative of Personal
Experience (1874)
James Morgan Hart

James Morgan Hart (1839–1916) studied law at the University of Göttingen from 1860–64. After a stint in professional legal practice, he became professor of modern languages at Cornell University (1868–72), an illustration of the frequent commerce between the legal and language-teaching professions in this period. Hart moved to the faculty of the University of Cincinnati (1876–90) and later returned to Cornell (1890–1907). A scholar of French, German, and Italian, as well as English, Hart was the author of a *Syllabus of Anglo-Saxon Literature* (1881) and compiled an Anglo-Saxon dictionary which he did not live to complete.

Hart's comprehensive book, *German Universities*, was published in 1874, at a time when growing numbers of Americans were going to Germany for the graduate programs that still did not as yet exist here. Many more Americans were beginning to consider this option, and it was this new interest that Hart's book met and stimulated. Only two years after its publication, the founding of Johns Hopkins University would initiate the great transformation of American Universities in the 1870s and 1880s. Hart emphasizes the heroism of the German university professor, who searches for truth "wholly irrespective of utilitarian application" and exercises a freedom of inquiry (*Lehrfreiheit*) that American college teachers at this time could only envy. It was such laudatory accounts as Hart's which encouraged reformers of American colleges to look to Germany for their principal model.

What is a University?

To the German mind the collective idea of a university implies a *Zweck*, an object of study, and two *Bedingungen*, or conditions. The object is *Wissenschaft*; the conditions are *Lehrfreiheit* and *Lernfreiheit*. By *Wissenschaft* the Germans mean knowledge in the most exalted sense of that term, namely, the ardent, methodical, independent search after truth in any and all of its forms, but wholly irrespective of utilitarian application. *Lehrfreiheit* means that the one who teaches, the professor or *Privatdocent*, is free to teach what he chooses, as he chooses. *Lernfreiheit*, or the freedom of learning, denotes the emancipation of the student from *Schulzwang*, compulsory drill by recitation.

If the object of an institution is anything else than knowledge as above defined, or if either freedom of teaching or freedom of learning is wanting, that institution, no matter how richly endowed, no matter how numerous its students, no matter how imposing its buildings, is not, in the eye of a German, a *university*. On the other hand, a small, out-of-the-way place like Rostock, with only thirty-four professors and docents, and one hundred and thirty-five students, is nevertheless as truly a university as Leipsic, where the numbers are one hundred and fifty and three thousand respectively, because Rostock aims at theoretical knowledge and meets the requirements of free teaching and free study. The difference is one of size, not of species.

If we examine the list of lectures and hours of universities like Leipsic, Berlin, and Vienna, we shall be overwhelmed, at first sight, with the amount and variety of literary and scientific labor announced. The field seems boundless. All that human ingenuity can suggest is apparently represented. On examining more closely, however, we shall find that this seemingly boundless field has its limits, which are very closely traced and which are not exceeded. Strange as it may sound to the American, who is accustomed to gauge spiritual greatness by big numbers and extravagant pretensions, a German university, even the greatest, perceives what it can do and what it *can not do.*

It is not a place "where any man can study anything." Its elevated character makes it all the more modest. It contents itself with the theoretical, and leaves to other institutions the practical and the technical. The list of studies and hours for Leipsic in the semester 1872–3 fills thirty octavo pages. In all that list we shall discover scarcely one course of work that can be called in strictness practical. A German university has one and only one object: to train thinkers. It does not aim at producing poets, painters, sculptors, engineers, miners, architects, bankers, manufacturers. For these, the places of instruction are the Art Schools of Dresden, Munich, Düsseldorf, the Commercial Schools at Bremen, Hamburg, Berlin, Frankfort, the Polytechnicums at Hanover, Frankenberg, Stuttgart, etc. Even in the professions themselves, theory and practice are carefully distinguished, and the former alone is considered as falling legitimately within the sphere of university instruction. . . . The reader will probably say: Is not this the case in America also? Are not our college professors all college graduates? To which the answer must be: Not in the same way, not to the same extent.

How many of our college professors have been professors, and nothing else? How many have qualified themselves directly for the respective chairs which they occupy, by a life of special study? How many of them formed the resolve while still students, to lead a college life forever, to devote themselves exclusively to instructing others in turn, either at their own Alma Mater or at some other college? I do not have in view such institutions as Yale and Harvard, old, well endowed, fed from the rich soil of New England culture. I mean the typical American college as it exists in the Middle, Southern, and Western States. How many of the professors have been in business, or tried their skill at farming, engineering, journalism? Has or has not the professor of Latin served an apprenticeship as mathematical tutor, or kept a boarding-school for young ladies? How few of the hundreds and thousands of men, from New York to San Francisco, calling themselves professors, can say with a comfortable degree of pride: I selected my specialty in youth, I have pursued it without intermission, without deviation ever since, and I have produced such and such tangible evidences of my industry as a specialist.

No, the reader may rest assured that the character and atmosphere of a German university differ radically from the character and atmosphere of the typical American college. It is a difference of kind, not merely of degree. Comparisons, according to the popular adage, are odious. Yet, even at the risk of giving offense, I take the liberty of drawing a comparison that may serve, perhaps, to throw some light on this vital point. At all events, the comparison shall be a just one. Marburg, in Hesse, has at present 430 students; Princeton, my Alma Mater, has 420. The numbers, then, are almost identical. Each is located in a small country town. Yet Princeton has, all told, not more than 18 professors and tutors; Marburg has 62. Among them are men renowned throughout the world for their original investigations. The same might be said, indeed, of the Princeton faculty, but only with grave restrictions. No one professor at Princeton has the opportunity of working either himself or his student up to his or their full capacity. The instruction goes by routine, each professor contributing his quota to the supposed general development of all the students in a body. At Marburg there is the fourfold division of faculties; there are students pursuing theology, law, medicine, classic philology, modern philology, the natural sciences, history, orientalia. Each instructor has his select band of disciples, upon whom he acts and who re-act upon him. There is the same quiet, scholarly atmosphere, the same disregard for bread-and-butter study, the same breadth of culture, depth of insight, liberality of opinion and freedom of conduct, that one finds in the most favored circles of Leipsic, Berlin, Heidelberg, or Vienna. During every hour of the two months that I passed at Marburg, I was made to feel that a German university, however humble, is a world in and for itself; that its aim is not to turn out clever, pushing, ambitious graduates, but to engender culture.

This condition is both cause and effect. Many of the students who attend the university do so simply with a view to becoming in time professors. The entire *personnel* of the faculty is thus a close corporation, a spiritual order perpetuating itself after the fashion of the Roman Catholic hierarchy. Inasmuch as every professional man and every school-teacher of the higher grades has to pass through the university, it follows that the shaping of the intellectual interests of the country is in the hands of a select few, who are highly educated, perfectly homogeneous in character and sympathies, utterly indifferent to the turmoils and ambitions of the outer-world, who regulate their own lives and mould the dispositions of those dependent upon them according to the principles of abstract truth. The quality of university education, then, is determined by its object, and that object is to train not merely skillful practitioners, *but also future professors.* In fact, the needs of the former class are subordinated to the needs of the latter. In this respect, the faculty acts, unconsciously, in accordance with the promptings of the instinct of self-preservation. If thorough scientific culture is an essential element in national life, it must be maintained at every cost. The slightest flaw in the continuity of spiritual descent would be as dangerous as a break in the apostolic succession of the church. Every inducement therefore, must be held out to young men to qualify themselves in season for succeeding to their present instructors. The lectures and other instruction must be adapted to train and stimulate *Privat-docenten*, for they are the ones who are to seize and wear the mantles of the translated Elijahs. For every professor dead or removed, there must be one or two instantly ready to fill his place.

This is not the *avowed* object of the university course. One might pass many years in Germany without perceiving it stated so bluntly. Yet I am persuaded that it is at bottom the determining factor in the constitution of university life. It will explain to us many incidental features for which there is elsewhere no analogy; for instance, the sovereign contempt that all German students evince for everything that savors of "bread-and-butter." The students have caught, in this respect, the tone of their instructors. Even such of them as have no intention of becoming *Privat-docenten* pass three and four years of their life in generous devotion to study pure and simple, without casting a single forward glance to future "business." All thought of practical life is kept in abeyance. The future practitioners and the future theoreticians sit side by side on the same bench, fight on the same *Mensur*, drink at the same *Kneipe,*[*] hear the same lectures, use the same books, have every sentiment in common; hence the perfect *rapport* that exists in Germany between the lawyer and the jurist, the pastor and the theologian, the practicing doctor and the speculative pathologist, the gymnasial teacher of Latin and Greek and the professed philologist. Hence the celerity with which innovating ideas spread in Germany. Let a professor in the university of Tübingen, for instance, publish a work on some abstruse, difficult topic, in which he threatens to overturn previous theories and notions. Why is it that in a month or two the book provokes a tempest of assent or dissent from far and near? Simply because every practical man in that line, every lawyer, or doctor, or pastor, as the case may

* *Mensur*, student's duel; *Kneipe*, public house. [ed.]

be, has been initiated so far into the theory of his profession as to be able to detect at a glance the full purport of the new departure. Let the book contain but a single mis-statement of an historic fact or an established principle of natural science, and a hundred angry reviewers pounce upon it and hold it up to public condemnation. Whereas, in this country, and even in England also, the grossest blunders pass unchallenged. Our reviewers are either ignorant or indifferent.

To repeat, the university instruction of Germany does not attempt to train successful practical men, unless it be indirectly, by giving its students a profound insight into the principles of the science and then turning them adrift to deduce the practice as well as they can from the carefully inculcated theory. Its chief task, that to which all its energies are directed, is the development of great thinkers, men who will extend the boundaries of knowledge.

Viewed from this point, then, the two conditions, *Lehrfreiheit* and *Lernfreiheit*, are not only natural and proper, but are absolutely essential. Were the object of higher education merely to train "useful and honorable members of society," to use the conventional phrase of the panegyrists of the American system, the German universities might possibly change their character. In place of professors free to impart the choicest results of their investigations, they might substitute pedagogues with text-books and class-books, noting down the relative merits and demerits of daily recitations. In place of students free to attend or to stay away, free to agree with the professor or to differ, free to read what they choose and to study after their own fashion, they might create a set of undergraduates reciting glibly from set lessons and regarding each circumvention of the teacher as so much clear gain. But the Germans know perfectly well wherein the value of their university education lies. They know that speculative thought alone has raised Germany from her former condition of literary and political dependence to the foremost rank among nations. The gain is not without its sacrifice. Many a young man who, under another method, might be drilled into a tolerable alumnus, falls by the way-side through idleness and dissipation. For one who succeeds, two or three fail. Yet the sacrifice is unavoidable. If German thought is to continue in its career of conquest, if the universities are to remain what they are, the training-ground of intellectual giants, the present system of freedom must be maintained. The professor has but one aim in life: scholarly renown. To effect this, he must have the liberty of selecting his studies and pushing them to their extreme limits. The student has but one desire: to assimilate his instructor's learning, and, if possible, to add to it. He must, therefore, be his own master. He must be free to accept and reject, to judge and prove all things for himself, to train himself step by step for grappling with the great problems of nature and history. Accountable only to himself for his opinions and mode of living, he shakes off spiritual bondage and becomes an independent thinker.

He *must* think for himself, for there is no one set over him as spiritual adviser and guide, prescribing the work for each day and each hour, telling him what he is to believe and what to disbelieve, and marking him up or down accordingly.

The universities occupy, then, an impregnable position. Recruiting their tuitional forces (*Lehrkräfte*) from among themselves, they are independent of the outer world. . . .

Professors

The character of the German professor will be best understood by first disposing of the preliminary question: What is he not?

The professor is not a teacher, in the English sense of the term; he is a specialist. He is not responsible for the success of his hearers. He is responsible only for the quality of his instruction. His duty begins and ends with himself.

No man can become a professor in a German university without having given evidence, in one way or another, that he has pursued a certain line of study, and produced results worthy to be called novel and important. In other words, to become a professor, he must first have been a special investigator. Professional chairs are not conferred "on general principles," or because the candidate is "a good teacher," or "well qualified to govern the young." Neither is there such springing about from one department of study to another as we observe in America. . . .

The chief attraction in the professorial career . . . is the nature of the work itself. No human lot, it is true, is without its trials. The life of a professor is anything but a bed of roses. It means severe intellectual toil from morning till evening, from manhood to declining years. But there is a freedom about it that is inexpressibly fascinating. The professor is his own master. His time is not wasted in cudgeling the wits of refractory or listless reciters. His temper is not ruffled by the freaks or the downright insults of mutinous youths. He lectures upon his chosen subject, comments upon his favorite Greek or Roman or early German or Sanscrit author, expounds some recently discovered mathematical theorem, discusses one or another of the grave problems of history or morals, and is accountable only to his own conscience of what is true and what is false. He lectures only to those who are willing and able to hear. He is sustained by the consciousness that his words are not scattered by the wayside, but that they fall upon soil prepared to receive them, and will bring forth new fruit in turn. His relation to his hearers is that of one gentleman speaking to another. He is not in perpetual dread of hearing himself nicknamed, of seeing his features caricatured; his domestic repose is not disturbed by midnight serenades. He addresses his pupils as men who know perfectly well what they are about, and whom he must seek to enlighten or convince. . . .

As a class, the professors of Germany are hard-workers. One who has never tried the experiment might suppose that it is not so very difficult to lecture eight or ten hours a week. The mere reading-off is perfectly easy; but the labor of preparing a set of lectures that shall be acceptable to a community so fastidious in its tastes, as a university, is immense. The professor being a specialist, it is expected of him that he shall produce something especially good, that he shall be up to the times. There are a few "old fogies," men who live on the reputation that they acquired twenty or thirty years ago. But they form a very small minority. A professor who has any ambition whatever, who is anxious to spare himself the mortification of reading to empty benches, must recast his lectures continually, striking out exploded errors, incorporating new discoveries. The German brain is prolific. The sight of the semi-annual catalogue of new publications in Germany is enough to unhinge the strongest mind. The professor must keep abreast with the swelling tide. He must study each new work in his own department, at least to the extent of knowing what novelties it contains, and how they agree or disagree with his own views. If he does not, if he falls behind, some ambitious rival, some aspiring *Privat-docent*, will overtake and pass him. In this respect, the students are quick-witted and exacting. No sooner do they discover that one professor represents the state of investigation as it was ten or only five years ago, while another gives it as it actually is, than they desert in a body to the younger man. Herein lies the real strength of the German professorial system and the check upon the abuses of *Lehrfreiheit*. A professor is free to lecture upon what topics he chooses; he is not compelled to modify his views. But if he persists in offering stale matter, in selecting topics that have ceased to interest, he does so at the peril of losing his prestige and his hearers. . . .

The chief defect in the character of the German professors as a class is one that arises of necessity from their mode of life. Devoted to a narrow range of study, living in comparative seclusion, they are unpractical in many ways and intolerant of dissent. What a German professor teaches, he teaches with an intensity of conviction that leaves no room for doubt or hesitancy. I should be loth to call this trait fanaticism. Certainly it is not the fanaticism of ignorance, or of one-sidedness; the professor, it may be safely assumed, has looked at the question from every side and weighed the evidence. It is rather the intolerance inherent in one who is not troubled with doubts and who fails to understand why another should stumble over what is to him so plain. It springs from want of familiarity with the world, want of appreciation of the complex motives that determine human opinion no less than human action. Man is not a purely intellectual being; the individual status of each one is the resultant of all sorts of forces, prejudices, temptations, inherited sentiments. Yet things are judged in Germany too exclusively by the standard of pure intellect. The Germans neglect the glorious example set them by their national genius, Goethe, and overlook in their criticisms the individuality of the person criticized. Of course there are many bright exceptions, but as a rule German critics judge everything by some exalted, ideal standard of what is absolutely right and absolutely wrong. Does a literary production come up to this standard? Well and good. If it does not,—off with the fellow's head! Hence the sweeping condemnations that one finds in every list of book reviews, the bitter literary feuds that have been waged and are still waged over debatable points where one might expect some degree of charity, some latitude of belief. Not all critics are professors, but all professors are critics. Notices and reviews of publications not purely belletristic or ephemeral in their nature are generally written by professors or docents, who thus give the tone.

The relation between professor and student is, if not positively friendly, at least pleasant. The chief drawback to the lot of a professor in America, namely, police-duty and discipline, does not exist in Germany. The professor, as such, has nothing to do with the university discipline. Unless he happens to be a member of the university court, and this he cannot be unless he is a jurist, or the rector for the time being, he is not called upon to pass sentence upon a student's conduct. He is not obliged to fritter away many hours a week of his valuable time in deciding whether Smith was really suffering from the measles or only shamming, whether Jones ought to be sent home for three months or six months for breaking a tutor's windows. He has nothing to do with the students as a body, does not know more than a tenth of them by sight or by name; his dealings are exclusively with the few who sit in his lecture-room. If the exercises are of a colloquial nature, as for instance in the numerous *practica, exegetica, seminaria,* and cliniques, he makes naturally an informal estimate of each pupil's capacities. But he keeps no record either of their performances or of their attendance. In consequence, neither professor nor student has any inducement to chicane each the other. They hold the relation of giver and receiver.

2

"Recollections of Language Teaching," *PMLA* (1893)

Francis A. March

Francis August March (1825–1911) became one of the earliest founders of English studies when he installed a program in English at Lafayette College in 1857, some thirty years before the subject would be widely established in American colleges. March's professorship in English Language and Comparative Philology was the first chair of its kind in any American or European university—though it is reflective of conditions at the time that in addition to English March taught not only French, German, Latin, and Greek, but also law, political economy, philosophy, and botany. March was a leading philological scholar,, the author of *Method of the Philological Study of the English Language* (1865) and *Comparative Grammar of the Anglo-Saxon Language* (1870).

These "Recollections of Language Teaching" were transcribed from a talk March delivered at the Modern Language Association convention of 1892, by which time the speaker was already a semi-legendary figure. The earliest college teaching of English copied the method which had been used to teach the classical languages (after the popular maxim that "English should be studied as Greek is"). As March's recollections make clear, this method involved heavy concentration on linguistic and etymological technicalities, with virtually no attention to the patterns of meaning that would later become central objects of literary pedagogy.

Noah Webster was one of the founders of Amherst College, and the Professor of Rhetoric and Oratory in my day, W. C. Fowler, LL. D., was his son-in-law. The professor lectured on Anglo-Saxon among other things. He had imported Anglo-Saxon books, then curiosities. He held them up and exhibited them to us, as he lectured, exactly as the natural history men did precious shells, or minerals. He said there were only two or three men living who knew anything about the language. He was working on one of the Webster dictionaries, and I became interested in the philological side of English.

In 1845, as a teacher in Leicester Academy, Massachusetts, I made my experiment of teaching English like Latin or Greek—hearing a short Grammar lesson, the rest of the hour reading Milton as if it were Homer, calling for the meaning of words, their etymology when interesting, the relations of words, parsing when it would help, the connection of clauses, the mythology, the biography and other illustrative matter, suited to the class.

In 1855 similar studies were begun at Lafayette College, but on a higher plane. Students who had nearly finished their Latin, Greek, French and German took two terms of Anglo-Saxon and Modern English. A professorship was established for this study. It was thought that it was the first of the kind. The most important peculiarity of the teaching in the mind of the professor was, that it was work upon Anglo-Saxon and English texts to read and understand them; not lectures about the languages, not lessons in descriptive or critical discourse about them, not a rhetorical but a linguistic study. There were no good text-books in 1855. Anglo-Saxon was studied for some years in Barnes's *Delectus*. In 1861 the difficulty of importing text-books led to the making of American books. Love of the work led to the making of a *Comparative Grammar of Anglo-Saxon*, beyond the ken of publishers of that day. The Modern Language Association of America will welcome a word of commemoration of the Trustees of Lafayette College, who had before set apart time for these studies and funds for procuring the apparatus of research, and who now personally paid the principal cost of publication. The *Grammar and Reader* came out in 1869–70.

In 1875 the United States Commissioner of Education sent out a circular to our colleges inquiring about their study of Anglo-Saxon. Twenty-three colleges then claimed to be reading some of it; the University of Virginia (1825), Harvard (1851), Lafayette (1856), Haverford (1867), St. John's College (1868), Cornell University (1871), Columbia College, the University of Wisconsin, Yale, in the Sheffield School and post-graduate course. Most of the others were just beginning. The University of Michigan was "sorry to say that the study is not pursued at all;" so was Dartmouth. Princeton said it might be introduced hereafter; so did the Central University at Richmond, Kentucky, and Vanderbilt University. Eight claimed to study it incidentally. Only sixteen were content with simply stating that they did not study Anglo-Saxon. Slight as this showing seems now, there was at that time, probably, nowhere else so much of this study as in America. Professor Child says, in his answer to the circular of the bureau, that "Anglo-Saxon is *utterly* neglected in England—at present there is but one man in England that is known to know anything of it—and not *extensively* pursued anywhere in America." The Germans, he adds, "cannot do their best for want of properly edited texts. Two or three American scholars, devoted to Anglo-Saxon, would have a great field to distinguish themselves in, undisputed by Englishmen."

The eighteen years since 1875 have seen great advances; Sweet's *Anglo-Saxon Reader* appeared in 1876, The Early English Text Society began to furnish materials for the Germans, and the press has teemed with critical studies as well as text-books. This Anglo-Saxon study, delightful and important in itself to specialists, seems also to be necessary for a solid and learned support to the study of Modern English in college. The early professors had no recondite learning applicable to English, and did not know what to do with classes in it. They can now make English as hard as Greek.

The introduction of studies of research in which looking up and reporting the contents of books is prescribed, and evidence of having examined books is taken instead of original thinking or mastery of thought, has greatly affected the study of English. Programs of researches of various kinds abound, so that a college class can be put through English literature very happily. The old teachers make light of this substitute for original thinking; but it is good, for all that, and is leading forward. We are having an outcry just now against stopping to study particular passages in literature, urging rapid emotional reading, the seeking to produce love of reading rather than knowledge of books,—love of reading all the new magazines, I suppose, and newspapers, and novels, and facts that are stranger than fiction, instead of spending days and nights with the great authors.

But professors who aim at the highest usefulness and the most honored positon must labor to give profound knowledge, and excite lasting love of great books and devotion to great thoughts. Their linguistic studies must be scientific as well as historical, deep and not vulgar. Their literary studies must be mainly upon great authors.

What books, what works shall we choose for study in schools and colleges? Those which contain weighty truths, important facts, close packed, expressed in musical simplicity, or with rhythmic distinction.

3

"How Far Should Our Teaching and Text-books Have a Scientific Basis?" PMLA (1884–85)

H. C. G. Brandt

Herman Carl George Brandt (1850–1920) was born in Germany and studied at the Universities of Göttingen, Freiburg, and Strassburg. Brandt received his Ph.D. at the Johns Hopkins University in 1886, around the time American Ph.D. programs were starting to surpass the German ones which they had emulated. He was a member of the heroic first generation of Hopkins graduates who would go on to propagate the gospel of scientific study of the modern languages in the formative years between 1880 and 1900.

Brandt taught German at Hamilton College (1874–76), at Hopkins (1876–82), and again at Hamilton (1883–1920). He authored a *German Science Reader* (1897), collaborated on a German and English dictionary, and edited Gotthold Lessing's *Nathan the Wise* (1895). It was Brandt who transcribed March's "Recollections of Language Teaching" (see Chapter 2) for publication in *PMLA*.

The present selection was delivered at the Modern Language Association's first meeting in 1883. It is of particular interest because of the candid way it addresses the "image-problem" of studies in English and modern languages, which were regarded by many at the time as not susceptible to the rigorous demands of Greek and Latin or the emerging sciences. Brandt's warning that unless language studies can be made scientific, the general view will continue to be that "any body can teach English," illustrates the professional status considerations which helped make philological science the basic methodology of early departments.

At a meeting of Natural Science Men, held a couple of years ago at Berlin, the question which I have proposed to ourselves was discussed. Much to the surprise of the adherents of Darwinism, Prof. Virchow maintained, that the doctrine of Darwin should not be taught in any institution lower than the University, that it should not enter the text-book of natural history used in a school of any grade from the volks schule up to the Gymnasium and

Realschule. I am not able to judge whether Virchow's view is too conservative in the field of natural science. But it is possible in any branch of learning to set before students theories and generalizations when they ought to be fed upon the old, hard and dry facts and laws. This method is the more vicious; the newer these theories and the vaguer these generalizations. But when the latest results consist of new facts and new laws of language well established, conservatism in the adoption and in the teaching of them becomes a great fault and a great injustice. I admit, that there is danger in going too fast and too far in adopting and teaching the new results, but in the department of Modern Languages as in many other departments the danger lies in the other direction, not merely in ultra-conservatism in appropriating and digesting the new results, not merely in ignoring them, but in unpremeditated, unconscious, down right ignorance of them.

I am ready to lay down and defend the following proposition: All teaching should start from a strictly scientific basis, and all aids in teaching, the text-books, reference books, etc., should be constructed upon a strictly scientific basis.

It may seem to some of you that I am re-asserting what nobody denies, and want to defend what nobody attacks. But let us not be deceived:

1. There are plenty of Classical Philologists—claiming to be the philologists par excellence, sneering at the same time at Comparative Philology and its results—who deny that there is a scientific basis to Modern Philology. They assert, that the study of Modern Languages is hardly worthy of the serious pursuit of students and investigators.

2. There are many, who may not deny the claim of a science to the study of Modern Language, but they do not care whether it is or not. They want to learn how to read or to speak a little French or German or Italian, because the ability to do so is of great value to them. They are the utilitarians taking the "bread and butter view" of our study. Even if they are the devotees of another science, they do not hesitate to put themselves on a level with the merchant and the traveller, who want a little French and German, "just enough to get along, you know." They do not object to learning even "a little Latin and less Greek," because the vocabulary of their branch of learning is largely made up of words derived from Latin and Greek.

3. There are even teachers of modern languages, who do not realize, that their department is a science. They teach at random, some with a text-book, some without any. At best they satisfy the utilitarian's demands, and even this they could do better, if they took a strictly scientific starting-point.

I believe, therefore, that I am not asserting the obvious, when I declare that our department *is* a science, and that its teaching must be carried on accordingly.

Were this proposition accepted, it would not be very difficult to fix the extent, to which the latest results reached in our science should be taught in the class-room or—what amounts to the same thing—how far these results should be embodied in the text-books. In fact, were our Association not as limited as it is—for very good reasons, to be sure—and were our papers intended to be brought before the general public, I am not sure but it would be worth our while to state the reasons, why our department is a science. But among us this will hardly be necessary. I need only recall such names as ten Brink, Sweet, Skeat, Scherer, the father of the "Jung grammatiker," tho Saturn-like he would now devour his own children, Sievers, Paul, Verner, Braune, Kluge, Gröber, Tobler, Förster, Neumann. We recognize these men as the foremost among those who have developed within the last fifteen years the old humdrum, empirical treatment of living languages into the scientific study of them of to-day. They have done even more than that. Investigating the phenomena of *living* languages they have reached results which are valuable contributions to the science of language and comparative philology. They have started a new branch of philology, viz., Phonetics, invented new methods of investigation, and gained deep insight into the nature of language—I refer to Paul's *Principien der Sprachzenhihte*. These men are modern-language men. They are Professors of either English, German or French (excepting Sweet) in England and Germany. And yet we are told, that these men and we, their pupils and humble followers, have no science as the basis and the goal of our endeavors!

Let us be bold enough to take for granted that we have a science and inquire now, why and how we should resort to this science in our teaching.

Let me give first a few reasons why:

1. By basing our instruction and text-books upon a scientific ground-work, our department and our profession gain dignity and weight. It has been often remarked, with how much justice I do not care to discuss that the still prevailing method of teaching Latin and Greek is old-fashioned, stale and stereotyped. The trouble with our teaching of modern languages is, that it is loose, random, unsystematic. This trouble is partly due to the fact, that our students come to us with such various objects in view. One wants to *speak* French only, the other to *read* it only, and only Prose at that, so that he can read French scientific books and journals. The third wants to study it thoroughly, the fourth wants its literature and its philology. We naturally vary our methods in teaching these groups of students. But we can go too far in this. The student who wants only to speak French, that is, to acquire a couple hundred phrases and a vocabulary to talk about the weather and all kinds of "small talk," has little claim upon the instructor in a high-school, college or university. Even the *natural method* can hardly save him at his age. He should have begun in the nursery, when the mother as the "bonne" was all in all to him, primer, grammar, dictionary and literature. We cannot bring back to him in our class-rooms the conditions in which the *natural method* is the only proper one. The *natural* method can have no claim upon us. I distinguish

between the natural and the *oral* method, which combined with grammar and exercises, is the best preparation for acquiring a speaking knowledge. It is even quite feasible to accustom a large class to the spoken word and train the *ear* as well as the *eye*. But the *natural* method we cannot use. For all other methods the ground-work should be scientific. I mean by that, that for instance the systems of inflection which the students learn should be such as can be traced to older systems, and be compared with those of related languages. Even if the student never study the language in its older periods, and only wants to acquire ability to read ordinary prose, the lowest purpose anyone can have. As another instance, taken from German, the terminology should be scientific, though we never go so far as to study the nature and history of Ablaut, Umlaut and other phonetic laws, the scientific terms can be used in the most elementary section of the grammar.

A scientific basis dignifies our profession. I do not wish to hurt any body's feelings, or bite off my own nose—for I am a foreigner myself—but our calling suffers from a large number of foreign-born teachers, who have never gone through any course of preparation and training for their work. The foreigner too often knows English very imperfectly, is a violent advocate of the natural method and takes to teaching, because he thinks he is naturally fitted for teaching his mother-tongue. The American teacher too often neglects the phonetics of the foreign tongue, teaches German or French because he has happened to sojourn a while in Germany or France, or because in the department for which he has really prepared himself abroad, there happens to be no vacancy at home. In short, the feeling is, *any body* can teach French or German or what is just as dangerous, any body can teach English. By introducing scientific methods, we shall show before very long that every body cannot so teach, that the teacher must be as specially and as scientifically trained for his work in our department as well as in any other.

2.   A scientific basis for our instruction and text-books is easiest, even for the beginner and for the student, who never goes farther into the language than is usually required in college or for admission to college. The so-called "practical" arrangements are often so fanciful, the rules so weighed down with exceptions, the groupings so arbitrary, that even with the large amount of exercises after the Ollendorfian system, the student might as well learn the inflection of each noun and each verb by itself. When the student advances to the elective and maximum courses of the college, and to the historical and comparative work of the university, the advantage of the scientific ground-work of his elementary course is apparent to every instructor able to conduct higher studies.

3.   A scientific basis affords a valuable discipline, otherwise, not attained from the study of a living language. There is a great deal of prejudice still on this score against our department, strongest, perhaps, against the study of English. But the prejudice that if any discipline is to be gained from the study

of languaes, Greek and Latin are *the* ones to be studied, has been shaken somewhat of late. But I want to say frankly that I cannot go the whole length that some of us and representatives of other departments have gone in the opposition to Greek and Latin. Our friends representing the Romance languages and English cannot do without Latin under any circumstances.

I am not in favor of throwing Greek overboard and taking on any amount of Modern Language to replace it. I always feel misgivings when we speak of a modern language as "replacing," as a "substitute for," or as an "equivalent of" Greek. But I do think, that French "im aller weitsten Sinn" ["in any broad sense," ed.] scientifically studied is worth as a disciplinary study, any amount of the old-fashioned syntactical gymnastics, which generally stands for Latin or Greek.

When "English" meant, and too often still means a certain amount of orthœpy, elocution, style and literature, when we teach French and German as if they were accomplishments like dancing, fencing, or final touches to be put on (to) young ladies in their seminaries at an extra charge, and on (to) young gentlemen, who have not brains enough to get into college, our department is justly charged with affording no mental discpline. Let "English" mean as it should and as it is bound to mean more and more, the historical scientific study of the language, Beowulf and Chaucer. Let "German" for students of the grade with which we have mainly to do mean an intelligent acquisition of its sounds, a drill in the various laws of its phonology, Ablaut, Umlaut, Grimm's Law, English and German corresponderes and cognates, syntactical analysis of Lessing's and Schiller's Prose, and of the difficult parts of Faust and of Nathan der Weise, the reading of the masterpieces of German literature, speaking and writing the language, and we claim without presumption, that the discipline acquired by going through such courses, while *different* from the discipline afforded by the study of Greek is not *inferior* to it. More than that. Two sides of this discipline Greek cannot afford at all, viz.:

1.   That gained from the exact analysis and reproduction of foreign sounds or in the case of English of the Old English pronunciation. The Greek and Latin sounds are difficult to reconstruct.

2.   That gained from so entering into the spirit of a foreign language as to be able not merely to appreciate its best literature which is the utmost attained in studying Greek, but to speak the language, to think in it, live in it, dream in it. Is it logical to claim that it trains the mental powers to reproduce the ancient Latin and to deny this to the reproduction of Neo-Latin? I have taken for granted that our department is a science and tried to give some reasons, *why* our instruction should have a scientific basis.

I will now briefly return to the question how far the latest scientific results shall enter our instruction. It seems clear, that when the results are pretty safely established, we should make use of them. They may not have been generally accepted yet. We cannot always wait for that. We *must* keep abreast of the latest research and sift its results. Every department will have its own tests.

In English and German, I think that Grassmann's and Verner's investigations, which have explained the two large groups of exceptions to Grimm's Law, should be made use of. I should leave alone all speculations about the cause and starting-point of the General Teutonic shifting, but the facts of Grimm's Law, including those of Verner's Law, ought to be taught. It is to be regretted that Sweet in his Anglo-Saxon Primer and Reader does not state the laws in the Phonology. He says, "s becomes r in the preterite plurals and past participles of strong verbs; th–d under the same conditions." Of course, these transitions take place according to Verner's Law, and why not state it? A student does not get that clear-cut impression from such separate statements of facts as Sweet gives. In the very next paragraph, he says, "r is often transposed," which means the transposition of r is no law. But the student ought to be made to understand clearly the difference between such an unexplained sporadic change as this and the interchange of s–r, th–d, which *must* take place, if there is such a thing as Verner's Law in the Teutonic Languages, which no one yet has ventured to gain say. In my opinion, there is nothing more stimulative of thinking and investigating than this conviction, that phonetic laws like physical laws, are not liable to unexplainable exceptions.

Of very few laws, it is true, *all* exceptions have been accounted for, but if the laws are firmly established and apparent exceptions are still unexplained, the greater is the benefit derived from studying and applying them. The fruitful work that has lately been done upon ablaut and accent can be made to tell in our treatment of strong verbs and word formation in a modern language, without shooting over the heads of students and entering too much into comparative philology. The strong-verb-classes should be based upon the now well established ablaut series. It is a mistake to expect students of college grade to learn the strong verbs individually and separately. They are learned more easily in the groups, into which they naturally fall according to their ablaut.

In conclusion, I will mention a very important subject, concerning which we ought, in my opinion, to teach the latest results, viz.: Phonetics. The analysis and synthesis of sounds is no mean branch of General Philology, though poohed at by many philologists. It certainly forms a large part of our work. We ought to employ above all the analysis of vowels by their articulation and not by the effect upon the ear, according to the Bell-Sweet system, now also adopted by Sievers. Persons from 14 to 20 years old ought not to be expected to learn foreign sounds by the almost unconscious imitation, proper enough in the nursery. Sounds can be acquired without knowing the movements of the organs of speech, just as I can raise my arm without knowing the movements of muscles. But by scientific instruction we can save time, and attain an accuracy otherwise never reached by adults. Think also of the large number of our students who have no aptitude for acquiring new sounds. By imitation alone they never acquire them. If we teach them the articulation according to a scientific system, it is possible to redeem some from their awkwardness and helplessness.

4

"The College Course in English Literature, How it May Be Improved," *PMLA* (1884–85)

James Morgan Hart

Most early professors of English saw themselves primarily as teachers of language, not of literature. Yet some of them had begun to question this restriction of scope as early as the first Modern Language Association meeting in 1883. Though a trained philologist and an enthusiastic promoter of the German model of higher education, Hart at that meeting offered a plea for the teaching of literature by trained professionals, versed in philology. But he also argued for the separation of language and literature classes, and mapped out one of the earliest proposals for a systematic pursuit of literary study. Hart's argument for the importance of organizing that study in *periods* according to "the great lines of division" illustrates the early hold of this idea as well as some of the perplexities it would soon lead to.

The possibility of bettering the present curriculum in English literature will depend in great measure upon the proportion of time allowed to it. So long as the classics and mathematics retain for themselves the lion's share of time and interest, the hopes of our professors of literature will never become unduly exalted. If I may express myself with thorough frankness, the customary quota of English literature, say less than two hours per week for less than two years, is so insufficient that I cannot look upon it as capable of improvement. The study will remain perforce hurried and superficial. Now the course that I have in mind is one of two full hours (better three) throughout three entire years. It is the course which has been required since 1880 for the B. L. degree in the University of Cincinnati, vis., three years, three hours a week. The classical students are now (beginning with 1884) compelled to take two of the three years, and the Scientifics one year. Perhaps this last requirement will be hereafter raised to two years.

How is this amount of time to be best utilized? I confess that at more than one point I am in doubt; at least, my past experience is still to some extent only experimental.

1. What does *not* rightfully pertain to English Literature? Settling this preliminary question will help us greatly. The main question resolves itself into three: What are we to do with Logic, with Rhetoric, with English Philology (Anglo-Saxon and Early English)? Fortunately the Logic question is fast settling itself. The growth of this study has been so rapid of late, its drift towards mathematics and the experimental sciences so unmistakable, that no disciplined mind of the present day can look upon logic and literature as having anything in common. As to Rhetoric, the course is not so clear. There are still only too many persons of influence and culture who persist in looking upon the instructor of English literature as necessarily the instructor of rhetoric. I am unable to share this opinion. To me rhetoric is a purely formal drill, having no more connection with the literature of England than it has with the literature of Greece, Rome, France, Germany, or Arabia. The canons of the art were laid down two thousand years ago by Aristotle, and quite one thousand years before there was an English literature in any sense.

To my way of thinking, the study of English literature means the study of the great movement of English life and feeling, as it is reflected in the *purest* prose of representative men; those men who have led their people's sympathies. Rhetoric always savors to me of the school-bench. It is, if we look into it scrutinizingly, little more than verbal jugglery. And however clever we may be at it ourselves, however quick we may be at perceiving it in others, we shall be none the wiser in *understanding* an author, the influences that moulded him, his peculiar mission, his hold upon us. The proper object of literary study, in one word, is to train us to *read*, to grasp an author's personality in all its bearings. And the less rhetoric here, the better—in my judgment. Rhetorical exercises are, of course, useful. So are the parallel bars and dumb-bells of a gymnasium. Need I push the comparison farther?[*]

In the next place, how is it with Anglo-Saxon and Early English? I think that here most of us have confounded two radically distinct matters, vis., literature and language. Literature is thought. Were, now, the connection of thought between our King Alfred of pious memory and our Queen Victoria an unbroken continuity, I could spare my time. I should say at once, unhesitatingly, that it would be our *duty* to master Beowulf and Elene just as

---

[*] I do not wish to be understood as arguing in general against the utility of training in Rhetoric and Composition. In fact, such training seems to me an indispensable part of the school-curriculum. The above strictures are aimed solely at Rhetoric and Compositon, as they are often taught in College. In my experience, college-students have a positive dislike of such drill, while they are almost invariably attracted to literature proper. It seems to me that Rhetoric, if taught at all in College, should be taught by the professor of Philosophy. It should come *after* the instruction in literature, should be treated in a very liberal spirit, in fact, as a national mode of *envisager* the subject, and especially should the instruction be of a kind to contrast ancient methods and tastes with modern, English with continental. It will be perceived that all this is very different from recitation upon Tropes, Introduction, and Arguments and from the writing of Themes.

the Athenians and Alexandrians mastered the Iliad and the Odyssey. But alas, the case is quite otherwise. However unpleasantly the confession may go against my own personal interest and sympathy, as a devoted specialist in Anglo-Saxon philology, I must confess that everything anterior to the Conquest is as foreign to our way of thinking as if it had been expressed in a foreign tongue. It is more foreign even than the thought of the Greeks and Romans. I do not see what literary *culture* our undergraduates can possibly derive from any English writings anterior to Chaucer's. And even Chaucer, whom I sincerely and heartily relish, is—shall I say—*double-faced?* He is a colossal sphinx. We look at him from one side, and his smile is sunny and inviting, and we hail him as one of ourselves, as indeed our literary father. But when, by dint of patient exploration, we have struggled around to the other side, we discover that our so-called father is the veriest *enfant perdu* of all the grossness, folly, superstition, and prattle that go by the name of the Middle Ages. By all means let us read our Chaucer. He is too poetical a poet to be ignored. But when we read, let us remember that he is not wholly one of us. There is a gulf between him and the meanest of the great Elizabethans.

I have expressed doubt as to the utility of Anglo-Saxon in a course of English literature. But if Anglo-Saxon be taught, let me make one suggestion. Our present method is a wrong one. We put our students into the most difficult and archaic poetry, and ignore the easy prose vernacular. This is anything but wise. Granting that Beowulf is a spirited poem, the noblest relic of ancient Germanic spirit, is it not too obscure for the non-specialist? And if, by dint of commentaries, we help the student over the hard places, have we given him the best insight into the language, which is—after all—the chief object of the study? . . .

On one point, at least, I have no doubts, viz., that every *teacher* of our literature should have made careful study of Anglo-Saxon and Early English. There are in modern speech hundreds of linguistic survivals which the trained eye sees through at a glance, but which are a perpetual stumbling block to the empiric. . . .

2. Passing from this preliminary discussion of negatives to the more positive question: How is English literature, as literature, to be taught, I wish to say a word or two upon the importance of teaching it by *periods*. Whatever be the amount of time at our disposal, we shall not do our whole duty by our pupils, if we neglect to impress upon their minds the observance of the great lines of division. They are only two—the first ends with the death of Milton; the second, with the death of Samuel Johnson. Of course these lines are not the hard, fixed lines of the geometrician or the statistician. They are ideal lines, merely serving to keep us within proper bounds. What does it matter that Dryden's authorship overlaps Milton's? Such juxtaposition only heightens the contrast. Matthew Arnold has called Milton "the last of the Immortals." In general I do not subscribe to Mr. Arnold's literary dicta. But this once

certainly he hit the mark. Milton is the direct successor and last survivor of Sidney, Spenser, and Shakespeare. So far as he is of any age and not for all time, he is of the great Elizabethan age. . . . With regard to the first great period, although it begins with Spenser and ends with Milton, we are to remember that its typical form is the drama, and our chief efforts should be directed towards the proper treatment of Shakespeare. For the study of Shakespeare himself there is no lack of appliances. Yet I do not believe that the great dramatist is rightly studied. He is isolated too much. We put our students into reading him before they are prepared. Thanks to Mr. Ward's excellent history of the English drama (now supplemented by Mr. Symonds on the Predecessors of Shakespeare), the teacher can give, by lecture, an adequate treatment of the origin of the English drama. But this is not enough. The student should catch the tone and temper of the pre-Shakespeareans by reading them. Just here, alas, we break down. Mr. Morley's English Plays is not only an unwieldy and expensive book, but it is wretchedly planned and swarms with errors of every kind, yet it is the only book that attempts to cover the ground. The selections made by Charles Lamb, fifty years ago, are palpably inadequate. What we need is two volumes of selections, of equal size, say corresponding to Lamb's selections, one giving the quintessence of the best pieces prior to Shakespeare (but excluding Marlowe), the other treating in like manner Ben Jonson and the others down to the reign of Charles I. I exclude Marlowe for the reason that his two leading plays, Faustus and Edward II, are now procurable in very good shape.

I have often tried to imagine to myself what results a year of this work might produce. A year that should include the first book of the Faery Queen, and some of Sidney's Sonnets, selections from Gorboduc, from Lyly, Greene, Kyd, three entire plays by Shakespeare, selections from Ben Jonson, Chapman, Webster, Ford, down to Shirley, and Milton's Comus. Such a year, would make, I think, an indelible impression upon the class. The second section, beginning with Dryden and ending with Samuel Johnson, is less interesting, because less poetic, but is perhaps more directly useful. With the aid of Mr. Hales's book, Arnold's selections from Johnson's Lives, and Mr. Minto's Manual of English Prose, the teacher can scarcely fail to make his pupils understand how the founders of our modern style thought and expressed themselves.

The third section, again, is difficult, but not for lack of books or good material. The difficulty consists in knowing precisely where and how to begin. I have been for years in the habit of training my pupils to look upon Wordsworth, and especially upon his Tintern Abbey, as the starting-point of our nineteenth century poet. Even this meets with objection from some quarters, I have perceived. Yet I cannot give up the position until some one offers me a better . . .

5

"The Place of English in the College Curriculum," PMLA (1884–85)

Theodore W. Hunt

Theodore Whitfield Hunt (1884–1930) graduated from Princeton University in 1865 and was licensed as a Presbyterian minister by the Princeton Theological Seminary in 1869. Instead of the ministry, Hunt chose to study Old English at the University of Berlin and at Lafayette College, where he took his Ph.D. in 1880. Hunt became the first chairman of the Princeton English Department, where he taught until 1918. Hunt's writings include *Principles of Written Discourse* (1884); *Ethical Teachings in Old English Literature* (1892); and *Studies in Literature and Style* (1890).

Like H. C. G. Brandt, Hunt in the present selection urges the need to upgrade English from its status of "decided inferiority" in order to become a worthy competitor to the classics. Unlike Brandt, however, Hunt believes that this upgrading would best be accomplished by the development of a "study of literature and style" having the same systematic method as linguistic criticism. In Hunt's aggressive vision, such a change would not be simply internal to the academy. As he puts it, "Literary culture should be more and more a scholarly culture," and the college should hold "a control over national culture and furnish the main material for its propagation."

Taken together, then, the selections from Brandt, Hart, and Hunt suggest that as early as the mid-1880s modern language scholars had already begun to disagree about whether philology or what Hunt calls "general literary culture" should be the primary model of literary study.

It is now customary among the most advanced students of modern education to divide the area of collegiate studies into the three great departments of Science, Philosophy, Language and Literature. Although within the sphere of a liberal training there are some studies not strictly included in this division, it is for all practical purposes a convenient and comprehensive one. It is with the last of these three departments that the present paper will deal. We mean by English,—the English Language and Literature as including, also, the subject of English style and criticism. The place of English as thus defined among other collegiate branches is one of the many open questions before the educators and the educated public of to-day. It is a quetsion so prominent and so urgently pressing for discussion and adjustment, that it must in some way be met. In the recent Modern Language Convention held at Columbia College, N.Y., it elicited special interest and clearly indicated the drift of modern opinion regarding it. It is the object of the present informal discussion to say a word on its behalf, if so be the department of English in our American Colleges may be more truly appreciated and a more generous provision be made for its needs.

The Present Place of English (in our Collegiate System)

It is patent to every careful observer of our educational methods that this place is one of decided inferiority. A cursory examination of the catalogues of our leading institutions will clearly reveal such an inferiority. In the oldest and what may be supposed to be the best regulated college of the country, we are told "that less than one-half as much instruction is offered in English as in the ancient tongues." A more extreme statement may be made as to most of our important colleges. There are a few institutions indeed that constitute a pleasing exception. Such is Lafayette, "the first American College," as Prof. Owen states "that fully recognized the claims of English studies." This was as early as 1857. Such is Cornell University. Such, also, is The University of California, where the English schedule is especially full. Such, strange to say, are some of the smaller and weaker colleges of the South and West. In the great body of our colleges, however, the place of English is quite subordinate to that of all other related departments. This is true as to the time allotted it, and the results expected from it so that the average graduate knows everything else among liberal studies better than he knows his own language and literature, and can do almost anything else better than express his ideas in clear, vigorous and elegant English. Todhunter, in his Conflict of Studies—makes no reference to English whatever, as if, indeed, it had no place at all in an educational scheme. Mr. Staunton, in his Great Schools of England, laments this neglect as he says, "Of all the chief modern languages, English is, perhaps, the worst spoken and written by educated men." Mr. Thwing in his "American Colleges" writes, "Most colleges offer very meagre opportunities for the study of the origin and growth of either our language or our literature." In a carefully prepared table showing the number of hours assigned to the different departments in twenty of our best colleges, he clearly proves this strong assertion.—(Amer. Colleges, p. 23). *

* Hunt here and later makes reference to the views of several of the most influential reformer-presidents of late nineteenth century American colleges: Charles Franklin Thwing (1853–1937) of Western Reserve; Charles William Eliot (1834–1926) of Harvard; Noah Porter (1811–1892) of Yale; James McCosh (1811–1894) of Princeton; and Andrew D. White (1832–1918) of Cornell.

It is in point to allude to one or two causes of this neglect: as seen in Defective Teaching and Want of Appreciation.

No department of college work has so suffered as the English at the hands of novices. In no department is there greater need of what might be called, Collegiate Service reform. Men are often appointed to English chairs apparently for no other reason than that they are able to speak the language grammatically and have a general society knowledge of the literature. Men who are still experimenting as to what their life-work is to be are willing, in the mean time, to do English work as a means to a higher end and on such terms are accepted by Boards of Trustees. Shamefully prevalent as this is in the lower schools, it is not without frequent illustration in our higher institutions. Hence the department is committed to those who have had no experience in conducting it; who do not and cannot appreciate its scope; who know nothing of its best methods and whose presence in it is mainly for personal ends. The anathemas of Alfred, of Chaucer and of Addison should rest upon them. The common sentiment, that any one can teach his vernacular, has been a curse to the English Department and largely accounts for what we see in the line of neglect and accepted inferiority. We agree with President Eliot "that there is no subject in which competent guidance and systematic instruction are of greater value." In this day of specialties, English is no exception. Its sphere is unique and it calls for special preparation. It may be noted further, that the inferior place assigned to English is partly due to that strange depreciation of the department which obtains so generally among parents, preparatory teachers, Boards of Trustees, Faculties of Arts, and with the general public. Some of this is comparatively thoughtless and innocent. Much of it, however, is blameworthy and is none the less so because it is based on educational traditions. It is the habit to underrate the vernacular. It is not one of the "substantial and necessary" departments as we are told. Its philology, it is said, takes us back to the barbarous days of the Anglo-Saxons; its literature ranks among the self-acquired accomplishments of the student rather than among the difficult and "regular" studies, while its actual expression in composition and literary criticism must be left to natural methods. It occurs to us that there is nothing more trying to a sensitive English scholar than the attitude which many college professors in other departments are pleased to assume, relative to the English. This attitude is at times one of indifference. At times it is patronizing and cynical. The reference here is not to scientific men whose interests as instructors are in widely different lines but to those who are identified with the departments of philosophy and the ancient languages and who are thereby presumed to have a just appreciation of all that pertains to the humanities. The English Department in our colleges has had to fight its way not only against illiteracy and ignorant prejudice but, also, against the persistent opposition of those from whom better things were expected. Whatever the causes, however, of the fact may be, the fact itself remains, that the historical place of English in our higher institutions has been a mere apology for a place, and it now claims a more generous acknowledgment. It insists, moreover, that its claims are reasonable and should at once be heeded.

The Rightful Place of English (in the Curriculum)

This, we hold, should be a *prominent* one, not meaning by this a place of precedence or supremacy, but an equitable position among other important linguistic and literary studies. President Eliot, in his suggestive article on "Liberal Education" (Century, June, '84), makes, perhaps, some extreme assertions. The drift of the paper, however, is in the right direction, and approaching changes in educational methods will prove the wisdom of most of his propositions. Among the statements not extreme is this: "The first subject which is entitled to recognition as of equal academic value with any subject now most honoured is, 'The English Language and Literature.' " These words may be accepted as the text of our discussion in this paper. It states just the truth, and in the most concise form. It is not traditional as to say with the ultra conservative classicist that no change in the adjustment of the ancient and the modern is to be for a moment tolerated, nor is it so erratic as to insist that the old landmarks must be erased and the newer studies take precedence of all else. President Eliot is not arguing against the older so much as he is arguing in favor of the more recent regime. He is contending for the interests of modern history, of social, political and natural science and of English. The claim is that English should have "equal academic value" in the schedule with any other department of value. Instead of retaining that grossly unjust disproportion of time which Mr. Thwing's tabulated statement reveals, being, in some cases, ten hours to one in favor of the foreign tongues, the proposal would secure something like a fair adjustment. It is not our purpose to discuss at this juncture the open question of classical teaching now before the American colleges. It touches the English question, however, just at this point and needs a passing notice. The question is not, Must the classics go? nor is it the more specific question, Must the Greek go? It is only the bigot and charlatan who would entertain, for a moment, either of these questions as related to college courses. The question is, will the classics as taught in our colleges make any concessions of their large amount of time to the modern languages appealing for such time? More specifically, will they make such concession to the English? We are within the department of language and literature. In that department, the place of English has been almost a cipher. The ancient languages have had the field. English now applies for more space in the department—for its rightful place. Inasmuch as the modern European tongues are themselves in need of similar allowances, these concessions must be made on the classical side. From the outside departments of science and philosophy it is evident that nothing can be justly asked. It may be said, therefore, that the acknowledgment of this claim depends on the attitude of the classical brotherhood and on the strength of the English movement behind the claim. If such concessions are made voluntarily by classicists, the question will be solved beneficiently to all concerned. If such concessions are stoutly denied, then the desired result will be secured more slowly and irregularly, but will still be secured, by the simple pressure of the modern upon the ancient. This has already been partially illustrated. The elective classical courses in our colleges are, in the main, a reluctant concession to educational pressure from without and these courses are increasing rather than lessening, beginning in Harvard even in the first year, and in some other institutions not later than the second. The demand of the English in common with that of some other studies is,—Give us a fair place in the general adjustment. Let us work together as languages on a common ground and for a common end, but no longer on this enormous disproportion. Such a claim is made, partly, because of what the English is in itself as a language and literature and partly because we are living in an era when the vernacular must be understood as never before,—when all that is English must have "ample room and verge enough" to give it its proper expression in the national history.

Within the general sphere of college studies, science made such a claim, and being denied, has established its separate schools of a professional order. Within the general department of philosophical study, similar claims are made by teachers of historical, political, and social science, and as these claims are unheeded, movements are even now in progress looking to the founding of separate schools, as in Columbia and the University of Pennsylvania.

Similar claims are made and similar schemes are agitated as to the French and German. It is not impossible that a persistent denial of the reasonable demands of English may lead to the organization of special schools where it can be taught with sufficient fulness. Whatever might be true of other departments, such an order of things would not be well as to English, in that the various branches of the one department of language and literature are so coordinated as to make their combined study logically necessary. In that "Renovated Curriculum" to which Professor Bain refers, a desirable adjustment can be reached on more rational methods. In some way or another the claims of the vernacular, so long and so urgently pressed, must be heeded and adjusted. Such an adjustment, we believe, will be practically effected within the experience of men now living.

Consequent Changes and Benefits

a. It is evident, at once, that from such a reconstruction of the English curriculum important results would ensue. There would be, as first in order, A *more serious attention to elementary English in our preparatory schools.* Up to the present time there may be said to have been no well-established English course in the large majority of such schools. The colleges have not required it and the schools have had no occasion of furnishing it. . . .

If asked what specific modification of preparatory English the rightful place of English in college would secure, we answer, the *remanding of the first year of collegiate English to the lower schools.* This would effect the double end of arranging English justly both in school and at college and place the entering student at once upon a basis from which the best results would be reached. In addition to a more thorough knowledge of what is at present required, the student should appear tolerably well acquainted with the history of the English language in its outline facts and periods: with a fair knowledge of English etymology and structure; with a substantial familiarity with the composite elements of the English vocabulary and conversant with, at least, the primary facts of historical English literature from the time of Bacon. All this is elementary, but essential. It would at once awaken new impulses in the student's mind, would open out a wide and an attractive field of study and would start him on his college work with an impartial judgment as to the claims of this or that department of activity. Mr. Hales, in his Essays on Liberal Education, contends for this in reference to the schools of England. President Porter pleads for it in reference to the schools of America. Nothing will secure it but the proper position of English in the colleges. Could a few of our first colleges have the wisdom and the heroism to state these high terms of entrance and hold to them, the problem would be solved. In the present unseemly rivalry as to numbers among our leading institutions, it is Utopian, we fear, to expect this. Here, again, public opinion may compel educators to do what they refuse voluntarily to do. Perchance, the lower schools themselves, under the influence of such popular pressure, may compel the colleges to elevate their standards.

b.   Closely connected with this result attendant upon a rightful adjustment of collegiate English there would ensue, A *healthful change in the methods and benefits of the teaching itself.* Instruction purely primary and limited having had its proper place in the elementary course, would now give way to a more advanced order of work. The purely historical method of dates and names, incidents and events, would now be secondary to the philosophic and critical methods. By safely gradationed stages the study of the English language would rise from a somewhat formal examination of phraseology and structure to a real philological study of the tongue in its content and its great linguistic changes, its inner spirit, and its possibilities. The study of mere grammatical laws as formulated by Brown would yield to the higher methods of such masters as Earle and Morris. Words would become, in Baconian phrase, "the footsteps and prints of reason." Principles and processes would take the place of mere detail and the interest resulting be commensurate with the increased profit. So as to the study of literature and style. This at once would become critical and comprehensive in distinction from being merely chronological.

The main facts being already in the possession of the student, an advance could at once be made to something like the process of generalization. The inductive principle in literary study is as valuable as it is in other realms and can be fully applied only in the event of assigning a larger place to English work. The current errors, that English literature is a subject for the desultory reader in his leisure hours rather than an intellectual study for serious workers; that it ranks as an accomplishment only, and that the terms literary and philosophic, are mutually exclusive, are errors that have been strengthened by the superficial methods on which the subject has been taught in most of our institutions. The enlargement of the collegiate course in English will correct all this. It will substitute the disciplinary for the aesthetic method and give true literary inspiration rank above mere verbal finish. The soul of the authorship will determine its excellence. The study will become psychological. It is this order of study and teaching that President Eliot has in mind when he insists that the purely disciplinary value of English literary study has been greatly underrated. If it begin and end with fact only, it is easy to see that apart from the training of the memory, there is no exercise of the intellectual powers in it. If, however, by reason of preceding drill in the schools, the collegiate teaching may at once assume high ground, the study will take its place thereby with all other studies of a philosophic order and the result will be mental breadth and vigor. As President Porter remarks, "The critical study of English Literature cannot be overestimated. It is thus that the spirit of independent activity can be most effectively directed."

As a natural result of this better method our college classes would receive what could justly be called a thorough English education. As a matter of fact, they are, at present, greatly deficient in this regard. Nor are we speaking here of an ignorance of that general English knowledge which is obtained by all students from the various branches of their collegiate work, but of those specific subjects formally falling under the English Department. Such deficiency on the part of the average graduate is greater than in any other important branch. Upon leaving college, he knows less of his vernacular than of any other language that has come before him and knows that little with less thoroughness. He has never been called to master the speech and letters of England as he has mastered those of other lands. Assuming an innate knowledge of these subjects not really possessed, he is led to depreciate and neglect them. For such a state of things the present narrowness of the English course is responsible, and the remedy lies in enlargement and thoroughness. The pupil would then have time under the guidance of judicious instruction to make himself substantially conversant with First English Philology in Cædmon, Bêowulf and Alfred; to study its characteristics and structure; to mark its transition through the middle English of Layamon and Langlande to

Chaucer and Spenser; to mark the great historical periods of Modern English from the Elizabethan to the Victorian; to study it in its relation to other Teutonic tongues—in fine to take up for the first or more minutely a thousand questions on which the college student should be informed and in virtual ignorance of which he is, at present, compelled to graduate.

So, in the province of English criticism and Literature, as the field here is still wider, the deficiencies of the average graduate and the benefits of an enlargement of the course are all the more marked. In such leading institutions as Yale and Princeton, it would seem to be in the line of travesty to assign to the professor of English Literature not more than two hours a week for one-half of the course and expect him to ground his classes therein. An application of Dr. Taylor's classical method or of Professor March's Philological method to the study of Shakespeare alone would scarcely conduct the student beyond the first half-dozen plays in the two years. Any proper study of the grand department of English Prose Authors would more than fill up such an allotment of time. What a host of topics—historical, linguistic, legendary, poetic and rhetorical—gathers about one such poem as the Faerie Queen or Comus! What deep and broad reaching questions of theology, metaphysics, social economy and literature center in The Essay on Man! Who could study the Dunciad and not make himself familiar with a vast amount of English biography and history? The study of the great forms of poetry, of the principles of poetic art, of the leading canons of style as illustrated in English classics, of the life and times of an author as related to his literary productions, of the influence of other literatures upon the English—the study of such germinal topics as these now necessarily passed with discursive comment, would by the readjustment of the course receive something like the attention they deserve and "furnish forth" the student with the knowledge he so much needs. Every graduate of an American college should be thoroughly conversant at his graduation with just such a body of English teaching as we have outlined. He owes it to himself as an English-speaking man to be thus "thoroughly furnished" and so prepared to do his work in the world among his English fellows.

c. It is pertinent here to remark that it is only by such a widening of the course in English that the *important problem as to efficient English teachers can be solved.* In no surer way would the training of a body of high class English instructors be secured. It is often said by way of adverse criticism that despite the urgent need of competent teachers of English, the English department in our colleges fails to provide them. The charge is a just one and the explanation lies in the direct line of our discussions. The course is too restricted to do anything more than give the barest outline and introduction of the subject. Certainly, nothing can be done in the way of making teachers or awakening in students such a desire. The only remedy is, in that expansion of the course by which the student would be truly educated in English. Dr. Porter, in his article on Preparatory Schools, makes timely allusion to this duty of the college. It is one of the first obligations of every important department of college study to furnish competent teachers in that department. One of the best tests of the efficiency of a department is found at this point. No pastor should more certainly look for converts under his preaching and pastoral care than should the college professor look among his classes for those desirous of becoming teachers and able to do so. The departments of classics, mathematics and philosophy have partially succeeded in this from the fact that what has been denied the English has been accorded them. If the trustees of our colleges desire a succession of superior English professors, then must the English course be made by them "of equal academic rank" with any other department. The curse of Jehovah is still on the theory of bricks without straw. Students properly educated in English would call at once for graduate courses in such studies, by the agency of which a continuous body of high class English scholars would be ready on demand. The reactionary influence of this upon the colleges and the lower schools would be stimulating in the extreme.

d. We allude to a single further benefit of the rightful adjustment of English.—The *marked increase of English Literary Culture in our colleges and in the country*. As to the special absence of this, at present, nothing need be said. The need is obvious to every observer. It would scarcely be aside from the truth to say that with the exception of one or two of our American institutions, our colleges are, in no true sense, literary centers. We are using the term literary in its specific sense as related to the study of English, quite distinct from that other literary influence connected with classical studies or from that general literary culture which results from the pursuit of the liberal arts. General literary culture and special classical culture are often found where a definite English literary culture is lacking and this we are bound to maintain, is for English speaking students the highest form of culture. In speaking of our colleges as the literary institutions of the country, special emphasis is to be given to that form of literary culture which is distinctively English. No amount of general culture and no amount of any specific culture from other sources than English study will give it. It must have the home flavor. In the sphere of English literary criticism what lamentable failures are daily seen on the part of those critics who bring no special English culture to their work but come to it only as general students, or as those conversant with the foreign tongues— ancient and modern. We insist that every American College should be instinct with English literary thought and life, so that faculty and students alike should feel it; so that those who come from the outside world to these institutions should feel it, and so that the effect of it upon the national life would be potent and elevating. We are speaking now to a point second to no other in the department of English as it stands related to academic and public life. We can but express our meaning here by raising the question so often raised, What are our colleagues doing specifically for English Literature in America—for

American Prose and Poetry? We are told on every hand that our literature is on the decline; that the heroic age of American Letters has no counterpart in modern times, and that in the main our literature is confined to fiction, periodicals and lighter verse, rather than to the great departments of creative prose and song. These questions are worth heeding. It is said by those acknowledging the charges, that the mission of America is not literary but industrial; that we are to expect an inferior order of literary art and a sluggish popular interest therein. It is stated, also, by way of palliation that the country is too young as yet for any decided development along these higher lines of national endeavor. These replies are partial and evasive. The difficulty lies deeper. Most of it is found in the want of a more distinctive literary English culture in our colleges. Students are not kept long enough in contact with the inner life of English Letters to take on something of that spirit which is resident therein. They fail to receive that literary bent and impulse which is the result of abiding, "communion with the visible forms" of English authorship. They are not sufficiently indoctrinated.

Hence, the large majority of our graduating classes go forth quite indifferent to the claims upon them of doing subsequent literary work, quite ignorant of the meaning and methods of such work, and quite uninterested, also, in the success or failure of the chosen few who may devote themselves to such activities. It is certainly not too much to say that in every graduating class of one hundred members there should be a goodly number of special English literary students—men who would be willing to survey, at least, the literary outlook in America and insist upon the assignment of good reasons why they should not make the attempt to do something in the field of national letters. What Milton terms "a complete and generous education" surely includes more fully that culture of the English mind and taste and heart, through the agency of which those possessing it will know all that is true and beautiful and good of an English character and be enabled to furnish such literary product for the appreciation of others. It is interesting to note that in the case of some of our earlier American authors, the high literary work of their maturity was somewhat anticipated in their collegiate days. It was thus with Motley, Prescott, Emerson, Everett, and Ticknor at Harvard. It was eminently so with Hawthorne and Longfellow at Bowdoin, as with Willis at Yale and with Bryant in his partial course at Williams. These and other writers that might be mentioned may be said to have begun their literary career at college. In addition to all that they owed to natural gifts, they owed something to that distinctive culture which was more prominent then in academic cirles than it is now.

It were highly desirable that more of our graduates might go forth with a similar preparation and purpose. If it is answered here, that the profession of literature is not lucrative, we have but to turn to the lives of some of these very authors, as Hawthorne and Bryant, or to such non-collegiate men as

Irving, Halleck, Cooper, and Bayard Taylor, to note through what personal struggles they went to realize their aims. It is surprising to mark how many of them reached literature through law, journalism and even business, or combined one of these pursuits with authorship itself. American literature is looking, as never before, to our colleges for her literary men,—her writers and critics, and this result, we repeat, will mainly depend upon a more serious attention in colleges to English work.

The place of English, therefore, in the college curriculum should be that of prominence. As the department of language and literature should rank with that of science or of philosophy, so, within the language department itself, the invidious distinctions that have so long had sway against the vernacular should yield by gradual concessions to a more equitable regime. In a division of hours among the Latin, Greek, French, German, and English, let the honest one-fifth of the time be set apart to each. President McCosh, in his last report to the trustees of Princeton College, writes: "As much as we appreciate other languages, we should set the *highest value* on our own."

President White, of Cornell, remarks: "It is impossible to find a reason why a man should be made B. A. for good studies in Cicero and Sophocles which does not equally prove that he ought to have the same distinction for good studies in Corneille, Schiller, Dante and Shakespeare." Recent statistics tell us "that notwithstanding the largely increased number of colleges in our country, the students in proportion to the population have been steadily decreasing for the last thirty years." The reference here is to colleges giving the degree of A. B. Among the assignable causes for such an anomaly it might not be amiss to ask whether an ultra conservative protest against the enlargement of the modern studies, and most especially of the vernacular, is not a possible one. Such an enlargement is at present before the American colleges with justifiable claims. It is noticeable that its attitude is becoming ever bolder and its educational and popular backing ever more formidable. Careful observers will not fail to note cheering signs of promise. Not only is it true, as Mr. Thwing asserts, "that the facilities for learning modern languages have vastly improved," but special facilities are at hand in the sphere of English. At no former period have such means been available. English philology has already taken its place in scholarly esteem side by side with that of any other tongue, while in English literature and criticism better and better results are realized. The question is practically before the colleges—whether this literary development is to be made safe and reputable by being under collegiate guidance. It lies, we believe, within the province and the high privilege of our liberal institutions to hold such a control over national culture and furnish the main material for its propagation. Literary culture should be more and more a scholarly culture. In the timely proposal that a larger place should be given to the modern studies, we press the claims of the native speech "to equal academic rank" with any other study of value. This should be done for its own sake as a language and literature, for the sake of our historical and providential relations to it as our vernacular, and by reason of the present era as eminently modern and English. On the ground, also, of those various benefits which such an expansion of English in the college curriculum will secure to the lower schools, to the colleges themselves, to the general American public and to American letters—we commend its temperate claims to the intelligent judgment and practical support of all those among us who have to do with educational reform.

6

Two English Programs in the 1890s, From *English in American Universities* (1895), Edited by William Morton Payne

Martin Wright Sampson and Charles Mills Gayley

In 1894, *The Dial*, a Chicago-based periodical, published a series of articles by professors of English reporting on the current state of English programs in American universities. Collected and published in 1895 by *Dial* editor William Morton Payne under the title *English in American Universities*, these papers provide the single most illuminating source of information on the form and rationale of college English studies just before the turn of the century. The *Dial* exchange testifies to the wide public interest at this time in the controversies of academic literary studies.

The selections from the collection presented here represent the thinking of two of the more advanced departments in the profession at the time. Both statements advocate a broad, critically oriented approach to English literature, and emphasize the need to elevate the analytic study characteristic of the professional over amateur appreciation and sentimentality.

Martin Wright Sampson (1866–1930) received an M. A. from the University of Cincinnati, where he studied English under James Morgan Hart. After a year at the University of Munich, he taught English at the State University of Iowa (1889–91), Stanford University (1892–93), Indiana University (1893–1906), where he chaired the department, and Cornell University (1906–30). An amateur poet and playwright, Sampson specialized in Elizabethan drama, English romantic poetry, and Milton. It is interesting to note how many of Sampson's observations in this selection anticipate ideas which we now tend to associate with the program of New Criticism some forty years later.

Charles Mills Gayley (1858–1932) received his B. A. from the University of Michigan in 1878 and studied at the Universities of Geissen and Halle in 1886–87. He taught Latin at Michigan from 1880–84, English from 1884–86 and 1887–89, and went to the University of California at Berkeley in 1889, where he served as chairman of the English Department and later Dean of Faculties, until his retirement in 1920. He was author (with Fred Newton Scott) of *A Guide to the Literature of Aesthetics* (1890), *Classic Myths in English Literature* (1893), and (with Scott) *Methods and Materials of Literary Criticism* (1899). As his statement indicates, Gayley, who at Berkeley became an enormously popular undergraduate lecturer, foresaw the educational potential of a more critically oriented approach to literature. For a more caustic view of Gayley's approach, however, see the memoir in Part III by his student, Frank Norris.

English at the University of Indiana

In September, 1893, the English department of the University of Indiana was completely reorganized. Six men—a professor, and five instructors—were appointed to carry on the work. The present course is our attempt to meet existing conditions. Each department must offer a full course of study leading to the bachelor's degree. Our students graduate in Greek, in mathematics, in sociology, in English, or in any one of the dozen other departments, with the uniform degree of A. B. About a third of the student's time is given to required studies, a third to the special work of the chosen department, and a third to elective studies. The department of English, then, is required to offer a four years' course of five hours a week; as a matter of fact, it offers considerably more.

The English courses fall into three distinct natural groups—language, composition, and literature,—in each of which work may be pursued for four or more years. One year of this work is required of all students; the rest is elective. With two exceptions, all our courses run throughout the year.

The linguistic work is under the charge of Mr. Harris. The elementary courses are a beginning class in Old English prose, and one in the history of the language. Then follow a course in Chaucer, the mystery plays, and Middle English romances and lyrics; an advanced course in Old English poetry, including a seminary study of *Béowulf*; the history of Old and Middle English literature; and a course in historical English grammar, which makes a special examination of forms and constructions in modern prose. In these classes the intention is to lead the student into independent investigation as soon as he is prepared for it.

In compositon, the work is as completely practical as we can make it. Writing is learned by writing papers, each one of which is corrected and rewritten. There are no recitations in "rhetoric." The bugbear known generally in our colleges as Freshman English is now a part of our entrance requirement, and university instruction in composition begins with those fortunate students who have some little control of their native language when a pen is between their fingers. We are still obliged, however, to supply instruction to students conditoned in entrance English, and the conditioned classes make the heaviest drain upon the instructors' time. The first regular class receives students who write clearly and can compose good paragraphs. The subjects of the year's work are narration, description, exposition. In the next year's class, an attempt is made to stimulate original production in prose and verse. A certain amount of criticism upon contemporary writing enters into this course—the object being to point out what is good in (for example) current magazines and reviews, and thus to hold before the student an ideal not altogether impossible of attainment. A young writer confronted with the virtues and defects of Macaulay and De Quincey is likelier to be discouraged or made indifferent, than inspired, as far as his own style is concerned. If he is shown wherein a "Brief" in *The Dial* is better than his own review of the book, he is in a fair way to improve. And so with the sketches, stories, and even poems. Of course current magazine writing is not held up as ideal literature; nor, on the other hand, is the production of literature deemed a possible part of college study. The work in this branch of English is rounded off by a class for students who intend to teach composition. The theory of rhetoric is studied, and something of its history; school texts in rhetoric are examined; and finally the class learns the first steps in teaching by taking charge of elementary classes.

In the literary courses the required work comes first. Many students take no more English than these prescribed three terms of five hours a week; many others continue the study; and the problem has been to arrange the course so as to create in the former class the habit of careful and sympathetic reading, and at the same time to give the latter class a safe foundation for future work. The plan is to read in the class, with the greatest attention to detail, one or more characteristic works of the authors chosen (Scott, Shakespeare, Thackeray, George Eliot), and to require as outside work a good deal of rapid collateral reading. . . .

The course in English prose style begins in the second year, and follows the method of the late Professor Minto. Macaulay, De Quincey, Carlyle, Ruskin, and Arnold are the writers taken up. A course in American authors finds then a place. Then comes a course in poetry: Coleridge, Wordsworth, Byron, Shelley, Keats, Tennyson, Browning. Complete editions of all the poets, except the last, are used, and the year's work is meant to serve as an introduction to the critical reading of poetry. A separate course of one term in metrics accompanies the poetry course. In the drama there is a full course in Shakespeare and other Elizabethans (which presupposes the first year's work in Shakespeare), and also a course in classical drama, Greek and French, studied in translation. The dramatic courses begin with a discussion of Professor Moulton's books on Shakespeare, and on the Greek drama, and then take up independent study of as many plays as possible. The last regular course is the literary seminary, which during the coming year will investigate, as far as the library will allow, the rise of romantic poetry in England. Special research courses are arranged for students who wish to pursue their English studies. It may be added that, in order to graduate in English, work must be taken in each of the three groups of the Department.

It has been my effort, naturally, to arrange the courses in a logical order, advancing from the simple to the more difficult, and covering as wide a range as is consistent with thoroughness; this latter quality being an ideal kept always in view—would we might say as confidently, in reach. And as to the method of conducting classes, each instructor teaches as he pleases; any man's best method is the one that appeals to him at the time.

And now, as to that vexed question, How shall literature be taught? Classroom methods vary in the Department, but our ultimate object is the same. The aim, then, in teaching literature is, I think, to give the student a thorough understanding of what he reads, and the ability to read sympathetically and understandingly in the future. If we use the phrase "to read intelligently," we name the object of every instructor's teaching. But in the definition of this ideal we come upon so many differences of opinion that in reality it means not one thing but a thousand. To touch upon a few obsolescent notions—to one teacher it meant to fill the student full of biography and literary history; to another it meant to put the student in possession of what the best critics, or the worst ones, had said about the artist and his work; to another it meant making a pother over numberless petty details of the text (a species of literary parsing); to another it meant harping on the moral purposes of the poet or novelist; anything, in short, except placing the student face to face with the work itself, and acting as his spectacles when his eyesight was blurred.

The negations of all these theories have become the commonplaces of today—truisms along a certain class of teachers. To repeat those principles that have thus become truisms of theory (not yet of practice—the difference is profound), we have first the truth that the study of literature means the study of *literature*, not of biography nor of literary history (incidentally of vast importance), not of grammar, not of etymology, not of anything except the works themselves, viewed as their creators wrote them, viewed as art, as transcripts of humanity,—not as logic, not as psychology, not as ethics.

The second point is that we are concerned with the *study* of literature. And here is the parting of the ways. Granting we concern ourselves with pure literature only, just how shall we concern ourselves with it? There are many methods, but these methods are of two kinds only: the method of the professor who preaches the beauty of the poet's utterance, and the method of him who makes his student systematically approach the work as a work of art, find out the laws of its existence as such, the mode of its manifestation, the meaning it has, and the significance of that meaning—in brief, to have his students interpret the work of art and ascertain what makes it just that and not something else. Literature, as every reader profoundly feels, is an appeal to all sides of our nature; but I venture to insist that as a *study*—and this is the point at issue—it must be approached intellectually. And here the purpose of literature, and the purpose of studying literature, must be sharply discriminated. The question is not, Apprehending literature, how shall I let it influence me? The question most definitely is, How shall I learn to apprehend literature, that thereby it may influence me?

As far as class study is concerned, the instructors must draw the line once for all between the liking for reading and the understanding of literature. To all who assert that the study of literature must take into account the emotions, that it must remember questions of taste, I can only answer impatiently, Yes, I agree; but between taking them into account, and making them the prime object of the study, there is the difference between day and night. It is only by recognizing this difference that we professors of English cease to make ourselves ridiculous in the eyes of those who see into the heart of things, that we can at all successfully disprove Freeman's remark—caustic and four-fifths true— "English literature is only chatter about Shelley."* As a friend of mine puts it: To understand literature is a matter of study, and may be taught in the class-room; to love literature is a matter of character, and can never be taught in a class-room. The professor who tries chiefly to make his students love literature wastes his energy for the sake of a few students who would love poetry anyway, and sacrifices the majority of his class, who are not yet ripe enough to love it. The professor who tries chiefly to make his students understand literature will give them something to incorporate into their characters. For it is the peculiar grace of literature that whoso understands it loves it. It becomes to him a permanent possession, not a passing thrill.

To revert to our University work in English, we have been confronted with a peculiar local condition. Some time ago, Professor Hale of the University of Iowa said in *The Dial*, that in the West there was comparatively little feeling for style. That certainly applies to the Indiana students I have met. But the Iowans, it was my experience, were willing to study style and develop their latent feeling. Widespread in Indiana, however, I find the firm conviction that style is unworthy of serious consideration. A poem is simply so much thought; its "form-side," to use a favorite student expression, ought to be ignored. And of the thought, only the ethical bearing of it is significant. Poetry is merely a question of morals, and beauty has no excuse for being. The plan of procedure is: believe unyieldingly in a certain philosophy of life; take a poem and read that philosophy into it. This is the "thought-side" of literature. Our first year has been largely an attempt to set up other aims than these.

English at the University of California

The teaching force in English in the University of California consists of seven men: three instructors, Messrs. Syle, Sanford, and Hart; an assistant professor

---

* E. A. Freeman (1832–1892), Regius Professor of Modern History at Oxford, who opposed the establishment of English as a university subject. [ed.]

of English literature, Mr. W. D. Armes; an associate professor of English philology, Dr. A. F. Lange; a professor of rhetoric, Mr. C. B. Bradley; and a professor of the English language and literature, who is head of the Department. For the year 1894–5 the Department offers thirty-one courses. Of these, twenty-four, covering seventy-five hours of work (slightly more than three hours a week each for half the year), are designed for undergraduates, and seven (of two hours a week each) for graduates. In 1893–4 there were in the University 1,383 students, of whom 815, attending the Academic and Technical Colleges in Berkeley, fell to a greater or less extent within the jurisdiction of the English Department. Including the class of 317 Freshmen, there were, during the first term, sixty per cent of the students in Berkeley in the English classes; during the year there were about seventy per cent. The total enrollment of students in English courses during the first term was 873, of whom 397, or forty-eight per cent of the students in Berkeley, were taking more than one course in English. [At the date of the revision of this article, June, 1895, the University has 1,781 students to 1,124 of whom, in the Colleges in Berkeley, the English courses are open. Including the Freshman class, which numbers about 400, the total enrolment in the English courses at present amounts to 951.] . . .

The administration of the Department is republican. Each instructor is independent within his sphere of activity. When, as in the matter of texts or methods, concerted action is necessary, the decision is made by the instructors concerned, subject to the approval of the head of the Department. The advisability of new courses, the scope and form of the annual announcement, and matters of general departmental policy, are discussed at the appropriate monthly meeting of the English faculty. Ordinarily, and primarily, however, the Department meets as a Critical Thought Club. The purpose of the club is to keep abreast of recent contributions in comparative literature, philology, aesthetics, and educational theory. The field of reading is apportioned among the members, and informal reports are had on books and articles bearing in any way upon the study of English.

The organization of studies in a department is perhaps a surer index of the purpose of instruction than any carefully formulated statement of aims. The English courses are classified as preliminary and advanced. The preliminary courses, whether prescribed or elective, are prerequisite to all advanced work. They attempt to furnish (1) the principles of style and the practice of written and oral composition; (2) the commonplaces of literary tradition; (3) a synoptic view of English literature by the study of the principal authors.* The advanced courses are subdivided in the usual way, as primarily for juniors and seniors, and primarily for graduates.

---

* Beginning with 1895–6 a year's course in Old English will be preliminary to all advanced work.

The preliminary courses are announced as types of English prose style, supplementary reading, practical rhetoric, English masterpieces, general history of English literature, and argumentation. The first is required, at the rate of four hours a week through the year, of all Freshmen in the Academic Colleges; the second (one hour any two consecutive terms) of non-classical students in these Colleges. The third and the fourth are prescribed in the colleges of Chemistry and Agriculture. All other English courses are elective; and in the Engineering Colleges English is altogether elective. Of prescribed preliminary courses, that in English prose style aims to acquaint the student, at first hand, with the features and elements of effective workmanship in prose-writing, and to train him to discern the salient qualities of any well-marked prose style presented for his consideration. The course is based upon the direct study of selected groups of authors. The course of supplementary reading extends, as far as time will permit, the acquaintance of the student with the Hellenic, Teutonic, or Romance epics, or other classics in translation. It serves as an introduction to the common and traditional store of literary reference, allusion, and imagery, and as a basis for paragraph-writing. The best translations of the *Iliad*, the *Odyssey*, the *Béowulf*, the *Jerusalem Delivered*, Morris's *Sigurd the Volsung*, etc., are studied. These courses, and the course in practical rhetoric for scientific students, in general serve to stimulate constructive effort and practical skill in writing *pari passu* with analytical effort and the acquisition of information. They accordingly include first the weekly exercise in paragraph-writing, written in the class-room upon some topic not previously announced, but involving acquaintance with the supplementary reading assigned for the week; and, secondly, a carefully supervised series of compositions. Three themes have been required each term. The supervision, which is personal, extends to methods of using the library, of securing material and of taking and arranging notes; to the limitation and definition of subject; to construction of a scheme of presentation in advance of the writing, as well as to careful criticism of the finished work. . . . It should be added that essays are required in connection with all work in the English Department. The course in English masterpieces for scientific students, given by Mr. Armes, involves the careful reading in class of representative poems and essays of the foremost writers, and supplementary reading out of class. Of elective preliminary courses, that in the general history of English literature is the *sine qua non* for all higher work. It presents a synoptical view of English literature as the outcome of, and the index to, English thought in the course of its development. It is accordingly based upon a text-book of English history, and the copious reading of authors illustrative of social and literary movements. It runs as a three-hour course throughout the Sophomore year, and involves the reading by each student, and the discussion in class, of some thirty masterpieces. The course in argumentation comprises the analysis of masterpieces, the preparation of briefs, and the delivery of arguments exemplifying the use of the syllogism and the exposure of fallacies. It must be preceded by a course in formal logic, and is introductory to a course in forensics.

The advanced courses for undergraduates are grouped as (1) Rhetoric and the theory of criticism: four courses; (2) Linguistics: four courses, including, besides grammar, history, and criticism, the comparative study of the Germanic sources of English culture, and Germanic philology; (3) The historical and critical study of literature: eleven courses in chronological sequence, by (a) periods, (b) authors, (c) literary movements, (d) the evolution of types. The first of these groups is essential to the other two. It involves the differentiation, for advanced work, of rhetoric into its species (exposition, including methods of literary research and interpretation, argumentation, narration, etc.), and an introduction to the comparative and aesthetic methods. A course in poetics outlines the theory of art, the theory and development of literature, the relations of poetry and prose, the principles of versification, and the canons, inductive and deductive, of dramatic criticism. It is usually accompanied by lectures on the æsthetics of literature. This course is followed by the problems of literary criticism: a comparative inquiry into the growth, technique, and function of literary types other than the drama. The attempt is made to arrive by induction at the characteristics common to the national varieties of a type, and to formulate these in the light of æsthetic theory. The resulting laws are applied as canons of criticism to English masterpieces of that type. The method has been described by a former student in the Century Magazine, January 1891. The reading and discussions are guided by questions, suggestions, and reference lists—part of a manual of literary criticism now in press (Ginn & Co., Boston). For lack of space the courses in linguistics and literature cannot be enumerated. Students making English their principal study must include in their elections linguistics, poetics, criticism, and the intensive study of at least one literary master and of one literary type or movement. For the teacher's certificate linguistics is indispensable.

The courses primarily for graduates have a twofold aim: first, to impart information; secondly, and principally, to encourage original research. This differentiation by purpose is necessarily relative. Under the former heading, however, falls one of the philological courses, Old Icelandic (Lange). Under the latter falls another philological course, First Modern English, an investigation into the orthographic, phonetic, and syntactical changes of sixteenth century English (Lange), and various literary courses which may be classified as æsthetic, comparative, and critical. The course in the history of æsthetic theory, which, by the courtesy of the professor of philosophy, is at present in my hands, is a study at first hand of the principal authorities in æsthetics, and of the literary art that chiefly influenced them. The course may be said to deal with fundamental literary forces. It is given both terms and extends through three years. In 1893–4 Plato and Aristotle were studied and

Plotinus begun. In 1894–5 we came down as far as Hegel. Next year we shall make a special study of Coleridge and Wordsworth. The courses which I have called comparative deal with *literary movements*. They are four in number: the mediæval spirit was related to art, its chief exponents in English literature and its modern revivals (Bradley); the influence of Germany on English literature of the eighteenth and nineteenth centuries (Lange); the development of the English essay (Bradley); and problems in the growth of English comedy (Gayley). A purely critical course, dealing with *literary methods*, is offered by Professor Bradley, in the study of the entire production of some author of limited scope.

To graduate courses of information and of research might legitimately be added courses having a third purpose: the encouragement of literary creation.* We have as yet none such in the University of California, unless that denominated special study, under which we announce ourselves ready to assist and advise competent graduates in approved plans of work, may be construed as sufficient for the emergency. Academic scholarship does not look with favor upon the attempt to stimulate or foster creative production. But, if charily advised, sagaciously circumscribed, and conducted under the personal supervision of a competent critic, constructive literary effort may surely find a place in the curriculum of an exceptional graduate,—never, of course, unattended by other study with informative or disciplinary purpose in view. There is, nowadays, no reason why genius should be untutored, or its early productions unkempt.

With regard to methods of introduction no stereotyped habit obtains. In our lower classes the text-book is not always used. When used it is treated as a guide, not as a bible. In both lower and higher classes, recitations, reports on reading, discussion of topics, informal or formal lectures, interpretative reading, and personal conference prevail, in such combination or with such preference as the instructor may deem wise. Students, however, are always put to work on the masterpieces themselves.

With regard to methods of investigation, we believe that a certain catholicity of attitude—not inconsistent with alertness—should be observed. The present anarchy, sometimes tyranny, of method is due generally to a deficient organization of studies; and that, in turn, to an incomprehensive view of the field. Hence, the uncertainty of aim with which instruction in English is frequently reproached. This lack of system is, however, indicative only of the fact that literary science is in a transitional stage: no longer static, not yet organic, but genetic. The study of literature in the sentimental, the formally stylistic, or the second-hand-historical fashion, is out of date. Scholars in philology—narrowed to linguistics—have set a new pace by making of their

---

* Such a course under the title "Literary Composition," is offered for 1895–6.

branch a genetic study: a study of sources, causes, relations, movements, and effects. Professors of literature and criticism are now, as rapidly as may be, adapting progressive methods, whether historical or æsthetic, to their lines of research. But each is naturally liable to urge the method that he favors or thinks that he has invented. One, therefore, advocates ethical and religious exegesis, another æsthetic interpretation, another comparative inquiry, another the historical study of style. This is to be expected; and our genetic, and frequently sporadic, stage of literary science cannot fulfil its promise until, by elimination, attrition, and adjustment of results, the way has been prepared for something organic. Hospitality to ideas and conservative liberality of method will hasten the advent of systematic investigation. Even now there are those who study the masterpiece, not only in dynamic relation to author and type, but also in organic relation to the social and artistic movements of which author and type are integral factors. The sum of the methods of any literary inquiry in any college course should be exhaustive so far as circumstances permit. The exigencies of time, training, and material are however, such that due regard, in turn, for historical criticism (linguistic, textual, genetic), technical criticism (distinctive of the type: its evolution, characteristic, and function), and literary criticism (ethical, psychological, æsthetic) can rarely be observed in the study of one specimen with one class. The method, moreover, adapted to one author, masterpiece, or type, is not necessarily of universal applicability. But the duty of the English Department in the teaching of literature is fulfilled if the student, after mastering the prime courses, with their appropriate means and ends, has acquired a comprehensive view of literary art and science, a rational method of study, and a critical sensitiveness to good literature—no matter in what intensive spirit it be approached. To this end, it is essential that the synthesis of the courses and the methods of a department furnish a system.

With these considerations in mind it is evident that the attempt to limit the teaching of English literature to "literary history, literary æsthetics, the theory and analysis of style, versification, and rhetoric, and the necessary philological apparatus" would, though attractive in its apparent simplicity, end in formalism: that is, remand the science to its static stage. But the limitation would be impossible. For form and thought are as inseparable in literature as in life: the expression is inherent in the idea. To appreciate the art of *Dis Aliter Visum** is to understand the ethics of Browning: that is, to be a philosopher. Sociological, metaphysical, and ethical themes are within the function of the belles-lettrist as soon as, emotionalized and clad in æsthetic form, they enter the field of letters. Nay, further, the methods of the laboratory, chemical or biological, are within his function as soon as their adaptation may assist him to

---

* The title of Robert Browning's poem means "Heaven Thought Not So." [ed.]

weigh æsthetic values or to trace the development of literary organisms. It is, consequently, unwise to contemn scientific methods, even though in the hands of enthusiasts they appear to countervail æsthetic interpretation and discipline. Monomaniacs are forces in periods of transition. It is for those of far gaze and patient temper to compute results and perform the synthesis.

One thing is certain: that, for the determination of critical principles and methods, organized effort is necessary. . . .

7

From *Shakespeare as a Dramatic Artist: A Study of Inductive Literary Criticism* (1888)

Richard G. Moulton

Richard Green Moulton (1849–1924) was raised and educated in England, graduating from London University in 1869 and taking a Ph.D. from Christ Church, Cambridge, in 1874. While at Christ Church, he was involved in the founding of the Cambridge University extension movement, which put the reading of literature at the center of middle- and working-class education. Moving to the United States in 1890, Moulton received a Ph.D. in English at the University of Pennsylvania in 1891 and was Professor of Literature at the University of Chicago from 1892 to 1919. Though a specialist in Shakespeare, ancient drama, and the Bible, Moulton saw himself as a generalist and aesthetician, working out the theory that a set of universal principles of "world literature" could be derived inductively from the classics, and that these principles should guide the teaching of literature.

Moulton's writings include *The Ancient Classical Drama: A Study of Literary Evolution* (1890), *The Literary Study of the Bible* (1895), *World Literature and its Place in General Culture* (1911), and *The Modern Study of Literature* (1915). The present selection is from *Shakespeare as a Dramatic Artist: A Study of Inductive Literary Criticism* (1888). It represents an ambitious attempt to furnish a systematic philosophical rationale for the new academic criticism, a rationale that sharply separates traditional "judicial" criticism based on taste from "inductive" criticism based on the scientific study of the changing "laws" of art. Moulton's plea is for "a branch of criticism separate from the criticism of taste" and "in harmony with the spirit of other modern sciences" that would "systematize the laws and principles" by which "the phenomena of literature . . . are moulded and produce their effects."

In the treatment of literature the proposition which seems to stand most in need of assertion at the present moment is, *that there is an inductive science of literary criticism.* As botany deals inductively with the phenomena of vegetable life and traces the laws underlying them, as economy reviews and systematises on inductive principles the facts of commerce, so there is a criticism not less inductive in character which has for its subject-matter literature.

The presumption is clearly that literary criticism should follow other branches of thought in becoming inductive. Ultimately, science means no more than organised thought; and amongst the methods of organisation induction is the most practical. To begin with the observation of facts; to advance from this through the arrangement of observed facts; to use à priori ideas, instinctive notions of the fitness of things, insight into far probabilities, only as side-lights for suggesting convenient arrangements, the value of which is tested only by the actual convenience in arranging they afford; to be content with the sure results so obtained as 'theory' in the interval of waiting for still surer results based on a yet wider accumulation of facts: this is a regimen for healthy science so widely established in different tracts of thought as almost to rise to that universal acceptance which we call common sense. Indeed the whole progress of science consists in winning fresh fields of thought to the inductive methods.

Yet the great mass of literary criticism at the present moment is of a nature widely removed from induction. The prevailing notions of criticism are dominated by the idea of assaying, as if its function were to test the soundness and estimate the comparative value of literary work. Lord Macaulay, than whom no one has a better right to be heard on this subject, compares his office of reviewer to that of a king-at-arms, versed in the laws of literary precedence, marshalling authors to the exact seats to which they are entitled. And, as a matter of fact, the bulk of literary criticism, whether in popular conversation or in discussions by professed critics, occupies itself with the merits of authors and works; founding its estimates and arguments on canons of taste, which are either assumed as having met with general acceptance, or deduced from speculations as to fundamental conceptions of literary beauty.

It becomes necessary then to recognise two different kinds of literary criticism as distinct as any two things that can be called by the same name. The difference between the two may be summed up as the difference between the work of a judge and of an investigator. The one is the enquiry into what ought to be, the other the enquiry into what is. Judicial criticism compares a new production with those already existing in order to determine whether it is inferior to them or surpasses them; criticism of investigation makes the same comparison for the purpose of identifying the new product with some type in the past, or differentiating it and registering a new type. Judicial criticism has a mission to watch against variations from received canons; criticism of investigation watches for new forms to increase its stock of species. The criticism of taste analyses literary works for grounds of preference or evidence on which to found judgments; inductive criticism analyses them to get a closer acquaintance with their phenomena.

Let the question be of Ben Jonson. Judicial criticism starts by holding Ben Jonson responsible for the decay of the English Drama.

Inductive criticism takes objection to the word 'decay' as suggesting condemnation, but recognises Ben Jonson as the beginner of a new tendency in our dramatic history.

But, judicial criticism insists, the object of the Drama is to pourtray human nature, whereas Ben Jonson has painted not men but caricatures.

Induction sees that this formula cannot be a sufficient definition of the Drama, for the simple reason that it does not take in Ben Jonson; its own mode of putting the matter is that Ben Jonson has founded a school of treatment of which the law is caricature.

But Ben Jonson's caricatures are palpably impossible.

Induction soon satisfies itself that their point lies in their impossibility; they constitute a new mode of pourtraying qualities of character, not by resemblance, but by analysing and intensifying contrasts to make them clearer.

Judicial criticism can see how the poet was led astray; the bent of his disposition induced him to sacrifice dramatic propriety to his satiric purpose.

Induction has another way of putting the matter: that the poet has utilised dramatic form for satiric purpose; thus by the 'cross-fertilisation' of two existing literary species he has added to literature a third including features of both.

At all events, judicial criticism will maintain, it must be admitted that the Shakespearean mode of pourtraying is infinitely the higher: a sign-painter, as Macaulay points out, can imitate a deformity of feature, while it takes a great artist to bring out delicate shades of expression.

Inductive treatment knows nothing about higher or lower, which lie outside the domain of science. Its point is that science is indebted to Ben Jonson for a new species; if the new species be an easier form of art it does not on that account lose its claim to be analysed.

The critic of merit can always fall back upon taste: who would not prefer Shakespeare to Ben Jonson?

But even from this point of view scientific treatment can plead its own advantages. The inductive critic reaps to the full the interest of Ben Jonson, to which the other has been forcibly closing his eyes; while, so far from liking Shakespeare the less, he appreciates all the more keenly Shakespeare's method of treatment from his familiarity with that which is its antithesis.

It must be conceded at once that both these kinds of criticism have justified their existence. Judicial criticism has long been established as a favourite pursuit of highly cultivated minds; while the criticism of induction can shelter itself under the authority of science in general, seeing that it has for its object to bring the treatment of literature into the circle of the inductive sciences. It is unfortunate, however, that the spheres of the two have not been kept distinct. In the actual practice of criticism the judicial method has obtained an illegitimate supremacy which has thrown the other into the shade; it has even invaded the domain of the criticism that claims to be scientific, until the word *criticism* itself has suffered, and the methodical treatment of literature has by tacit assumption become limited in idea to the judicial method.

Explanation for this limited conception of criticism is not far to seek. Modern criticism took its rise before the importance of induction was recognised: it lags behind other branches of thought in adapting itself to inductive treatment chiefly through two influences. The first of these is connected with the revival of literature after the darkness of the middle ages. The birth of thought and taste in modern Europe was the Renaissance of classical thought and taste; by Roman and Greek philosophy and poetry the native powers of our ancestors were trained till they became strong enough to originate for themselves. It was natural for their earliest criticism to take the form of applying the classical standards to their own imitations: now we have advanced so far that no one would propose to test exclusively by classical models, but nevertheless the idea of *testing* still lingers as the root idea in the treatment of literature. Other branches of thought have completely shaken off this attitude of submission to the past: literary criticism differs from the rest only in being later to move. This is powerfully suggested by the fact that so recent a writer as Addison couples science in general with criticism in his estimate of probable progress; laying down the startling propositon that 'it is impossible for us who live in the later ages of the world to make observations in criticism, in morality, *or in any art or science*, which have not been touched upon by others'!

And even for this lateness a second influence goes far to account. The grand literary phenomenon of modern times is journalism, the huge apparatus of floating literature of which one leading object is to review literature itself. The vast increase of production consequent upon the progress of printing has made production itself a phenomenon worthy of study, and elevated the sifting of production into a prominent literary occupation; by the aid of book-tasters alone can the ordinary reader keep pace with production. It is natural enough that the influence of journalism should pass beyond its natural sphere, and that the review should tend to usurp the position of the literature for which reviewing exists. Now in journalism testing and valuation of literary work have a real and important place. It has thus come about that in the great preponderance of ephemeral over permanent literature the machinery adapted to the former has become applied to the latter: methods proper to journalism have settled the popular conception of systematic treatment; and the bias already given to criticism by the Renaissance has been strengthened to resist the tendency of all kinds of thought towards inductive methods.

History will thus account for the way in which the criticism of taste and valuation tends to be identified with criticism in general: but attempts are not wanting to give the identification a scientific basis. Literary appreciation, it is said, is a thing of culture. A critic in the reviewer's sense is one who has the literary faculty both originally acute and developed by practice: he thus arrives quickly and with certainty at results which others would reach laboriously and after temporary misjudgments. Taste, however arbitrary in appearance, is in reality condensed experience; judicial criticism is a wise economy of appreciation, the purpose of which is to anticipate natural selection and universal experience. He is a good critic who, by his keen and practised judgment, can tell you at once the view of authors and works which you would yourself come to hold with sufficient study and experience.

Now in the first place there is a flaw in this reasoning: it omits to take into account that the judicial attitude of mind is itself a barrier to appreciation, as being opposed to that delicacy of receptiveness which is a first condition of sensibility to impressions of literature and art. It is a matter of commonest experience that appreciation may be interfered with by prejudice, by a passing unfavourable mood, or even by uncomfortable external surroundings. But it is by no means sufficient that the reader of literature should divest himself of these passive hindrances to appreciation: poets are pioneers in beauty, and considerable activity of effort is required to keep pace with them. Repetition may be necessary to catch effects—passages to be read over and over again, more than one author of the same school to be studied, effect to be compared with kindred effect each helping the other. Or an explanation from one who has already caught the idea may turn the mind into a receptive attitude. Training again is universally recognized as a necessity for appreciation, and to train is to make receptive. Beyond all these conditions of perception, and including them, is yet another. It is a foundation principle in art-culture, as well as in human intercourse, that *sympathy is the grand interpreter:* secrets of beauty will unfold themselves to the sunshine of sympathy, while they will wrap themselves all the closer against the tempest of sceptical questionings. Now a judicial attitude of mind is highly unreceptive, for it necessarily implies a restraint of sympathy: every one, remarks Hogarth, is a judge of painting except the connoisseur. The judicial mind has an appearance of receptiveness, because it seeks to shut out prejudice: but what if the idea of judging be itself a prejudice? On this view the very consciousness of fairness, involving as it does limitation of sympathy, will be itself unfair. In practical life, where we have to act, the formation of judgments is a necessity. In art we can escape the obligation, and here the judicial spirit becomes a wanton addition to difficulties of appreciation already sufficiently great; the mere notion of condemning may be enough to check our receptivity to qualities which, as we have seen, it may need our utmost effort to catch. So that the judicial attitude of mind comes to defeat its own purpose, and disturbs unconsciously the impression it seeks to judge; until, as Emerson puts it, 'if you criticize a fine genius the odds are that you are out of your reckoning, and instead of the poet are censuring your caricature of him.'

But the appeal made is to experience: let it go. It will be found that, speaking broadly, *the whole history of criticism has been a triumph of authors over critics:* so long as criticism has meant the gauging of literature, so long its progress has consisted in the reversal of critical judgments by further experience. I hesitate to enlarge upon this part of my subject lest I be inflicting upon the reader the tedium of a thrice-told tale. But I believe that the ordinary reader, however familiar with notable blunders of criticism, has little idea of that which is the essence of my argument—the degree of regularity, amounting to absolute law, with which criticism, where it has set itself in opposition to freedom of authorship, has been found in time to have pronounced upon the wrong side, and has, after infinite waste of obstructive energy, been compelled at last to accept innovations it had pronounced impossible under penalty of itself becoming obsolete.

Shakespeare-criticism affords the most striking illustration. Its history is made up of wave after wave of critical opposition, each retiring further before the steady advance of Shakespeare's fame. They may almost be traced in the varying apologetic tones of the successive *Variorum* editors, until Reed, in the edition of 1803, is content to leave the poet's renown as established on the basis which will 'bid defiance to the caprices of fashion and the canker of time. . . .'

The critics may themselves be called as chief witnesses against themselves. Those parts of their works in which they apply themselves to analysing and interpreting their authors survive in their full force: where they judge, find fault, and attempt to regulate, they inevitably become obsolete. Aristotle, the founder of all criticism, is for the most part inductive in his method, describing poetry as it existed in his day, distinguishing its different classes and elements, and tabulating its usages: accordingly Aristotle's treatise, though more than two thousand years old, remains the text-book of the Greek Drama. In some places, however, he diverges from his main purpose, as in the final chapter, in which he raises the question whether Epic or Tragic is more excellent, or where he promises a special treatise to discuss whether Tragedy is yet perfect: here he has for modern readers only the interest of curiosity. Dr. Johnson's analysis of 'metaphysical poetry,' Addison's development of the leading effects in *Paradise Lost*, remain as true and forcible to-day as when they were written: Addison constructing an order of merit for English poets with Cowley and Sprat at the head, Dr. Johnson lecturing Shakespeare and Milton as to how they ought to have written—these are to us only odd anachronisms. It is like a contest with atomic force, this attempt at using ideas from the past to mould and limit productive power in the present and future. The critic peers into the dimness of history, and is found to have been blind to what was by his side: Boileau strives to erect a throne of Comedy for Terence, and never suspects that a truer king was at hand in his own personal friend Molière. It is in vain for critics to denounce, their denunciation recoils on themselves: the sentence of Rymer that the soul of modern Drama was a brutish and not a reasonable soul, or of Voltaire, that Shakespeare's Tragedy would not be tolerated by the lowest French mob, can harm none but Rymer and Voltaire. If the critics venture to prophesy, the sequel is the only refutation of them needed; if they give reasons, the reasons survive only to explain how the critics were led astray; if they lay down laws, literary greatness in the next generation is found to vary directly with the boldness with which authors violate the laws. If they assume a judicial attitude, the judgment-seat becomes converted into a pillory for the judge, and a comic side to literary history is furnished by the mockery with which time preserves the proportions of things, as seen by past criticism, to be laid side by side with the true perspective revealed by actual history. . . .

It may be well to recall the exact purpose to which the present argument is intended to lead. The purpose is not to attack journalism and kindred branches of criticism in the interests of inductive treatment. It would be false to the principles of induction not to recognise that the criticism of taste has long since established its position as a fertile branch of literature. Even in an inductive system journalism would still have place as a medium for fragmentary and tentative treatment. Moreover it may be admitted that induction in its formal completeness of system can never be applied in practical life; and in the intellectual pursuits of real life trained literary taste may be a valuable acquisition. What is here attacked is the mistake which has identified the criticism of taste and valuation with the conception of criticism as a whole; the intrusion of methods belonging to journalism into treatment that claims to be systematic. So far from being a standard of method in the treatment of literature, criticism of the reviewer's order is outside science altogether. It finds its proper place on the creative side of literature, as a branch in which literature itself has come to be taken as a theme for literary writing; it thus belongs to the literature treated, not to the scientific treatment of it. Reviews so placed may be regarded almost as the lyrics of prose: like lyric poems they have their completeness in themselves, and their interest lies, not in their being parts of some whole, but in their flashing the subjectivity of a writer on to a variety of isolated topics; they thus have value, not as fragments of literary science, but as fragments of Addison, of Jeffrey, of Macaulay. Nor is the bearing of the present argument that commentators should set themselves to eulogise the authors they treat instead of condemning them (though this would certainly be the safer of two errors). The treatment aimed at is one independent of praise or blame, one that has nothing to do with merit, relative or absolute. The contention is for a branch of criticism separate from the criticism of taste; a branch that, in harmony with the spirit of other modern sciences, reviews the phenomena of literature as they actually stand, enquiring into and endeavouring to systematise the laws and principles by which they are moulded and produce their effects. Scientific criticism and the criticism of taste have distinct spheres: and the whole of literary history shows that the failure to keep the two separate results only in mutual confusion.

Our present purpose is with inductive criticism. What, by the analogy of other sciences, is implied in the inductive treatment of literature?

The inductive sciences occupy themselves directly with facts, that is, with phenomena translated by observation into the form of facts; and soundness of inductive theory is measured by the closeness with which it will bear confronting with the facts. In the case of literature and art the facts are to be looked for in the literary and artistic productions themselves: the dramas, epics, pictures, statues, pillars, capitals, symphonies, operas—the details of these are the phenomena which the critical observer translates into facts. A picture is a title for a bundle of facts: that the painter has united so many figures in such and such groupings, that he has given such and such varieties of colouring, and such and such arrangement of light and shade. Similarly the *Iliad* is a short name implying a large number of facts characterising the poem: that its principal personages are Agamemnon and Achilles, that these personages are represented as displaying certain qualities, doing certain deeds, and standing in certain relations to one another.

Here, however, arises that which has been perhaps the greatest stumbling-block in the way of securing inductive treatment for literature. Science deals only with ascertained facts: but the details of literature and art are open to the most diverse interpretation. They leave conflicting impressions on different observers, impressions both subjective and variable in themselves, and open to all manner of distracting influences, not excepting that of criticism itself. Where in the treatment of literature is to be found the positiveness of subject-matter which is the first condition of science?

In the first place it may be pointed out that this want of certainty in literary interpretation is not a difficulty of a kind peculiar to literature. The same object of terror will affect the members of a crowd in a hundred different ways, from presence of mind to hysteria; yet this has not prevented the science of psychology from inductively discussing fear. Logic proposes to scientifically analyse the reasoning processes in the face of the infinite degrees of susceptibility different minds show to proof and persuasion. It has become proverbial that taste in art is incapable of being settled by discussion, yet the art of music has found exact treatment in the science of humour. In the case of these well-established sciences it has been found possible to separate the variable element from that which is the subject-matter of the science: such a science as psychology really covers two distinct branches of thought, the psychology that discusses formally the elements of the human mind, and another psychology, not yet systematised, that deals with the distribution of these elements amongst different individuals. It need then be no barrier to inductive treatment that in the case of literature and art the will and consciousness act as disturbing forces, refracting what may be called natural effects into innumerable effects on individual students. It only becomes a question of practical procedure, in what way the interfering variability is to be eliminated.

It is precisely at this point that *à priori* criticism and induction part company. The *à priori* critic gets rid of uncertainty in literary interpretation by confining his attention to effects produced upon the best minds: he sets up *taste* as a standard by which to try impressions of literature which he is willing to consider. The inductive critic cannot have recourse to any such arbitrary means of limiting his materials; for his doubts he knows no court of appeal except the appeal to the literary works themselves. The astronomer, from the vast distance of the objects he observes, finds the same phenomenon producing different results on different observers, and he has thus regularly to allow for personal errors: but he deals with such discrepancies only by fresh observations on the stars themselves, and it never occurs to him that he can get rid of a variation by abstract argument or deference to a greater observer. In the same way the inductive critic of literature must settle his doubts by referring them to the literary productions themselves; to him the question is not of the nobler view or the view in best taste, but simply what view fits in best with the details as they stand in actual fact. He quite recognises that it is not the objective details but the subjective impressions they produce that make literary effect, but the objective details are the *limit* on the variability of the subjective impressions. The character of Macbeth impresses two readers differently: how is the difference to be settled? The *à priori* critic contends that his conception is the loftier; that a hero should be heroic; that moreover the tradition of the stage and the greatest names in the criticism of the past bear him out; or, finally, falls back upon good taste, which closes the discussion. The inductive critic simply puts together all the sayings and doings of Macbeth himself, all that others in the play say and appear to feel about him, and whatever view of the character is consistent with these and similar facts of the play, that view he selects; while to vary from it for any external consideration would seem to him as futile as for an astronomer to make a star rise an hour earlier to tally with the movements of another star.

We thus arrive at a foundation axiom of inductive literary criticism: *Interpretation in literature is of the nature of a scientific hypothesis, the truth of which is tested by the degree of completeness with which it explains the details of the literary work as they actually stand.* That will be the true meaning of a passage, not which is the most worthy, but which most nearly explains the words as they are; that will be the true reading of a character which, however involved in expression or tame in effect, accounts for and reconciles all that is represented of the personage. The inductive critic will interpret a complex situation, not by fastening attention on its striking elements and ignoring others as oversights and blemishes, but by putting together with business-like exactitude all that the author has given, weighing, balancing, and standing by the product. He will not consider that he has solved the action of a drama by some leading plot, or some central idea powerfully suggested in different parts, but will investigate patiently until he can find a scheme which will give point to the inferior as well as to the leading scenes, and in connection with which all the details are harmonised in their proper proportions. In this way he will be raising a superstructure of expositon that rests, not on authority however high, but upon a basis of indisputable fact.

In actual operation I have often found that such positive analysis raises in the popular mind a very practical objection: that the scientific interpretation seems to discover in literary works much more in the way of purpose and design than the authors themselves can be supposed to have dreamed of. Would not Chaucer and Shakespeare, it is asked, if they could come to life now, be greatly astonished to hear themselves lectured upon? to find critics knowing their purposes better than they had known them themselves, and discovering in their works laws never suspected till after they were dead, and which they themselves perhaps would need some effort to understand? Deep designs are traced in Shakespeare's plots, and elaborate combinations in his characters and passions: is the student asked to believe that Shakespeare really *intended* these complicated effects?

The difficulty rests largely upon a confusion in words. Such words as 'purpose,' 'intention,' have a different sense when used in ordinary parlance from that which they bear when applied in criticism and science. In ordinary parlance a man's 'purpose' means his conscious purpose, of which he is the best judge; in science the 'purpose' of a thing is the purpose it actually serves, and is discoverable only by analysis. Thus science discovers that the 'purpose' of earthworms is to break up the soil, the 'design' of colouring in flowers is to attract insects, though the flower is not credited with foresight nor the worm with disinterestedness. In this usage alone can the words 'purpose,' 'intention,' be properly applied to literature and art: science knows no kind of evidence in the matter of creative purpose so weighty as the thing it has actually produced. . . .

The . . . most important of the . . . ideas . . . which bring judicial and inductive criticism into contrast. . . . is the idea that there exist 'laws' of art, in the same sense in which we speak of laws in morality or the laws of some particular state—great principles which have been laid down, and which are binding on the artist as the laws of God or his country are binding on the man; that by these, and by lesser principles deduced from these, the artist's work is to be tried, and praise or blame awarded accordingly. Great part of formal criticism runs on these lines; while, next in importance to comparisons of merit, the popular mind considers literary taste to consist in a keen sensitiveness to the 'faults' and 'flaws' of literary workmanship.

This attitude to art illustrates the enormous misleading power of the metaphors that lie concealed in words. The word 'law,' justly applicable in one of its senses to art, has in practice carried with it the associations of its other sense; and the mistake of metaphor has been sufficient to distort criticism until, as Goldsmith remarks, rules have become the greatest of all the misfortunes which have befallen the commonwealth of letters. Every expositor has had to point out the widespread confusion between the two senses of this term. Laws in the moral and political world are external obligations, restraints of the will; they exist where the will of a ruler or of the community is applied to the individual will. In science, on the other hand, law has to do not with what ought to be, but with what is; scientific laws are facts reduced to formulæ, statements of the habits of things, so to speak. The laws of the stars in the first sense could only mean some creative fiat, such as 'Let there be lights in the firmament of heaven'; in the scientific sense laws of the stars are summaries of their customary movements. In the act of getting drunk I am violating God's moral law, I am obeying his law of alcoholic action. So scientific laws, in the case of art and literature, will mean descriptions of the practice of artists or the characteristics of their works, when these will go into the form of general propositions as distinguished from disconnected details. The key to the distinction is the notion of external authority. There cannot be laws in the moral and political sense without a ruler or legislative authority; in scientific laws the law-giver and the law-obeyer are one and the same, and for the laws of vegetation science looks no further than the facts of the vegetable world. In literature and art the term 'law' applies only in the scientific sense; the laws of the Shakespearean Drama are not laws imposed by some external authority upon Shakespeare, but laws of dramatic practice derived from the analysis of his actual works. Laws of literature, in the sense of external obligations limiting an author, there are none: if he were voluntarily to bind himself by such external laws, he would be so far curtailing art; it is hardly a paradox to say the art is legitimate only when it does not obey laws. What applies to the term 'law' applies similarly to the term 'fault.' The term is likely always to be used from its extreme convenience in art-training; but it must be understood strictly as a term of education and discipline. In inductive criticism, as in the other inductive sciences, the word 'fault' has no meaning. If an artist acts contrary to the practice of all other artists, the result is either that he produces no art-effect at all, in which case there is nothing for criticism to register and analyse, or else he produces a new effect, and is thus extending, not breaking, the laws of art. The great clash of horns in Beethoven's Heroic Symphony was at first denounced as a gross fault, a violation of the plainest laws of harmony; now, instead of a 'fault,' it is spoken of as a 'unique effect,' and in the difference between the two descriptions lies the whole difference between the conceptions of judicial and inductive criticism. Again and again in the past this notion of faults has led criticism on to wrong tracks, from which it has had to retrace its steps on finding the supposed faults to be in reality new laws. Immense energy was wasted in denouncing Shakespeare's 'fault' of uniting serious with light matter in the same play as a violation of fundamental dramatic laws; experience showed this mixture of passions to be the source of powerful art-effects hitherto shut out of the Drama, and the 'fault' became one of the distinguishing 'laws' in the most famous branch of modern literature. It is necessary then to insist upon the strict scientific sense of the term 'law' as used of literature and art; and the purging of criticism from the confusion attaching to this word is an essential step in its elevation to the inductive standard. It is a step, moreover, in which it has been preceded by other branches of thought. At one time the practice of commerce and the science of economy suffered under the same confusion: the battle of 'free trade' has been fought, the battle of 'free art' is still going on. In time it will be recognised that the practice of artists, like the operations of business, must be left to its natural working, and the attempt to impose eternal canons of taste on artists will appear as futile as the attempt to effect by legislation the regulation of prices. . . .

To some, I know, it appears that literature is a sphere in which the strict sense of the word 'law' has no application: that such laws belong to nature, not art. The essence, it is contended, of the natural sciences is the certainty of the facts with which they deal. Art, on the contrary, is creative; it does not come into the category of objective phenomena at all, but is the product of some artist's will, and therefore purely arbitrary. If in a compilation of observations in natural history for scientific use it became known that the compiler had at times drawn upon his imagination for his details, the whole compilation would become useless; and any scientific theories based upon it would be discredited. But the artist bases his work wholly on imagination, and caprice is a leading art-beauty: how, it is asked, can so arbitrary a subject-matter be reduced to the form of positive laws?

In view of any such objections, it may be well to set up [a further] axiom of inductive criticism: *That art is a part of nature*. Nature, it is true, is the vaguest of words: but this is a vagueness common to the objection and the answer. The objection rests really on a false antithesis, of which one term is 'nature,' while it is not clear what is the other term; the axiom set up in answer implies that there is no real distinction between 'nature' and the other phenomena which are the subject of human enquiry. The distinction is supposed to rest upon the degree to which arbitrary elements of the mind, such as imagination, will, caprice, enter into such a thing as art-production. But there are other things in which the human will plays as much part as it does in art, and which have nevertheless proved compatible with inductive treatment. Those who hold that 'thought is free' do not reject psychology as an inductive science; actual politics are made up of struggles of will, exercises of arbitrary power, and the like, and yet there is a political science. If there is an inductive science of politics, men's voluntary actions in the pursuit of public life, and an inductive science of economy, men's voluntary actions in pursuit of wealth, why should there not be an inductive science of art, men's voluntary actions in pursuit of the beautiful? The whole of human action, as well as the whole of external nature, comes within the jurisdiction of science; so far from the productions of the will and imagination being exempted from scientific treatment, will and imagination themselves form chapters in psychology, and caprice has been analysed.

It remains to notice the [last] . . . of the ideas in relation to which the two kinds of criticism are in complete contrast with one another. It is a vague notion, which no objector would formulate, but which as a fact does underlie judicial criticism, and insensibly accompanies its testing and assaying. It is the idea that the foundations of literary form have reached their final settlement, the past being tacitly taken as a standard for the present and future, or the present as a standard for the past. Thus in the treatment of new literature the idea manifests itself in a secret antagonism to variations from received models; at the very least, new forms are called upon to justify themselves, and so the judicial critic brings his least receptive attitude to the new effects which need receptiveness most. In opposition to this tacit assumption, inductive criticism starts with a distinct counter-axiom of the utmost importance: *That literature is a thing of development.* This axiom implies that the critic must come to literature as to that in which he is expecting to find unlimited change and variety; he must keep before him the fact that production must always be far ahead of criticism and analysis, and must have carried its conquering invention into fresh regions before science, like settled government in the wake of the pioneer, follows to explain the new effects by new principles. No doubt in name literary development is recognised in all criticism; yet in its treatment both of old literature and new the *à priori* criticism is false to development in the scientific sense of the term. Such systems are apt to begin by laying down that 'the object of literature is so and so,' or that 'the purpose of the Drama is to pourtray human nature'; they then proceed to test actual literature and dramas by the degree in which they carry out these fundamental principles. Such procedure is the opposite of the inductive method, and is a practical denial of development in literature. Assuming that the object of existing literature were correctly described, such a formula could not bind the literature of the future. Assuming that there was ever a branch of art which could be reduced to one simple purpose, yet the inherent tendency of the human mind and its productions to develop would bring it about that what were at first means towards this purpose would in time become ends in themselves side by side with the main purpose, giving us in addition to the simple species a modified variety of it; external influences, again, would mingle with the native characteristics of the original species, and produce new species compound in their purposes and effects. The real literature would be ever obeying the first principle of development and changing from simple to complex, while the criticism that tried it by the original standard would be at each step removed one degree further from the only standard by which the literature could be explained. And if judicial criticism fails in providing for development in the future and present, it is equally unfortunate in giving a false twist to development when looked for in the past. The critic of comparative standards is apt to treat early stages of literature as elementary, tacitly assuming his own age as a standard *up to* which previous periods have developed. Thus his treatment of the past becomes often an assessment of the degrees in which past periods have approximated to his own, advancing from literary pot-hooks to his own running facility. . . . The inductive critic will accord to the early forms of his art the same independence he accords to later forms. Development will not mean to him education for a future stage, but the perpetual branching out of literary activity into ever fresh varieties, different in kind from one another, and each to be studied by standards of its own: the 'individuality' of authors is the expression in literary parlance which corresponds to the perpetual 'differentiation' of new species in science. Alike, then, in his attitude to the past and the future, the inductive critic will eschew the temptation to judgment by fixed standards, which in reality means opposing lifeless rules to the ever-living variety of nature. He will leave a dead judicial criticism to bury its dead authors and to pen for them judicious epitaphs, and will himself approach literature filled equally with reverence for the unbroken vitality of its past and faith in its exhaustless future.

To gather up our results. Induction, as the most universal of scientific methods, may be presumed to apply wherever there is a subject-matter reducible to the form of fact; such a subject-matter will be found in literature where its effects are interpreted, not arbitrarily, but with strict reference to the details of the literary works as they actually stand. There is thus an inductive literary criticism, akin in spirit and methods to the other inductive sciences, and distinct from other branches of criticism, such as the criticism of taste. This inductive criticism will entirely free itself from the judicial spirit and its comparisons of merit, which is found to have been leading criticism during half its history on to false tracks from which it has taken the other half to retrace its steps. On the contrary, inductive criticism will examine literature in the spirit of pure investigation; looking for the laws of art in the practice of artists, and treating art, like the rest of nature, as a thing of continuous development, which may thus be expected to fall, with each author and school, into varieties distinct in kind from one another, and each of which can be fully grasped only when examined with an attitude of mind adapted to the special variety without interference from without.

Part II
COUNTER-STATEMENTS AND REASSESSMENTS

8

From *The Study of English Literature* (1891)

John Churton Collins

John Churton Collins (1848–1908) was an Oxford-educated British man of letters,
who became famous for his zealous promotion of English literature as a university
subject and his attacks on narrow philological teaching. Disappointed in his
personal effort to secure the newly founded Chair in English Literature at Oxford
University, Collins accepted a professorship at the University of Birmingham. But
his strong polemic, *The Study of English Literature* (1891), was influential in its
Matthew Arnold-like defense of the humanistic value of literary study.

   We excerpt Collins's book here, not only because it documents the
transatlantic character of changes in literary studies, but also because it was widely
cited by Americans who objected to the philologists' stranglehold over English
departments. In a letter written in 1892, for example, William Hand Browne
wrote as follows to Johns Hopkins University President Daniel Coit Gilman:

> Have you seen Churton Collins's new book on the teaching of Eng. Lit. His objections to
> swamping literature in philology are well taken; but perhaps he is a little too *acharné* against
> the philologists. However, a man has to push hard against a leaning wall; and in England,
> apparently—at least in Oxford—knowledge of Fabian and Ulfilas ranks higher than
> knowledge of Shakespeare and Bacon. Yet it is the thoughts of great men and not the laws of
> Teutonic vowel-change that move and mould the world.

Browne, the University Librarian at Johns Hopkins, was the custodian of belles-
lettres, perhaps explaining these subversive sentiments in this intensely philological
department.

All who have watched the educational movements of the last few
years . . . must feel with much satisfaction that they are the earnest and
anticipation of a great revolution in advanced education. What they plainly
indicate is that the changed conditions under which we are now living are
necessitating corresponding changes in our systems of instruction. Partly owing
to vague notions that culture on its moral side is supplied by religious teaching,
and partly owing to our national habit of regarding politics in relation merely

to the public game, neither ethics nor politics have as instruments of culture, as subjects for discipline, received any systematic attention. With music and the fine arts associated for the most part with mere amusement, and poetry resolved into little more than an idle pastime without, and into pabulum for philology within our Schools and Colleges, what ought to represent æsthetic discipline has fared even worse. Generation after generation for ages have the best and wisest of our countrymen been directing attention to this deplorable deficiency in our systems of public instruction. And now the people are awakening to it. In all quarters and among all classes, men and women are beginning to feel that there is no reason why education should not, through a proper use of the same instruments, be directed to the same ends, as the ends to which the ancients directed it; why poetry, why history, why art and philosophy generally should not be brought into the same influential relation to the lives of English citizens as they stood to the lives of the citizens in Athens and Rome. . . . During the last few years, both Oxford and Cambridge have been petitioned, and petitioned over and over again, to take into consideration the serious deficiencies which confessedly exist in our system of advanced education. It has been pointed out that they are now standing face to face with new duties and new responsibilities; that the comparatively contracted sphere to which their direct influence was formerly confined is rapidly becoming co-extensive with the kingdom; that in an immense adult population there is no class with which they are not being brought into immediate and intimate contact; that the influence therefore which they have hitherto exercised on popular education, on its religious side, it is perfectly competent for them to extend to that education on its ethical, on its political, and on its artistic sides; that in Literature, if Literature include what it ought to include, they have the instrument, and in the interpretation of Literature the means, of affording such instruction. It has been pointed out that if Literature as a subject of teaching is to effect for popular culture what it is of power to effect; if, as an instrument of political education, it is to warn, to admonish, to guide; if, as an instrument of moral and æsthetic education, it is to exercise that influence on taste, on tone, on sentiment, on opinion, on character, on all, in fine, which is susceptible of educational impression, it must first hold that place in the training of its modern exponents which it held in that of the training of its exponents in ancient times; that it must be rescued from its present degrading vassalage to Philology, that its profession must not be regarded as the common property and makeshift of any graduate in any faculty whom accident may turn to it; that all that constitutes, or ought to constitute, a liberal academic education in Literæ Humaniores must be regarded as a foundation not less indispensable to the special and particular discipline of its teachers than a training in geometry was, according to the inscription on Plato's School, a preliminary indispensable to the study of his Philosophy; that its boundaries must be enlarged that the interpretation of such classical works in moral and political philosophy, in theology and metaphysics, as are not merely technical and esoteric, of such works, for example, as the *Republic*, the *Apology* and *Phædo*, the *Memorabilia*, the *Politics*, the *Ethics*, the *Analogy* and *Sermons* of Butler, the chief political treatises of Hobbes, of Burke, of De Tocqueville, should be as much the business of its missionaries as the interpretation of what is ordinarily included in *Belles Lettres*. Nor was this all. Attention was directed to the disastrous effects resulting from the refusal of the Unversities to distinguish between a literary and a philological study of the Greek and Roman Classics, between their interest as monuments of language, and their value as the expression of genius and art. If, it was pleaded, they were to maintain their place in modern education, they could maintain it only by virtue of their relation to Philosophy and Literature, and that regarded from this point of view there would be little danger of their supremacy being shaken. It was urged that what was needed was provision for a liberal study of the Classics of Greece and Rome side by side with the liberal study of our own Classics and the Classics of the Continent, as this would at once place the study of the Greek and Roman Literature on the only footing on which in modern times it is possible to justify it, and at the same time raise the study of English Literature to its proper level in education.

The result of this appeal is an excellent illustration of the fate of liberal movements in our Universities. There has never been wanting either at Oxford or at Cambridge a small minority which sees clearly the sort of reforms which are needed, and as clearly by what means and in what way they may best be effected. This minority, recognizing the reasonableness of the appeal, and anxious to introduce the study of Literature into the University, so far prevailed as to obtain the consent of Convocation to the foundation of an English Chair. A Chair of English Literature was accordingly founded and liberally endowed. A Board of Electors was appointed. As there was already a Chair of Celtic, a Chair of Anglo-Saxon, a Chair of Comparative Philology, and as, therefore, the philological study of English had been amply provided for, it was confidently anticipated that the choice of the electors would fall on the sort of teacher contemplated by the originators of the movement. Indeed, it was hoped and expected that Matthew Arnold would be invited to fill it. But Philology triumphed. The Board, discovering that though the language of Cædmon and the language of Oisin had received the attention they deserved, the dialect of Robert Gloucester and William of Shoreham had not, determined to seize this opportunity to remedy the defect. Availing themselves of a quibble on the word "language," for the statute authorizing the foundation of the Chair happened by a mere accident to couple the word "language" with "literature," they succeeded in ignoring the object for which the Chair was founded, and proceeded to elect, at a permanent salary of £900 a year, a professor for the interpretation of Middle English. But the perversion of this Chair was merely a preliminary step. A Professor elected on such a theory of the scope and functions of a Chair of Literature was to have been succeeded by a School framed in accordance with the same theory of the scope and functions of a School of Literature. What the constitution of the curriculum of that School was to have been has been explained by Professor Max Müller. It was

.:"to consist of three branches—Teutonic, Romanic, and Celtic. The Teutonic to be subdivided into an English, German and Scandinavian section: the Romanic into a Southern (Provençal and Italian), a Northern (French) and possibly a third section comprising Spanish and Portuguese. These are as yet *pia vota** only, but I have that faith in young Oxford that with certain modifications and possibly after some hesitation some such scheme will be carried."

This scheme, it may be added, is simply the counterpart of the scheme which has unhappily found embodiment in the Mediæval and Modern Languages Tripos at Cambridge. Let us consider for a moment what the effect of such a curriculum on the prospects of education and culture would be likely to be. In the first place, it would confer on a successful candidate the academic diploma of an Honour degree in "Literature." His "literary" qualifications would certainly be remarkable. In the leading and parent Literatures of the world he would have received no instruction. In the principles of criticism he would have received no instruction. Taught to approach literature purely in relation to philology, of literature in its relation to history, to ethics, to politics, to æsthetics, he would have been required to pay no attention at all. Of works which are the glory of the human race in poetry, in oratory, in philosophy, in criticism, he need never have read one line. With the barbarous and semi-barbarous experiments of the infancy of civilization and with the niceties of the various Romance and Teutonic dialects he would have been expected to be minutely acquainted; he would, indeed, have spent the three best years of his life in mastering them. What effect such discipline as this would be likely to have on taste, on tone, on temper, on all these faculties and powers, in fine, which take their ply and derive their quality from education, it is not difficult to see. Nor again is it difficult to foresee what would be likely to be the notions of a teacher, who emerged from such a training to represent and interpret Literature, on the scope and functions of Literature as an instrument of culture. And this is not all. What the Literature of Greece is to that of Rome, the Literatures of Greece and Rome are to that of England. A scholar would at once see the absurdity of separating the study of the Roman Classics from that of the Greek, for the simple reason that without a knowledge of the latter the former are historically and critically unintelligible. . . .

It remains to be seen whether those who would provide for the study of

* pious wishes. [ed.]

Literature in the proper sense of the term will be strong enough to thwart the efforts of the philological party—in other words, whether a School in which the interests of Literature will be subordinated to those of Philology, shall be established in the University. As the former attempt was defeated only by a casting vote, and as the University is almost completely under the dominion of those who would dissociate it from national education and national life by preserving it as a nursery for specialists and a centre of technical learning, there is too much reason to fear that the philologists will carry the day.

9

"Mere Literature," the Atlantic Monthly (1893)

Woodrow Wilson

Woodrow Wilson (1856–1924), a Virginian and son of a Presbyterian clergyman and teacher, was educated at Davidson College and Princeton University (B. A. 1879). He attended law school at the University of Virginia and took a Ph.D. at Johns Hopkins University (1886). It was at Johns Hopkins that Wilson had a taste of the new Germanic scholarship, against which—in essays like the present selection—he reacted as a perversion of humanistic values. After teaching stints at Bryn Mawr College and Wesleyan University, Wilson became professor of jurisprudence and political economy at Princeton (1890–1902), where he eschewed specialized research and instead cultivated general humanistic and inspirational themes in his well-attended undergraduate courses.

Wilson succeeded to the presidency of Princeton in 1902, where he made a strenuous but unsuccessful attempt to combat the growth of graduate specialization over general culture and the growing social snobbery of college social life. He ran successfully for the governorship of New Jersey in 1910 and became 28th President of the United States (1913–1921).

Wilson's magazine essay, "Mere Literature," which appeared in the *Atlantic Monthly* in 1893, was an American counterpart of John Churton Collins's *The Study of English Literature*. Like Collins, Wilson expressed the dismay of Arnoldian humanists inside and outside the university at the constricted research methods which had come to dominate literary study. But Wilson's insistence that the literary "expression of spirit" is "not pervious to research" and resists the "critical knowledge of language" comes close to rejecting any analytic treatment of literature.

A singular phrase this, "mere literature,"—the irreverent invention of a scientific age. Literature we know, but "mere" literature? We are not to read it as if it meant *sheer* literature, literature in the essence, stripped of all accidental or ephemeral elements, and left with nothing but its immortal charm and power. "Mere literature" is a serious sneer, conceived in all honesty by the scientific mind, which despises things which do not fall within the categories of demonstrable knowledge. It means *nothing but literature*, as who should say, "mere talk," "mere fabrication," "mere pastime." The scientist, with his head comfortably and excusably full of knowable things, takes nothing seriously and with his hat off except human knowledge. The creations of the human spirit are, from his point of view, incalculable vagaries, irresponsible phenomena, to be regarded only as play, and, for the mind's good, only as recreation,—to be used to while away the tedium of a railway journey, or to amuse a period of rest or convalescence; mere byplay, mere make-believe.

And so very whimsical things sometimes happen, because of this scientific and positivist spirit of the age, when the study of the literature of any language is made part of the curriculum of our colleges. The more delicate and subtle purposes of the study are put quite out of countenance, and literature is commanded to assume the phrases and the methods of science. It would be very painful if it should turn out that schools and universities were agencies of Philistinism; but there are some things which should prepare us for such a discovery. Our present plans for teaching everybody involve certain unpleasant things quite inevitably. It is obvious that you cannot have universal education without restricting your teaching to such things as can be universally understood. It is plain that you cannot impart "university methods" to thousands, or create "investigators" by the score, unless you confine your university education to matters which dull men can investigate, your laboratory training to tasks which mere plodding diligence and submissive patience can compass. Yet, if you do so limit and constrain what you teach, you thrust taste and insight and delicacy of perception out of the schools, exalt the obvious and the merely useful above the things which are only imaginatively or spiritually conceived, make education an affair of tasting and handling and smelling, and so create Philistia, that country in which they speak of "mere literature," I suppose that in Nirvana one would speak in like wise of "mere life."

The fear, at any rate, that such things may happen cannot fail to set us anxiously pondering certain questions about the systematic teaching of literature in our schools and colleges. How are we to impart classical writings to the children of the general public? "Beshrew the general public!" cries Mr. Birrell. "What in the name of the Bodleian has the general public got to do with literature?"* Unfortunately, it has a great deal to do with it: for are we not complacently forcing the general public into our universities, and are we not arranging that all its sons be instructed how they may themselves master and teach our literature? You have nowadays, it is believed, only to heed the suggestions of pedagogics in order to know how to impart Burke or Browning,

---

* Augustine Birrell (1850–1933), British politician and man of letters. [ed.]

Dryden or Swift. There are certain practical difficulties, indeed; but there are ways of overcoming them. You must have strength so that you can handle with real mastery the firm fibre of these men; you must have a heart, moreover, to feel their warmth, an eye to see what they see, an imagination to keep them company, a pulse to experience their delights. But if you have none of these things, you may make shift to do without them. You may count the words they use, note the changes of phrase they make in successive revisions, put their rhythm into a scale of feet, run their allusions—particularly their female allusions—to cover, detect them in their previous reading. Or if none of these things please you, or you find the big authors difficult or dull, you may drag to light all the minor writers of their time, who are easy to understand. By setting an example in such methods you render great services in certain directions. You make the higher degrees of our universities available for the large number of respectable men who can count, and measure, and search diligently; and that may prove no small matter. You divert attention from thought, which is not always easy to get at, and fix attention upon language, as upon a curious mechanism, which can be perceived with the bodily eye, and which is worthy to be studied for its own sake, quite apart from anything it may mean. You encourage the examination of forms, grammatical and metrical, which can be quite accurately determined and quite exhaustively catalogued. You bring all the visible phenomena of writing to light and into ordered system. You go further, and show how to make careful literal identification of stories somewhere told ill and without art with the same stories told over again by the masters, well and with the transfiguring effect of genius. You thus broaden the area of science; for you rescue the concrete phenomena of the expression of thought—the necessary syllabification which accompanies it, the inevitable juxtaposition of words, the constant use of particles, the habitual display of roots, the inveterate repetition of names, the recurrent employment of meanings heard or read—from their confusion with the otherwise unclassifiable manifestations of what had hitherto been accepted, without critical examination, under the lump term "literature," simply for the pleasure and spiritual edification to be got from it.

An instructive differentiation ensues. In contrast with the orderly phenomena of speech and writing, which are amenable to scientific processes of examination and classification, and which take rank with the orderly successions of change in nature, we have what, for want of a more exact term, we call "mere literature,"—the literature which is not an expression of form but an expression of spirit. This is a troublesome thing, and perhaps does not belong in well-conceived plans of universal instruction; for it offers many embarrassments to pedagogic method. It escapes all scientific categories. It is not pervious to research. It is too wayward to be brought under the discipline of exposition. It is an attribute of so many different substances at one and the same time that the consistent scientific man must needs put it forth from his company, as without responsible connections. By "mere literature" he means mere evanescent color, wanton trick of phrase, perverse departures from categorical statement,—something *all* personal equation, such stuff as dreams are made of. . . .

There is but one way in which you can take mere literature as an education, and that is directly, at first hand. Almost any media except her own language and touch and tone are non-conducting. A descriptive catalogue of a collection of paintings is no substitute for the little areas of color and form themselves. You do not want to hear about a beautiful woman, simply,—how she was dressed, how she bore herself, how the fine color flowed sweetly here and there upon her cheeks, how her eyes burned and melted, how her voice thrilled through the ears of those about her. If you have ever seen a woman, these things but tantalize and hurt you, if you cannot see her. You want to be in her presence. You know that only your own eyes can give you direct knowledge of her. When once you have seen her, you know her in her habit as she lived; nothing but her presence contains her life. 'T is the same with the authentic products of literature. You can never get their beauty at second hand, or feel their power except by direct contact with them.

It is a strange and occult thing how this quality of "mere literature" enters into one book, and is absent from another; but no man who has once felt it can mistake it. . . .

It is so with all essential literature. It has a quality to move you, and you can never mistake it, if you have any blood in you. And it has also a power to instruct you which is as effective as it is subtle, and which no research or systematic method can ever rival. 'T is a sore pity if that power cannot be made available in the classroom. It is not merely that it quickens your thought and fills your imagination with the images that have illuminated the choicer minds of the race. It does indeed exercise the faculties in this wise, bringing them into the best atmosphere, and into the presence of the men of greatest charm and force; but it does a great deal more than that. It acquaints the mind, by direct contact, with the forces which really govern and modify the world from generation to generation. There is more of a nation's politics to be gotten out of its poetry than out of all its systematic writers upon public affairs and constitutions. Epics are better mirrors of manners than chronicles; dramas oftentimes let you into the secrets of statutes; orations stirred by a deep energy of emotion or resolution, passionate pamphlets that survive their mission because of the direct action of their style along permanent lines of thought, contain more history than parliamentary journals. It is not knowledge that moves the world, but ideals, convictions, the opinions or fancies that have been held or followed; and whoever studies humanity ought to study it alive, practice the vivisection of reading literature, and acquaint himself with something more than anatomies which are no longer in use by spirits. . . .

It is doubtless due to the scientific spirit of the age that these plain, these immemorial truths are in danger of becoming obscured. Science, under the influence of the conception of evolution, devotes itself to the study of forms, of specific differences, of the manner in which the same principle of life manifests itself variously under the compulsions of changes of environment. It is thus that it has become "scientific" to set forth the manner in which man's nature submits to man's circumstances; scientific to disclose morbid moods, and the conditions which produce them; scientific to regard man, not as the centre or source of power, but as subject to power, a register of external forces instead of an originative soul, and character as a product of man's circumstances rather than a sign of man's mastery over circumstance. It is thus that it has become "scientific" to analyze language as itself a commanding element in man's life. The history of word roots, their modification under the influences of changes wrought in the vocal organs by habit or by climate, the laws of phonetic change to which they are obedient, and their persistence under all disguises of dialect, as if they were full of a self-originated life, a self-directed energy of influence, is united with the study of grammatical forms in the construction of scientific conceptions of the evolution and uses of human speech. The impression is created that literature is only the chosen vessel of these forms, disclosing to us their modification in use and structure from age to age. Such vitality as the masterpieces of genius possess comes to seem only a dramatization of the fortunes of words. Great writers construct for the adventures of language their appropriate epics. Or, if it be not the words themselves that are scrutinized, but the style of their use, that style becomes, instead of a fine essence of personality, a matter of cadence merely, or of grammatical and structural relationships. Science is the study of the forces of the world of matter, the adjustments, the apparatus, of the universe; and the scientific study of literature has likewise become a study of apparatus,—of the forms in which men utter thought, and the forces by which those forms have been and still are being modified, rather than of thought itself.

The essences of literature of course remain the same under all forms, and the true study of literature is the study of these essences,—a study, not of forms or of differences, but of likenesses, likenesses of spirit and intent under whatever varieties of method, running through all forms of speech like the same music along the chords of various instruments. There is a sense in which literature is independent of form, just as there is a sense in which music is independent of its instrument. It is my cherished belief that Apollo's pipe contained as much eloquent music as any modern orchestra. Some books live; many die: wherein is the secret of immortality? Not in beauty of form, nor even in force of passion. We might say of literature what Wordsworth said of poetry, the most easily immortal part of literature: it is "the impassioned expression which is in the countenance of all science; it is the breath of the finer spirit of all knowledge." Poetry has the easier immortality because it has the sweeter accent when it speaks, because its phrases linger in our ears to delight them, because its truths are also melodies. Prose has much to overcome,—its plainness of visage, its less musical accents, its homelier turns of phrase. But it also may contain the immortal essence of truth and seriousness and high thought. It too may clothe conviction with the beauty that must make it shine forever. Let a man but have beauty in his heart, and, believing something with his might, put it forth arrayed as he sees it, the lights and shadows falling upon it on his page as they fall upon it in his heart, and he may die assured that that beauty will not pass away out of the world.

Biographers have often been puzzled by the contrast between certain men as they lived and as they wrote. Schopenhauer's case is one of the most singular. A man of turbulent life, suffering himself to be cut to exasperation by the petty worries of his lot, he was nevertheless calm and wise when he wrote, as if the Muse had rebuked him. He wrote at a still elevation, where small and temporary things did not come to disturb. 'T is a pity that for some men this elevation is so far to seek. They lose permanency by not finding it. Could there be a deliberate regimen of life for the author, it is plain enough how he ought to live, not as seeking fame, but as deserving it.

> "Fame, like the wayward girl, will still be coy
> To those who woo her with too slavish knees;
> But makes surrender to some thoughtless boy,
> And dotes the more upon a heart at ease.
>
> .   .   .   .
>
> "Ye love-sick bards, repay her scorn with scorn;
> Ye love-sick artists, madmen that ye are,
> Make your best bow to her and bid adieu:
> Then, if she likes it, she will follow you."
> (From Keats's "Sonnet on Fame")

It behooves all minor authors to realize the possibility of their being discovered some day, and exposed to the general scrutiny. They ought to live as if conscious of the risk. They ought to purge their hearts of everything that is not genuine and capable of lasting the world a century, at least, if need be. Mere literature is made of spirit. The difficulties of style are the artist's difficulties with his tools. The spirit that is in the eye, in the pose, in mien or gesture, the painter must find in his color box; as he must find also the spirit that nature displays upon the face of the fields or in the hidden places of the forest. The writer has less obvious means. Word and spirit do not easily consort. The language that the philologists set out before us with such curious erudition is of very little use as a vehicle for the essences of the human spirit. It is too sophisticated and self-conscious. What you need is, not a critical knowledge of language, but a quick feeling for it. You must recognize the affinities between your spirit and its idioms. You must immerse your phrase in your thought, your thought in your phrase, till each becomes saturated with the other. Then what you produce is as necessarily fit for permanency as if it were incarnated spirit. . . .

It is in this way that we get some glimpse of the only relations that scholarship bears to literature. Literature can do without exact scholarship, or any scholarship at all, though it may impoverish itself thereby; but scholarship cannot do without literature. It needs literature to float it, to set it current, to authenticate it to the race, to get it out of closets, and into the brains of men who stir abroad. It will adorn literature, no doubt; literature will be the richer for its presence; but it will not, it cannot, of itself create literature. Rich stuffs from the east do not create a king nor costly trappings a conqueror. There is, indeed, a natural antagonism, let it be frankly said, between the standards of scholarship and the standards of literature. Exact scholarship values things in direct proportion as they are verifiable; but literature knows nothing of such tests. The truths which it seeks are the truths of self-expression. It is a thing of convictions, of insights, of what is felt and seen and heard and hoped for. Its meanings lurk behind nature, not in the facts of its phenomena. It speaks of things as the man who utters it saw them, not necessarily as God made them. The personality of the speaker runs throughout all the sentences of real literature. That personality may not be the personality of a poet: it may be only the personality of the penetrative seer. It may not have the atmosphere in which visions are seen, but only that in which men and affairs look keenly cut in outline, boldly massed in bulk, consummately grouped in detail, to the reader as to the writer. Sentences of perfectly clarified wisdom may be literature no less than stanzas of inspired song, or the intense utterances of impassioned feeling. The personality of the sunlight is in the keen lines of light that run along the edges of a sword no less than in the burning splendor of the rose or the radiant kindlings of a woman's eye. You may feel the power of one master of thought playing upon your brain as you may feel that of another playing upon your heart. . . .

Scholarship is the realm of nicely adjusted opinion. It is the business of scholars to assess evidence and test conclusions, to discriminate values and reckon probabilities. Literature is the realm of conviction and of vision. Its points of view are as various as they are oftentimes unverifiable. It speaks individual faiths. Its groundwork is not erudition, but reflection and fancy. Your thoroughgoing scholar dare not reflect. To reflect is to let himself in on his material; whereas what he wants is to keep himself apart, and view his materials in an air that does not color or refract. To reflect is to throw an atmosphere about what is in your mind,—an atmosphere which holds all the colors of your life. Reflection summons all associations, and they throng and move so that they dominate the mind's stage at once. The plot is in their hands. Scholars, therefore, do not reflect; they label, group kind with kind, set forth in schemes, expound with dispassionate method. Their minds are not stages, but museums; nothing is done there, but very curious and valuable collections are kept there. If literature use scholarship, it is only to fill it with fancies or shape it to new standards, of which of itself it can know nothing.

True, there are books reckoned primarily books of science and of scholarship which have nevertheless won standing as literature: books of science such as Newton wrote, books of scholarship such as Gibbon's. But science was only the vestibule by which such a man as Newton entered the temple of nature, and the art he practiced was not the art of expositon, but the art of divination. He was not only a scientist, but also a seer; and we shall not lose sight of Newton because we value what he was more than what he knew. If we continue Gibbon in his fame, it will be for love of his art, not for worship of his scholarship. We some of us, nowadays, know the period of which he wrote better even than he did; but which one of us shall build so admirable a monument to ourselves, as artists, out of what we know? The scholar finds his immortality in the form he gives to his work. It is a hard saying, but the truth of it is inexorable: be an artist, or prepare for oblivion. You may write a chronicle, but you will not serve yourself thereby. You will only serve some fellow who shall come after you, possessing, what you did not have, an ear for the words you could not hit upon, an eye for the colors you could not see, a hand for the strokes you missed. . . .

You can make no catalogue of [the] features of great writing; there is no science of literature. Literature in its essence is mere spirit, and you must experience it rather than analyze it too formally. It is the door to nature and to ourselves. It opens our hearts to receive the experiences of great men and the conceptions of great races. It awakens us to the significance of action and to the singular power of mental habit. It airs our souls in the wide atmosphere of contemplation. "In these bad days, when it is thought more educationally useful to know the principle of the common pump than Keats's Ode on a Grecian Urn," as Mr. Birrell says, we cannot afford to let one single precious sentence of "mere literature" go by us unread or unpraised. If this free people to which we belong is to keep its fine spirit, its perfect temper amidst affairs, its high courage in the face of difficulties, its wise temperateness and wide-eyed hope, it must continue to drink deep and often from the old wells of English undefiled, quaff the keen tonic of its best ideals, keep its blood warm with all the great utterances of exalted purpose and pure principle of which its matchless literature is full. The great spirits of the past must command us in the tasks of the future. Mere literature will keep us pure and keep us strong. Even though it puzzle or altogether escape scientific method, it may keep our horizon clear for us, and our eyes glad to look bravely forth upon the world.

10

From *The Aims of Literary Study* (1895)

Hiram Corson

Hiram Corson, a Philadelphian, worked as a reporter in the United States Senate, a librarian at the Smithsonian Institute, and an unattached lecturer and private teacher before his appointment as professor of moral science, history, and rhetoric at Girard College (1865–66) and St. John's College at Annapolis (1866–70). A personal friend both of Robert Browning and Walt Whitman, Corson organized Browning Clubs throughout the United States, wrote an introduction to the poet, and defended Whitman's poetry.

Corson became professor of English at the newly founded Cornell University in 1870, where he became famous for his spellbinding classroom style, in which he illustrated his theory that literature could be taught and comprehended only by declamatory oral reading. Corson expounded this theory in *The Aims of Literary Study* (1895) and particularly *The Voice and Spiritual Education* (1896), works which also included harsh denunciations of philological and historical ways of teaching literature. In later life Corson became absorbed in spiritualism, holding seances in which he claimed to have contacted the spirits of deceased writers.

A great impulse has, of late years, been imparted to the study of the English language and literature, and that study has been introduced into all our institutions of learning, from the highest down to the lowest grade; and in most of our Colleges and Universities it is represented by a special professor. Text-books on the English language abound, and so do Manuals and Histories of English Literature, and elaborately annotated editions of selected works of classic authors, poetical and prose. Methods are discussed *ad nauseam*, almost, in school institutes and educational conventions, and the opinions of prominent educators are solicited by journals of education, as to the best thing to be done for the study of English.

But the question is far from gratuitous whether all the means so strenuously employed for the end in view, prove correspondingly efficient. They certainly do not. The evidences against such result are too strong to leave much faith in the means employed. And the grand defect of those means may be said to be, that the language and its literary products are not sufficiently studied as living organisms. Words are too much studied as *completely significant individuals*, and the study of literary products is too much devoted to their *accidents*, and not enough, scarcely at all, indeed, to their *substances*. Perhaps it is not a rash statement to make, that many teachers think it the prime business of scholastic discipline to deal with accidents. In the words of Chaucer,

> These cookes, how they stampe, and streyne, and grynde,
> And turnen substaunce into accident!

The lamentable ignorance of the mother tongue which prevails in the lower schools, and not much less in the Colleges and Universities, will not be remedied by the study of text-books on the language, nor by any amount of technical instruction imparted by the teacher. There is, at present, a superabundance of such study and such instruction; but the results are certainly very far from gratifying. Little or no vital knowledge of the language is imparted or acquired by these means, and whatever susceptibility to literature any student might otherwise have, is more or less deadened by petty details, grammatical, philological, and other, and irrelevant matters of every kind, which drink up all the sap of the mind (*omnem sucum ingenii bibunt*, as Quintilian says of the treatises on rhetoric, in his time), make impossible all continuity of thought and feeling, and shut off all synthetic appreciation. Here is, no doubt, one explanation of the very limited stock of thought which many students possess, after having been for several years at school. It would seem that thought were not an object in 'literary' exercises, to say nothing of feeling, but formulæ and technical knowledge of various kinds. Students are taught methods, but comparatively few attain unto the proposed *objects* of the methods, which objects are often lost sight of, altogether, in the *grind* to which they are subjected.

It is the merest truism that the leading aim in the teaching of English should be, 1. to enlarge the student's vocabulary, and, 2. to cultivate a nice sense of the force of words which constitute a large proportion of every language, whose meanings are not absolute, but relative and conditional, being variously modified and shaded according to their organization in the expression of thought and feeling; and, 3. (the sole end of 1 and 2), to speak and write good live English, of the best verbal material and texture, and closely fitting the thought which it clothes. . . .

These three things can be secured (the capacity for them being postulated) only through an extensive and sympathetic reading of good authors, the subject-matter being made the prime object, and the *ne quid nimis** being

---

* nothing in excess. [ed.]

strictly observed in incidental instruction, that the student's thought and feeling be not kept disintegrated.

It is in their *social* life, so to speak, that a large proportion of words must be known, to be truly known. As solitaires, they are more or less opaque, reflect no variety of hue, do not come into relation with feeling. Their radical ideas may be learned from dictionaries, and these are all that the mere word-monger, who makes words an end to themselves, may know of them. They must be variously organized in the expression of thought and feeling before all their *moral* potentialities are brought out. . . .

Inspiring power must come from an author's or a teacher's *being*, and not from his brain.

Being is teaching, the highest, the only quickening mode of teaching; the only mode which secures that unconscious following of a superior spirit by an inferior spirit—of a kindled soul by an unkindled soul. 'Surely,' says Walt Whitman,

> Surely whoever speaks to me in the right
> voice, him or her I shall follow,
> As the water follows the moon, silently, with
> fluid steps anywhere around the globe.

And so, to get at the *being* of a great author, to come into relationship with his absolute personality, is the highest result of the study of his works. I have just said, *par parenthèse*, that a teacher without inspiring power should have nothing to do with conducting literary studies. The teacher who unites in himself a fulness of intellectual and spiritual vitality, in whom the 'what Knows' and the 'what Is' work harmoniously together, is an epistle known and read of all his students. The young are quicker, often, to discover such vitality, or the want of it, than adults are. After a recitation or a lecture, they feel their faculties refreshed or dulled, according to the vitality or non-vitality of their teacher. The inspiring power of personality is quite as much needed in scientific teaching. Many are the men still living, in whom the great naturalist, Professor Louis Agassiz, continues to live, in this world. And they are far superior as naturalists by reason of what he elicited from them of the 'what Is.' He thus brought them into a deeply sympathetic relationship with the animal kingdom—a relationsip which is the condition of sagacious insight. . . .

Again, reading must not be done in expectation of an examination on details. The teacher might talk with his class familiarly, and encourage the class to talk, about their reading—its subject-matter, of course. He could thus get a sufficient estimate of their varied appreciation, to grade them (if that were necessary); but he should not directly 'examine' them, to determine what each should be 'marked,' on a scale of ten, or a hundred, or any other scale which might be adopted in the school. They would then read for the examination, and would thus be more or less shut off from some of the best influences which might otherwise act upon them.

Examinations are the bane of literary study, for the reason that they largely determine the character of this study, in the schools. They *must* deal specially, if not exclusively, with the definite, with matters of fact, and these are accordingly made the main subject of study. Examinations on a play of Shakespeare, have generally nothing to do with the play as a play, with the dramatic action, with the *artistic expression* in its highest sense; they are rather examinations on Elizabethan English, and *de omnibus rebus et quibusdam aliis,* * except the *play.* But, as Hamlet says, in quite another connection, 'the play's the thing.'

The opinion is prevalent among educators, that clear, definite, intellectual conceptions are the only measure of true education; and that indefinite impressions, in order to be educating, must be intellectualized as far as possible; that truly to know really means this. On the contrary, it may be maintained, that in the domain of the spiritual (and to this domain the higher literature primarily belongs), it is all important that indefinite impressions, derived, for example, from a great creation of genius, should long be held in solution (to use a chemical figure), and not be prematurely precipitated into barren judgments which have no quickening power. They then cease to have a spiritual action. One should be well *charged* with a great author, through long, sympathetic, 'wisely passive' reading of his works, before any attempt be made at defining, formulating, precipitating, which 'refuse the soul its way.' But the tendency is strong in the other direction—so strong as to lead to the attempt to 'make square to a finite eye the circle of infinity.' In this respect, the squaring of the circle has not yet been given up.

We must long inhale the choral atmosphere of a work of genius before we attempt, if we attempt at all, any intellectual formulation of it; which formulation must necessarily be comparatively limited, because genius, as genius, is transcendental, and therefore outside of the domain of the intellect. The human spirit can be educated only through the concrete and the personal; and these may be said to constitute the vernacular language of genius. But if this language, in our educational systems, be translated into the abstract, into the language of the intellect, so far as it can be, its proper function is defeated. The spiritual man is not responsive to the abstract. The word must become flesh in order to be spiritually responded to. The response of the intellect to the abstract, does not quicken.

The intellect should be trained and habituated to clear, distinct, and adequate conceptions concerning all things that are objects of clear

---

* about everything and more besides. [ed.]

conceptions. But it must not be unduly fostered to the benumbing of the spiritual faculties. That such benumbing often results from such cause, is unquestionable.

The most *practical* education (but this, so considered, preëminently practical age does not seem to know it) is the education of the spiritual man; for it is this, and not the education of the intellectual man, which is, *must* be (or Christianity has made a great mistake) the basis of individual character; and to individual character (not so much to institutions, to the regulations of society, to the State, to moral codes) humanity chiefly owes its sustainment. . . .

The time must come, it is perhaps in the far future, when literary examinations will be through vocal interpretation which will reveal the extent of a student's assimilation of the intellectually indefinite elements of a literary work. But there will then have to be higher ideals of vocal culture than the educational world, at the present time, can boast of.

I have been present at literary examinations which brought out answers, acceptable indeed to the examiners, but which no more evidenced the students' knowledge of the works on which they were examined, than the boy Bitzer's definition of a horse, in the 2d Chapter of Dickens's 'Hard Times,' evidenced that he knew anything of the noble animal he defined, though it was entirely satisfactory to Thomas Gradgrind, the examiner on the occasion, who believed that 'facts alone are wanted in life. Plant nothing else, and root out everything else:'

> 'Quadruped. Graminivorous. Forty teeth, namely, twenty-four grinders, four eye-teeth, and twelve incisive. Sheds coat in the spring; in marshy countries, sheds hoofs, too. Hoofs hard, but requiring to be shod with iron. Age known by marks in mouth.'

Hereupon, Mr. Gradgrind said to poor little Sissy Jupe, who had been asked to define a horse, but who, in her trepidation, could not, 'Now, girl number twenty, you know what a horse is.' Yes, she *did* know, with a vengeance, if her knowledge was derived from Bitzer's definition.

Let it not be understood that there is implied in the foregoing remarks, any depreciation of grammatical, philological, rhetorical, or any other kind of instruction for which the work studied affords material. Philology, on its higher planes, is a great science, one of the greatest, indeed, which has been developed in modern times. But it is a science. It is not literature. And in literary study, the only true object of which is to take in the *life* of the work studied, that object must not be defeated by the teacher's false notions of thoroughness, which resulted in his obtruding upon the student's attention all manner of irrelevant things, even to the utter exclusion of the one thing needful. The irrelevant things may have their importance, but they must also have their proper time and place. A man of reputed wisdom once said, 'to everything there is a season, and a time to every purpose (or matter) under the heaven.' It is not in season, for example, for a teacher, while pretending to study, with a class, a poem, as a poem, to

> chase
> A panting syllable through time and space,
> Start it at home, and hunt it in the dark,
> To Gaul, to Greece, and into Noah's ark.

And yet such unreasonable things *are* done, in these philological days, in the name of literary study. If the poem were studied merely as a monument of the language, and the study were called philological, there would be no objection thereto. But when philological study sails under false colors, it does a wrong to what must certainly be considered the higher study, upon which it should never be obtruded, when that study is going on, except where its services are really in requisition; and they rarely are, in strictly literary study. All the philological knowledge which may really be needed, can be found in Webster's International, The Century, Skeat's Etymological, or any other good dictionary in present use.

11
"The Province of English Philology," PMLA (1898)
Albert S. Cook

Albert Stanburrough Cook (1853–1927) graduated from Rutgers University in 1872 and went on to Leipzig, Göttingen, and Jena Universities to study philology. He was appointed to the Johns Hopkins University faculty in 1879, where he organized the English Department. He became chairman of the department at the University of California at Berkeley in 1882 and moved to Yale University in 1889 where he stayed until retirement in 1927. He served as president of the Modern Language Assocation, 1898–99. Author of philological studies on the Bible and its influence and *Beowulf*, and editor for many years of *Yale Studies in English*, Cook is probably best known today for his editions of the great critical defenses of poetry by Horace, Sidney, Boileau, and Shelley.

Cook's essay, delivered as the presidential address at The Modern Language Association meeting of 1897, was an attempt to answer the attacks on philology mounted by the likes of Woodrow Wilson and Hiram Corson. Cook saw himself as a humanistic generalist who tried to embody the older, broader meaning of "philology" as the study of the whole of civilization, not a narrow linguistic study. As this selection illustrates, Cook was typical of many who identified with the philological scholars and defended them against detractors, yet who could not help conceding that such scholarship was falling short of what was needed in the sphere of education and general culture, Cook's defense of philology, then, in some ways constitutes a more damaging indictment than the outright attacks of men of letters.

Perhaps no reproach is oftener addressed to those who call themselves philologists than that they are unconcerned with that beauty which has furnished a distinctive epithet for the word 'literature' in the phrase *belles lettres*, that they lack imagination and insight, and that they are quite unfitted to impart to others a sense of the spiritual values which inhere in the productions that form the subject-matter of their studies. An eloquent writer, who is himself a capable investigator, has recently presented this view in an essay which deserves the attention of every teacher of literature, and especially of every teacher of English literature.

I make no apology for quoting a rather long extract from the essay in question, since the arraignment puts into definite form what a good many people have been feeling and intimating, and the philologist is bound to meet the attack either by mending his ways, or by showing that the critic, with the best intentions in the world, has not fully comprehended the purposes of philology, or has perhaps taken a part for the whole. Here, then, is the passage:

> "And so very whimsical things sometimes happen, because of this scientific and positivist spirit of the age, when the study of the literature of any language is made part of the curriculum of our colleges. The more delicate and subtle purposes of the study are put quite out of countenance, and literature is commanded to assume the phrases and the methods of science. . . . It is obvious that you cannot have universal education without restricting your teaching to such things as can be universally understood. It is plain that you cannot impart 'university methods' to thousands, or create 'investigators' by the score, unless you confine your university education to matters which dull men can investigate, your laboratory training to tasks which mere plodding diligence and submissive patience can compass. Yet, if you do so limit and constrain what you teach, you thrust taste and insight and delicacy of perception out of the schools, exalt the obvious and the merely useful above the things which are only imaginatively or spiritually conceived, make education an affair of tasting and handling and smelling. . . ."
> (Woodrow Wilson, *Mere Literature, and Other Essays*, 1896, p. 2.)

This is a stern indictment to bring against the philologist—the 'mere philologist,' as our author might say—and if it contains the whole truth, and nothing but the truth; if things are quite as bad as here represented, and the fault is the fault of certain innovators, who usurp the domain of better men with their science falsely so-called; then it behoves us to be on our guard, lest we also be entangled in the net they have woven for their own feet, and so become involved with them in a common destruction.

Let us first see, however, whether some of these matters are susceptible of being differently stated. And first, is it quite certain that the evils complained of are due to the scientific and positivist spirit of this age, and to the effort after universal education? It is more than two thousand years since Herodicus described the followers of the critic Aristarchus as 'buzzing in corners, busy with mono-syllables.' It is more than eighteen hundred years since Seneca thus declaimed against what he understood by the philological study of literature. . . .

But, unfortunately, the trail of the serpent is over philosophy even. Seneca can not help admitting that his very philosophers are not quite what they should be. "I speak," he says, "of liberal studies; how much of what is useless do philosophers possess, how much of what is unpractical! They also have descended to the distinction of syllables, and to the proprieties of conjunctions and prepositions, and to envy grammarians, to envy geometricians. . . . Thus it is come to pass that, with all their diligence, they know rather to speak than to live." . . .

There must, one would infer, be something inherently attractive and valuable about learning, which enables it to survive such attacks as those of Seneca; there must be something inherently attractive and valuable about the learning which occupies itself with literature, to make it the concern of so many magnanimous spirits, and to extort vindications from the antagonists who come out armed to destroy it. Perhaps the explanation is to be sought in Aristotle's famous sentence, "All men by nature desire to know." Perhaps the justification has been furnished by Seneca himself, who elsewhere asks why we instruct our children in liberal studies, and answers, "Not because they can give virtue, but because they prepare the mind to the receiving of it." Possibly, then, virtue may sometimes be best suggested by indirection; perhaps, too, the same is true of taste and insight; it may be that they come not with observation, or at least not exclusively with observation; it may be that they who devotedly study any aspect of great works receive of their spirit, even as one may approach the one spirit of Nature through the different channels of astronomy, chemistry, and zoology. A lover of literature and of all forms of beauty, too early lost to his University and the world—I refer to the late Professor McLaughlin—in an essay in which he pleaded for the recognition of the spiritual element in literature, was yet fain to admit: "The first steps toward the desired results must be prosaic; people must train themselves, or be trained, to see what is on the surface, to grow conscious of metrical differences, for instance; not to remain quite blind to the real meaning beneath a figurative turn; even to come to recognize that there is a figurative turn."

If we could take this view to heart, perhaps the difficulties which perplex so many earnest seekers after truth, as they consider the subject, would vanish away, or at any rate become less formidable. According to this mode of looking at the matter, taste and insight and delicacy of perception are by no means common in an era of universal education, nor indeed in any era whatever; the person who possesses them only in a rudimentary degree is as likely to be repelled as attracted by a sudden revelation of their austere charms; in this, as in everything else, the natural progress is by easy stages from the phenomenal to the noumenal, from the things of sense to the things of the spirit; and accordingly the science which undertakes to deal with the forms in which the human spirit has, in various epochs, manifested itself, especially through the medium of literature, must be prepared to take account of the phenomenal no less than the noumenal, and accompany the seeker along the whole scale of ascent from the one to the other.

But is there any such science? There is; its name is Philology; and in no other sense than as designating this science should the term 'philology' be used, unless with some qualifying term which limits its meaning in a specific and unmistakable manner.

The function of the philologist, then, is the endeavor to relive the life of the past; to enter by the imagination into the spiritual experiences of all the historic protagonists of civilization in a given period and area of culture; to think the thoughts, to feel the emotions, to partake the aspirations, recorded in literature; to become one with humanity in the struggles of a given nation or race to perceive and attain the ideal of existence; and then to judge rightly these various disclosures of the human spirit, and to reveal to the world their true significance and relative importance.

In compassing this end, the philologist will have much to do; much that is not only laborious, but that even, in itself considered, might justly be regarded as distasteful, or even repellent. He must examine and compare the records of the human spirit bequeathed us by the past, and, before doing this, must often exhume them, perhaps in a mutilated condition, from the libraries and monasteries where they may have been moldering for ages; he must piece them together, where they have been separated and dispersed; interpret them; correct their manifest errors, so far as this may safely be done in the light of fuller information; determine their meaning and their worth; and then deliver them to the world, freed, as far as may be, from the injuries inflicted by time and evil chance, with their sense duly ascertained, their message clearly set forth, and their contribution to the sum of human attainment justly and sympathetically estimated.

This is the work that has been done, and is still in process of doing, for the Sacred Scriptures; for Homer, Sophocles, and Pindar among the Greeks; for Virgil, Lucretius, Tacitus, and Juvenal among the Romans; for the Italian Dante and Ariosto; for the French *chansons de geste*, no less than for Ronsard, Molière, and Rousseau; for the *Nibelungenlied* and Goethe among the Germans; for Cynewulf, Chaucer, Shakespeare, and Milton among the English; and for a multitude of others of whom these may stand as types.

The ideal philologist is at once antiquary, palaeographer, grammarian, lexicologist, expounder, critic, historian of literature, and, above all, lover of humanity. He should have the accuracy of the scientist, the thirst for discovery of the Arctic explorer, the judgment of the man of affairs, the sensibility of the musician, the taste of the connoisseur, and the soul of the poet. He must shrink from no labor, and despise no detail, by means of which he may be enabled to reach his goal more surely, and laden with richer results. Before traversing unknown seas, he must appropriate every discovery made by his predecessors on similar quests, and avail himself of every improvement upon their methods which his imagination can suggest, and his judgment approve. He will be instant in season and out of season. Whatsoever his hand finds to do he will do with his might. He will choose the task which humanity most needs to have performed, and at the same time that in which his own powers and special equipment can be most fully utilized; and, when possible, he will give the preference to such labors as shall afford play and outreach to his nobler faculties, rather than to such as may dwarf and impoverish them.

According to the exigencies which circumstances create, or his own intuition perceives, he will edit dictionaries, like Johnson or Murray; make lexicons to individual authors, like Schmidt; compile concordances, like Bartlett or Ellis; investigate metre, like Sievers or Schipper; edit authors, as Skeat has edited Chaucer, Child the English and Scottish Ballads, and Furness Shakespeare; discourse on the laws of literature, like Sidney, or Ben Jonson, or Lewes, or Walter Pater; write literary biography, like Brandl or Dowden; or outline the features and progress of a national literature, like Ten Brink, or Stopford Brooke, or Taine.

The ideal philologist must, therefore, have gained him "the gains of various men, ransacked the ages, spoiled the climes." Yet withal he must be content, if fortune, or his sense of a potential universe hidden in his apparently insignificant task, will have it so, merely to settle *hoti's* business, properly base *oun*, or give us the doctrine of the enclitic *de*—sure that posterity, while it may ungratefully forget him, will at least have cause to bless his name, as that of one without whose strenuous and self-sacrificing exertions the poets, the orators, the historians, and the philosophers would have less completely yielded up their meaning, or communicated their inspiration, to an expectant and needy world.

That the philologist, as such, is not necessarily a creative literary artist, is no impugnment of his mission or its importance. Neither is he who expounds the law, or the doctrines of Christianity, necessarily a creative literary artist. Yet he may be; Erskine was, and Webster; and so were Robert South and Cardinal Newman in their sermons. To be learned is not necessarily to be dull, for Burke was learned, and Chaucer, and Cicero, and Homer. Petrarch was not dull; and all the philology of modern times goes back to Petrarch. . . .

But it has been observed that dull men crowd into the profession, men who can only count and catalogue, or who, to employ the language of Chapman in *The Revenge of Bussy d'Ambois,* are

> Of taste so much depraved, that they had rather
> Delight, and satisfy themselves to drink
> Of the stream troubled, wandering ne'er so far
> From the clear fount, than of the fount itself.

Alas, it is but too true! Heaven-sent geniuses are rare, and there is not room for all the dull men in the other professions. Moreover, great poets are sometimes averse to spending their lives in the professor's chair, when they can write *Idylls of the King* and *Men and Women.* Also, there is no recipe by which to convert dull men into heaven-sent geniuses, and the preponderance of the former class everywhere is an evil not sufficiently to be deplored. Then, too, some of us must do the intellectual hewing of wood and drawing of water for the rest, and how should this be were no dull men to interest themselves in literature? . . .

Philology is frequently considered to be identical with linguistics. This is an error which can not be sufficiently deprecated. It results in the estrangement of the study of language from that of literature, with which, in the interests of both, it should be most intimately associated. The study of language is apt to seem arid and repellent to those who do not perceive how essential it is to the comprehension of literature. The conception of linguistics as a totally independent branch of learning, and the bestowal upon it of the appellation which properly designates the whole study of the history of culture, especially through the medium of literature, is fraught with incalculable injury to the pursuit of both divisions of the subject. . . .

Why should not all thoughtful students of English call themselves philologists, and thus recognize that they are all virtually aiming at the same thing, notwithstanding that they approach the subject from different points of view, and in practise emphasize different aspects of their common theme?

It may perhaps be objected that this would be equivalent to attributing an arbitrary and novel signification to the word philology. In this presence, I need only advert to the fact that in Germany the meaning I advocate is recognized as the only tenable one by all the recent authorities. More than a hundred years ago, Wolf, acting in part under the inspiration of Goethe, outlined the conception which in more recent times has been developed by Boeckh, and from him has been adopted by all the chief authors or editors of systematic treatises dealing with the philology of the various nations or races.* . . . No one who has not reflected long and deeply upon the conception elaborated by Boeckh can realize how fruitful it proves, and how fully it satisfies the demand for a philosophy of our work which shall recognize at once the part played in its advancement by the intuitions of genius and by the humbler labors of the compiler and systematizer. . . .

We must never forget that the philologist is a lover. As Pythagoras was not willing to be called a wise man, but only a lover of wisdom, and thus coined the word philosophy, so the philologist may well be content to call himself a lover too, a lover of the thrilling and compelling voices of the past. He becomes a philologist, if he is worthy of the name, because they have thrilled and compelled him; and he would fain devise means, however circuitous in appearance, by which to insure that they shall thrill and compel others. His sensibility is the measure of his devotion; and his devotion, while it may not

---

* Friedrich August Wolf (1759–1824) and his student Philipp August Boeckh (1785–1867), classical scholars and pioneers in defining the broad cultural scope of philological discipline. [ed.]

be the measure of his success, is certainly its indispensable condition.

If then, philology, truly considered, enlists the head in the service of the heart; if it demands not only high and manifold discipline, but rich natural endowment; if its object is the revelation to the present of the spiritual attainments of the past; if it aims to win free access for the thoughts of the mightiest thinkers, and the dreams of the most visionary of poets; if it seeks to train the imagination to re-create the form and pressure of a vanished time, in order to stimulate our own age to equal or surpass its predecessors in whatever best illustrates and ennobles humanity; if there are not wanting numerous examples of poets who have been philologists, and philologists who have been essentially poets; and, finally, if philology is the only term which thus fully comprehends these various aspects of a common subject, and we have the most authoritative precedents for employing it in that signification; shall we willingly allow the word to be depreciated, and the largeness and unity of the corresponding conception imperiled, by consenting to employ it for the designation of a single branch of the comprehensive whole, and that the branch which, to the popular apprehension, least exhibits the real import and aim of the science? If not, and we are willing to be known as philologists in the truer and larger sense, can we not do something to make this sense the prevalent one, by consistently adhering to it in our practice, and, so far as possible, inducing others to accept and adopt it? By thus doing, we shall not only be recognizing a truth which is indisputable, but also be promoting that harmony of opinions and sentiments without which the most strenuous individual efforts are certain to prove in some degree nugatory.

12

From *The Amateur Spirit* (1904)
Bliss Perry

Bliss Perry (1860–1954) grew up in Williamstown, Massachusetts, attended
Williams College, and succeeded his father as a professor there upon taking his
M. A. in 1883. Accorded a leave, Perry studied philology for two years at the
Universities of Berlin and Strasbourg before returning to teach English at
Williams. Perry moved to the English department at Princeton University from
1893–1900, resigning to become editor of the *Atlantic Monthly* until 1909. He
taught English literature at Harvard University from 1909 until retirement in
1930. Perry was one of the early advocates of the teaching of American and
contemporary literature in college courses.

Perry's many books and editions include *The Spirit of American Literature*, *The
Amateur Spirit*, the Cambridge Poets series, and an autobiography, *And Gladly
Teach* (see selection in Chapter 16). The present selection from *The Amateur
Spirit* reflects the mixture of feelings experienced by figures like Perry at the eclipse
by the modern specialist of the all-around amateur man of letters. Though Perry
hopes that the best qualities of the amateur and professional spirit can be
combined within a liberal education, his own remarks frequently suggest that this
reconciliation seems to be an "impossible ideal." One symptom of this widening
division is the contrast between "the born investigator" and "the born teacher,"
combining in the same person according to Perry only by a "miracle."

In any particular art or sport, it is often difficult to draw a hard-and-fast line
between amateur and professional activity. The amateur athlete may be so
wholly in earnest as to take risks and to endure hardships which no amount of
money would tempt him to undergo. This earnestness has seldom, if ever, been
carried so far as it is in our American athletic contests of the present day. . . .

The athletic contests of zealous undergraduates are of course but one
illustration of the earnestness which the amateur may carry into every
department of life. Amateur philanthropy, for example, is of great and
increasing service in the social organism of the modern community. Many an

American brings to his amusement, his avocation,—such as yachting, fancy farming, tarpon fishing,—the same thoroughness, energy, and practical skill that win him success in his vocation.

And yet, as a general rule, the amateur betrays amateurish qualities. He is unskillful because untrained; desultory because incessant devotion to his hobby is both unnecessary and wearisome; ineffective because, after all, it is not a vital matter whether he succeed or fail. The amateur actor is usually interesting, at times delightful, and even, as in the case of Dickens, powerful; his performance gives pleasure to his friends; but, nevertheless, the professional who must act well or starve, acts very much better. In a country where there is a great leisure class, as the Warden of Merton points out, amateurism is sure to flourish. "The young Englishman of this great leisure class," he says, "is no dandy and no coward, but he is an amateur born and bred, with an amateur's lack of training, an amateur's contempt of method, and an amateur's ideal life." The English boy attends school, he adds, with other boys who are amateurs in their studies, and almost professionals in their games; he passes through the university with the minimum of industry; he finds professional and public life in Great Britain crippled by the amateur spirit; in the army, the bar, the church, in agriculture, manufacturing, and commerce, there is a contempt for knowledge, an inveterate faith in the superiority of the rule of thumb, a tendency to hold one's self a little above one's work. . . .

Amateurs, then, to borrow Mr. Brodrick's definition, "are men who are not braced up to a high standard of effort and proficiency by a knowledge that failure may involve ruin, who seldom fully realize the difficulties of success against trained competitors, and who therefore rebel against the drudgery of professional drill and methodical instruction." One may accept this definition, in all its implications, without ceasing to be aware of the charm of the amateur. For the amateur surely has his charm, and he has his virtues,—virtues that have nowhere wrought more happily for him than here upon American soil. Versatility, enthusiasm, freshness of spirit, initiative, a fine recklessness of tradition and precedent, a faculty for cutting across lots,—these are the qualities of the American pioneer. . . .

The amateur search for truth has always flourished, and is likely to flourish always, in the United States. That the quest is inspiriting, amusing, sometimes highly rewarded, one may readily admit. But if it promotes individualism, it also produces the crank. If it brevets us all as philosophers, it likewise brands many of us as fools. Who does not know the amateur economist, with his "sacred ratios," or his amiable willingness to "do something for silver"? The amateur sociologist, who grows strangely confused if you ask him to define Sociology? Popular preachers, who can refute Darwin and elucidate Jefferson "while you wait,"—if you do wait? Amateur critics of art and literature, who have plenty of zeal, but no knowledge of standards, no anchorage in principles? The lady amateur, who writes verses without knowing prosody, and paints pictures without learning to draw, and performs what she calls "social service" without training her own children either in manners or religion? Nay, are there not amateur teachers who walk gracefully through the part, but add neither to the domain of human knowledge nor to the practical efficiency of any pupil? . . .

What is true of the sport, of the art, is even more invariably true in the field of scientific effort. How secure is the course of the *Fachmann*,* who by limiting his territory has become lord of it, who has a fund of positive knowledge upon all the knowable portions of it, and has charted, at least, the deepening water where knowledge sheers off into ignorance! It is late in the day to confess the indebtedness of our generation to the scientific method. How tonic and heartening, in days of dull routine, has been the example of those brave German masters to whom our American scholarship owes so much! What industry has been theirs, what confidence in method, what serene indifference to the rivalry of the gifted amateur! I recall the fine scorn with which Bernhard ten Brink, at Strassburg, used to wave aside the suggestions of his pupils that this or that new and widely advertised book might contain some valuable contribution to his department. "Nay," he would retort, "*wissenschaftliche Bedeutung hats doch nicht.*" Many a pretentious book, a popular book, even a very useful book, was pilloried by that quiet sentence, "*It has no scientific significance.*" To get the import of that sentence thoroughly into one's head is worth all it costs to sit at the feet of German scholars. There speaks the true, patient, scientific spirit, whose service to the modern man was perhaps the most highly appraised factor when we of the western world tried to take an inventory of ourselves and our indebtedness, at the dawn of the twentieth century.

For to be able to assess the scientific bearing of the new book, the new fact, upon your own profession proves you a master of your profession. Modern competitive conditions are making this kind of expert knowledge more and more essential. The success of German manufacturing chemists, for example, is universally acknowledged to be due to the scientific attainments of the thousands of young men who enter the manufactories from the great technical schools. The alarm of Englishmen over the recent strides of Germany in commercial rivalry is due to a dawning recognition of the efficacy of knowledge, and of the training which knowledge recommends. It is the well-grounded alarm of the gifted amateur when compelled to compete with the professional. The professional may not be a wholly agreeable antagonist; he may not happen to be a "clubable" person; but that fact does not vitiate his record. His record stands.

Is it possible to explain this patent or latent antagonism of the amateur

---

* *Fachmann*, specialist. [ed.]

toward the professional? It is explicable, in part at least, through a comparison not so much of their methods of work—where the praise must be awarded to the professional—as of their characteristic spirit. And here there is much more to be said for the amateur. The difference will naturally be more striking if we compare the most admirable trait of the amateur spirit with the least admirable trait of the professional spirit.

The cultivated amateur, who touches life on many sides, perceives that the professional is apt to approach life from one side only. It is a commonplace to say that without specialized training and accomplishment the road to most kinds of professional success is closed. Yet, through bending one's energies unremittingly upon a particular task, it often happens that creation narrows "in man's view," instead of widening. Your famous expert, as you suddenly discover, is but a segment of a man,—overdeveloped in one direction, atrophied in all others. His expertness, his professional functioning, so to speak, is of indisputable value to society, but he himself remains an unsocial member of the body politic. He has become a machine,—as Emerson declared so long ago, "a thinker, not a man thinking." He is uninterested, and consequently uninteresting. Very possibly it may not be the chief end of man to afford an interesting spectacle to the observer. And yet so closely are we bound together that a loss of sympathy, of imagination, of free and varied activity, soon insulates the individual, and lessens his usefulness as a member of society. . . .

There are few observers of American life who believe that specialization has as yet been carried too far. Yet one may insist that the theory of specialized functions, necessitated as it is by modern conditions, and increasingly demanded as it must be while our civilization grows in complexity, needs examination and correction in the interests of true human progress. It is not that we actually meet on the sidewalk some scientific Frankenstein, some marvelously developed special faculty for research or invention or money-making, which dominates and dwarfs all other faculties,—though we often see something that looks very much like it. It is rather that thoughtful people are compelled to ask themselves, How far can this special development—this purely professional habit of mind—proceed without injury to the symmetry of character, without impairing the varied and spontaneous and abundant play of human powers which gives joy to life? And the prejudice which the amateur feels toward the professional, the more or less veiled hostility between the man who does something for love which another man does for money, is one of those instinctive reactions—like the vague alarm of some wild creature in the woods—which give a hint of danger.

Let us make the very fullest acknowledgment of our debt to the professional spirit. . . .

Ours must be, not "a nation of amateurs," but a nation of professionals, if it is to hold its own in the coming struggles,—struggles not merely for commercial dominance, but for the supremacy of political and moral ideals. Our period of national isolation, with all it brought of good or evil, has been outlived. The new epoch will place a heavy handicap upon ignorance of the actual world, upon indifference to international usages and undertakings, upon contempt for the foreigner. What is needed is, indeed, knowledge, and the skill that knowledge makes possible. The spirit with which we confront the national tasks of the future should have the sobriety, the firmness, the steady effectiveness, which we associate with the professional.

Yet is it not possible, while thus acknowledging and cultivating the professional virtues, to free ourselves from some of the grosser faults of the mere professional? The mere professional's cupidity, for instance, his low aim, his time-serving, his narrowness, his clannish loyalty to his own department only? How often he lacks imagination! How indifferent he may show himself to the religious and moral passion, to the dreams, hopes, futilities, regrets of the breathing, bleeding, struggling men and women by his side! It is not the prize-fighter only who brings professionalism into disrepute. The jockey who "pulls" a horse, the oarsman who "sells" a race, the bicyclist who fouls a rival, are condemned even by a mob of "sporting men." But the taint of professionalism clings also to the business man who can think only of his shop, the scholar who talks merely of letters, the politician who asks of the proposed measure, "What is there in this for me?" To counteract all such provinciality and selfishness, such loss of the love of honor in the love of gain, one may rightly plead for some breath of the spirit of the amateur, the amator, the "man who loves;" the man who works for the sheer love of working, plays the great complicated absorbing game of life for the sake of the game, and not for his share of the gate money; the man who is ashamed to win if he cannot win fairly,—nay, who is chivalric enough to grant breathing-space to a rival, whether he win or lose!

Is it an impossible ideal, this combination of qualities, this union of the generous spirit of the amateur with the method of the professional? In the new world of disciplined national endeavor upon which we are entering, why may not the old American characteristics of versatility, spontaneity, adventurousness, still persist? These are the traits that fit one to adjust himself readily to unforeseen conditions, to meet new emergencies. They will be even more valuable in the future than in the past, if they are employed to supplement, rather than to be substituted for, the solid achievements of professional industry. If we are really to lead the world's commerce,—though that is far from being the only kind of leadership to which American history should teach us to aspire,—it will be the Yankee characteristics, plus the scientific training of the modern man, that will enable us to do it. The personal enthusiasm, the individual initiative, the boundless zest, of the American amateur must penetrate, illuminate, idealize, the brute force, the irresistibly on-sweeping mass, of our vast industrial democracy.

The best evidence that this will happen is the fact that it is already happening. There are here and there amateurs without amateurishness, professionals untainted by professionalism. Many of us are fortunate enough to recognize in some friend this combination of qualities, this union of strict professional training with that free outlook upon life, that human curiosity and eagerness, which are the best endowment of the amateur. Such men are indeed rare, but they are prized accordingly. And one need hardly say where they are most likely to be found. It is among the ranks of those who have received a liberal education. Every higher institution of learning in this country now offers some sort of specialized training. To win distinction in academic work is to come under the dominion of exact knowledge, of approved methods. It means that one is disciplined in the mechanical processes and guided by the spirit of modern science, no matter what his particular studies may have been. The graduates whose acquisitions can most readily be assessed are probably the ones who have specialized most closely, who have already as undergraduates begun to fit themselves for some form of professional career. They have already gained something of the expert's solid basis of accurate information, the expert's sureness of hand and eye, the expert's instinct for the right method.

But this professional discipline needs tempering by another spirit. The highest service of the educated man in our democratic society demands of him breadth of interest as well as depth of technical research. It requires unquenched ardor for the best things, spontaneous delight in the play of mind and character, a many-sided responsiveness that shall keep a man from hardening into a mere high-geared machine. It is these qualities that perfect a liberal education and complete a man's usefulness to his generation. Taken by themselves, they fit him primarily for living, rather than for getting a living. But they are not to be divorced from other qualities; and even if they were, the educated American can get a living more easily than he can learn how to live. The moral lessons are harder than the intellectual, and faith and enthusiasm, sympathy and imagination are moral qualities. . . .

There are two professional types, assuredly, that are admirably adjusted to their environment; the born investigator, and the born teacher. Men belonging to the first of these classes find in research itself a sufficient recompense; their happiness is in widening the bounds of knowledge, and undermining stoutly intrenched stupidities, and adding to the effectiveness of human energy. Almost every college has one or more of these men. The larger institutions have many of them, and the college community is their rightful place. They deserve their bed and board,—and their cakes and ale besides—even if they are too absent-minded to remember their lecture hours, or too feebly magnetic to hold the attention of undergraduates. An unerring process of differentiation is constantly at work, making out these born scholars and scientists from those of their colleagues who possess scholarly and scientific tastes, but who learn by the time they are forty that they are never likely to produce anything. These latter men often make noteworthy drill-masters. Their respect for original scholarship grows as they come to recognize that it is beyond their own reach. Though they discover the futility of "doing something for" science or literature themselves, they touch elbows daily with men who can, and they reflect something of the glory of it, and impart to their pupils a regard for sound learning.

Not every teacher, of course, is an investigator *manqué*. Your born teacher is as rare as a poet, and as likely to die young. Once in a while a college gets hold of one. It does not always know that it has him, and proceeds to ruin him by over-driving, the moment he shows power; or to let another college lure him away for a few hundred dollars more a year. But while he lasts—and sometimes, fortunately, he lasts till the end of a long life—he transforms the lecture-hall as by enchantment. Lucky is the alumnus who can call the roll of his old instructors, and among the martinets and the pedants and the piously inane can here and there come suddenly upon a man; a man who taught him to think or helped him to feel, and thrilled him with a new horizon.

Sometimes it happens that the great teacher is also a great investigator, but that is a miracle. For a man to be either one or the other—not to speak of being both—requires singular vitality. Outsiders usually underestimate the obstacles to successful professorial work. With regard to one's own scholarly ambitions, particularly, the steady term-time strain, the thankless and idle sessions of committees, the variety of demands upon one's time and energy, combine to make one pay a heavy price for winning distinction. You must do, upon the average, as much teaching as your colleagues, and the time for your *magnum opus* must either be stolen from that due your classes, or you must accomplish two day's work in one. It is true that the number of hours of classroom instruction required of the professor varies greatly in different institutions. Sometimes a schedule of four hours per week is considered sufficient, in the case of men who have won the right to devote themselves to advanced research. In the smaller colleges, and for the younger men in the larger ones, the schedule is often sixteen or twenty hours. perhaps twelve would be a fair average for colleges and universities the country over. To teach college boys for two hours a day does not seem like a very severe task to one who has never tried it, but I have observed that most professors who have taught or lectured for two hours thoroughly well, putting their best powers into the task, are ready to quit. Few men can rivet the attention of fifty or a hundred students for one hour without feeling, five minutes after the end of it, that vitality has gone out of them. The emery wheel that wears out fastest cuts the diamond best; and when a man boasts that he teaches without effort and weariness, he has sufficiently described his teaching. Every college town has its own pitiful or tragic stories of professors who have broken down; they are usually the men whom the college could least afford to lose. It is no wonder that in the face of all this many professors cease trying to ride two horses at once; they either do their duty by their classes and let the dust gather on the leaves of the *magnum opus*, or else they get over their class work with as little expenditure of energy as possible, and give to the *magnum opus* their real strength. And the college would not be the microcosm it is if there were not some professors who abandon both ambitions after a little, becoming quite incurable though often very charming dead-beats; and this, I confess, is the most interesting type of all. . . .

13

From *Literature and the American College: Essays in Defense of the Humanities* (1908)

Irving Babbitt

Irving Babbitt (1865–1933) was possibly the most famous, and certainly the most caustic, of the humanistic generalists who attacked the overspecialization and pedantry of the new academic research establishment. Babbitt took a B. A. from Harvard University in modern languages in 1889, taught Greek and Latin for a year at the College of Montana, studied Sanskrit for a year in Paris and oriental studies at Harvard. After a stint teaching romance languages at Williams College (1893–94), Babbitt became an instructor in French at Harvard, where he remained until his death.

Babbitt became influential as an exponent (with Paul Elmer More, whom he met at Harvard) of the New Humanism, which asserted sternly classical literary, moral, and social ideals against the twin evils of romantic emotionalism (epitomized for Babbitt by Jean-Jacques Rousseau) and naturalism (epitomized by Sir Francis Bacon). Babbitt saw the narrow research spirit in modern language departments as a symptom of naturalism, though—as he notes in the present selection—the romantic and the naturalist often coexisted within the same intellectual type. Babbitt's books include *The New Laokoön*, *Rousseau and Romanticism*, and *Literature and the American College* (1908), from which the present selection is taken.

Literature and the Doctor's Degree

It is related of Darwin that after a morning of hard work in his study he was wont to come out into the drawing-room and rest on the sofa while listening to a novel read aloud. This anecdote may serve as a symbol not only of the scientific attitude toward literature, but of the place that literature is coming to occupy in life. The modern man reserves his serious energy for science or sociology or finance. What he looks for when he turns to pure literature is a soothing and mildly narcotic effect. Many people, of course, do not seek in books even the solace of their idle moments, but leave art and literature to women. "Poetry," as Lofty says, speaking for men of business, "is a pretty thing enough for our wives and daughters, but not for us." In the educational institutions, especially the large universities of the Middle West, the men flock into the courses on science, the women affect the courses in literature. The literary courses, indeed, are known in some of these institutions as "sissy" courses. The man who took literature too seriously would be suspected of effeminacy. The really virile thing is to be an electrical engineer. One already sees the time when the typical teacher of literature will be some young dilettante who will interpret Keats and Shelley to a class of girls. As it is, the more vigorous and pushing teachers of language feel that they must assert their manhood by philological research. At bottom they agree with the scientist—and the dilettante—in seeing in literature the source not of a law of life, but of more or less agreeable personal impressions.

The distinction between the dilettante and the philologist is closely related to the more general distinction we have already made between the sentimental and the scientific naturalist, or, as we have agreed to call them, between the Rousseauist and the Baconian. Many of the grammarians in ancient Alexandria did work very similar to that of our contemporary philologists. Evidently, however, they took a much more modest view of their profession, and this was because the Alexandrian was not like the modern philologist, exalted in his own eyes by the feeling that he was contributing by his research to the advancement of learning and pushing at the great car of progress. It is by their definite contribution to knowledge that our modern linguistic Baconians would wish to be esteemed; provided they can get at the precise facts in their study of language, and then disengage from these facts the laws that are supposed to govern them, they are content to turn the human values over to the Rousseauist and to the vagabondage of intellect and sensibility in which the Rousseauist delights.

Once more, however, we are arrested by the need of right definition. The word philology is used nowadays to cover everything from Vedic noun inflections to literary criticism and the Epistles of St. Paul.* By the very classifications they insert in university catalogues our philologists make clear that they look on literature itself as only a department of philology. We can scarcely hope to define this strangely elastic term in a way that will be generally acceptable, but we can at least define it for our present use.

In coming at our definition we need to return for a moment to Emerson's distinction between the two laws "not reconciled." So far as language falls under the "law for thing," it is philology; so far as it expresses the "law for man," it is literature. In following out the phenomenal relationships of language and literature, philology has a vast and important field. It becomes an abuse and a usurpation only when it would set up these phenomenal relationships as a substitute for the still more important relationships of language and literature to the human spirit. Again, the appeal of literature to the individual intellect and

* See *Harvard University Catalogue*, 1906–07, pp. 439, 440.

sensibility has a large and legitimate place. Impressionism and dilettanteism arise only when the individual would emancipate himself entirely from the discipline of more general standards.

The philologist as we know him nowadays is not always a grammarian who differs from his Alexandrian prototype merely in being puffed up by the Baconian sense of contributing to human progress. That variety of philologist, to be sure, is still extremely common, especially among our classical teachers. But there is another school of philology which has found full expression only in comparatively recent times and is more closely akin to history than to linguistics; or it would be more correct to say that the keener sense of historical relativity, of growth and development, that marked the nineteenth century has profoundly modified all forms of history, including the history of literature. Unfortunately it has proved extremely difficult in practice to combine the historical method with a due regard for intrinsic values. To do this properly is to mediate between the absolute and the relative, and this, as we have seen, is the most difficult of all the adjustments the humanist has to make. The great danger of the whole class of philologists we are discussing is to substitute literary history for literature itself—a danger that has been especially manifest in a field where literary phenomena are numerous and genuine literature comparatively scarce, that of the Middle Ages.* The interest of a certain type of mediævalist in the object of his study would often seem to be in inverse ratio to its real importance. The vital question, after all, is not whether one *chanson de geste* is derived from another *chanson de geste*, but whether either work has in itself any claim to the attention of a serious person. I have heard of Ph. D. examinations of candidates who were planning to teach modern literature, where the questions were almost entirely on the mediæval field; and on minute points of linguistics and literary history, at that, with only incidental mention of the mediæval authors who are important for the humanist,—Dante, Chaucer, Petrarch, Boccaccio.

Our modern philologists often accuse their classical brethren of being narrow and illiberal because they do not make a fuller use of the historical method. But the trouble lies deeper, and is not to be remedied by substituting one school of philology for another. The historical method is invaluable, but only when it is reinforced by a sense of absolute values.* In itself a great deal of the *Quellenforschung** that goes on at present is really on a lower level than good old-

---

* The Middle Ages had plenty of intellectual power, but this was largely diverted from the vernaculars into Latin and the scholastic philosophy. With the exception of Dante's poem, the Middle Ages hardly succeeded in expressing themselves so completely in literature as they did, for example, in the Gothic cathedral.

* What I say here on the historical and comparative methods needs to be completed by what I say on the same subject in the essays on the "Rational Study of the Classics" and on "Ancients and Moderns" [in *Literature and the American College*].

* *Quellenforschung*, source study. [ed.]

fashioned grammar or text criticism. The man who has that dry book-keeping habit of mind, which is perennial, wins repute as a scholar to-day by some study of origins and influences, much as he might have got on as a critic in neo-classic days by talking about the "rules" and cataloguing "beauties" and "faults." Comparative literature owes its sudden prosperity to the talismanic virtues that are supposed to belong to the historical and comparative methods. But comparative literature will prove one of the most trifling of subjects unless studied in strict subordination to humane standards. For instance, the relationship of Petrarch to the sonneteers of the Renaissance is interesting, but the weightier problem is how both Petrarch and his disciples are related, not to one another, but to the "constant mind of man." Comparative literature may become positively pernicious if it is allowed to divert undergraduates from gaining a first-hand acquaintance with the great classics, to a study of interrelationships and interdependencies either of individual authors or of national literatures. Besides, there is no necessary connection between an author's historical influence and significance and his true worth. Petrarch deserves on the whole a larger place in literary history than Dante, and yet is far inferior to Dante both as a writer and as a man.

The corruption of literature by historical philology resembles what has taken place in history itself. The historians, likewise, have been too exclusively occupied with the phenomena of their subject, and have failed to adjust the rival claims of the absolute and the relative. In one of his essays Bacon tries to get at some of the underlying laws of the human spirit as they are manifested in the phenomena of history, and at the same time warns us against fixing our gaze too intently on these phenomena themselves. "It is not good," he says, "to look too long on these turning wheels of vicissitude. As for the philology of them, that is but a circle of tales, and therefore not fit for this writing." Here is a correct use of the word philology by a great master of thought and language—so correct, indeed, as almost to seem a prophecy of our most recent scholarship and the excess into which it has fallen. The danger of a former type of scholar was to gloss over the infinite complexity of the facts with a few facile generalizations. The danger of the scholar of to-day is rather to philologize everything, to turn literature and history and religion itself into a mere "circle of tales,"—in other words, to make endless accumulations of facts, and then fail to disengage from these accumulated stores their permanent human values.

What has just been said may seem to some to echo the attacks of Carlyle on Dryasdust, and in general the attacks of the whole romantic school on the abuse of scientific analysis. But at bottom nothing could be more different from each other than the protests of the humanist and the romanticist against the excess of dry analysis and fact-collecting. The romanticist protests because this excess interferes with enthusiasm, with the free play of emotion; the humanist protests because it interferes with judgment and selection. In spite of the opprobrious epithets Carlyle heaped upon him, Dryasdust has prospered, and is now teaching history—and literature—in our American colleges. Indeed, one may go farther and say that Dryasdust has been helped rather than hindered by the romanticist. The excess of dry fact-collecting is the natural rebound from an excess of undisciplined emotion. How often Carlyle himself fails to distinguish between the "law for man" and what is simply law for Carlyle! But Carlyle, after all, is something more than a mere romantic impressionist. Our meaning will perhaps be better illustrated by a historian like Michelet, who was a thoroughgoing Rousseauist. A person who reads continuously Michelet's account of the French Revolution is tempted to exclaim at last: In Heaven's name, let us have the cold facts, unembroidered by these arabesques of a disordered fancy, and undistorted by the hallucinations of a revolutionary temperament! Since a man cannot put the human element into his work without thus being wantonly subjective, let him eliminate the human element entirely, and attain at least to the objectivity of the scientist. This is the reasoning that the whole of French literature went through after the riot of subjectivity indulged in by the romantic school of 1830. The great writers have known how to be at once objective and human; but the French writers who tried to escape from the romantic excess of emotion by scientific detachment, by subjecting man entirely to the "law for thing," fell, as a French critic expresses it, into a "stark inhumanity." And this is usually what happens to the fact-collecting, scientific historian. By selecting his facts and affirming a judgment he would, of course, run the risk of expressing nothing higher than his own temperament; but even this is better than to run the risk of expressing nothing human at all.

We have been talking all along as though the scientist and the impressionist, the philologist and the dilettante were necessarily separate and antagonistic persons; but this is very far from being the case. Philology and dilettanteism are in reality only the analytical and the æsthetic, or, as one would be tempted to say, the masculine and the feminine aspects of the same naturalistic movement. They are often combined in the same person, or rather exist alongside one another in him, as a special form of that unreconciled conflict between intellect and feeling that one finds in Rousseau and his descendants. As Renan says somewhat inelegantly of himself, one half of his nature made monkey faces at the other half. . . .

Most of our philologists, of course, are not Renans. The philological discipline is not in itself conducive either to ideas or to the art of expressing ideas, and Renan, after all, had both. There often exists, however, even in the average philologist, along with the scientific method, which is his masculine side, a feminine or dilettante side. He often combines his strict philologizing with that impressionism which is only the excess of the sympathetic and appreciative temper. The judicial and selective temper he neither possesses himself nor understands in others. What he admires next to philology is the cleverness of the dilettante, and he sometimes succeeds in attaining to it himself.

This curious interplay of philology and impressionism, sometimes united in the same person, but more often existing separately, runs through the whole of our language-teaching, but is most visible perhaps in the teaching of English. At one extreme of the average English department is the philological mediaevalist, who is grounded in Gothic and Old Norse and Anglo-Saxon; at the other extreme is the dilettante, who gives courses in "daily themes," and, like the sophists of old, instructs ingenuous youth in the art of expressing itself before it has anything to express.

The philologists are better organized than the dilettantes, and command the approaches to the higher positons through their control of the machinery of the doctor's degree. The dilettante is generally relegated to a subordinate place, and is often fitted for it by a pliant and subservient temper. Indeed, it might not be an exaggeration to say that a majority of the more important chairs of ancient and modern literature in this country are already held by men whose whole preparation and achievement have been scientific rather than literary. This situation is on the face of it absurd, and in some respects even scandalous. Yet the philological syndicate can scarcely be blamed for pushing forward men of its own kind; and the problem is in itself so difficult that one should sympathize with the perplexities of college presidents. The young doctor of philosophy has at least submitted to the discipline of facts and given evidence of some capacity for hard work. The dilettante has usually given evidence of nothing, except perhaps a gentle epicureanism. Temperamental indolence and an aversion to accuracy have been known to disguise themselves as a love of literature; so that the college president is often justified in his preference.

Yet it is this acceptance of the doctor's degree as proof of fitness for a chair of literature that is doing more than any one thing to dehumanize literary study and fix on our colleges a philological despotism. The degree as now administered puts a premium, not on the man who has read widely and thought maturely, but on the man who has shown proficiency in research. It thus encourages the student to devote the time he still needs for general reading and reflection to straining after a premature "originality." Any plan for rehabilitating the humanities would therefore seem to turn on the finding of a substitute for the existing doctorate. What is wanted is a training that shall be literary, and at the same time free from suspicion of softness or relaxation; a degree that shall stand for discipline in ideas, and not merely for a discipline in facts. Our language instruction needs to emphasize more than it is now doing the relationship between literature and thought, if it is to be saved from Alexandrianism. Alexandria had scholars who were marvels of æsthetic refinement, and others who were wonders of philological industry. Yet Alexandrian scholarship deserves its doubtful repute because of its inability to vitalize either its æstheticism or its philology,—because of its failure, on the whole, to make any vigorous and virile application of ideas to life. The final test of the scholar must be his power to penetrate his facts and dominate his impressions, and fuse them with a fire of a central purpose (*ergo vivida vis animi pervicit*).* What is disquieting about our teachers of language is not any want of scientific method or æsthetic appreciativeness, but a certain incapacity for ideas. Some of our classical scholars have done distinguished work of a purely linguistic kind. A number of scholars in the modern field have achieved eminence not only in linguistic work, but also in that investigation of literary history which passes with many for literature itself. But we do not get from our teachers of the classics any equivalent of such writing as that of Professor Butcher in England, or of M. Boissier in France—writing that should be almost the normal product of a humanistic scholarship; nor do our teachers of modern languages often attain to that union of finished form and mature generalization which is a common occurrence in the French doctor's thesis.

One of our scholars of German training, evidently alarmed at the growing dissatisfaction with the present Ph. D., admits that the American thesis should try to combine the solidity of German scholarship with the French finish of form. Satisfactory doctor's theses, however, are not to be compounded by any such easy recipe. Most German theses, on literary subjects, at least, are as flimsy in substance as they are crude in form; and finish of form in the French thesis has value only in so far as it is the outer sign of maturity of substance. One can scarcely contemplate the German theses, as they pour by hundreds into a large library, without a sort of intellectual nausea. American scholarship should propose to itself some higher end than simply to add a tributary to the stream.

Hope for literary study in this country would seem to lie in questioning the very things that to our philologists of German training seem self-evident. Thus they assume not only that the chief aim of our graduate schools should be to train investigators, but that our graduate students have as a rule a preparation sufficiently broad to justify them in embarking at once on their investigations. They assume—and this is perhaps the underlying assumption of the whole German school—that there are two kinds of scholars: the receptive scholar, who takes things on authority and is still in his intellectual nonage; and the originative scholar, who by independent research proves that he is intellectually of age. But this is to overlook the all-important intermediary stage when the mind is neither passively receptive nor again originative, but is assimilative in the active and masculine sense. It is this oversight which leads to the exaggerated estimate of the man who brings forward new material as compared with the man who has really assimilated the old. Nothing was more remarkable about Greek literature than the balance it maintained between the forces of tradition and the claims of originality,* so that Greek literature at its

* Thus the lively power of the mind prevailed—Lucretius. [ed.]
* This point is clearly made in a recent paper by Professor H. W. Smyth of Harvard on "Aspects of Greek Conservatism."

best is a kind of creative imitation. It is precisely the lack of this creative imitation that is the special weakness of our contemporary literature, just as the lack of creative assimilation is the special weakness of our contemporary scholarship. A pseudo-originality is equally the bane of both.

The trouble with most of our imitation of German scholarship is that it has not been creative, as all fruitful imitation must be, but servile. We should be grateful to the Germans for all we have learned from them, but at the same time we should not be their dupes. The uncritical adoption of German methods is one of the chief obstacles to a humanistic revival. The Germanizing of our classical study in particular has been a disaster not only to the classics themselves, but to the whole of our higher culture. It was not so very long ago that a man could win reputation as a classical scholar merely by editing some Greek or Latin text with notes mainly translated from the German. A feeling for form and proportion, good taste, measure and restraint, judgment and discriminating selection—these are the humanistic virtues that should be associated with a study of the classics. It can scarcely be claimed that these humanistic virtues are the ones in which the Germans chiefly excel. . . .

The new degree that we propose, though putting a diminished emphasis on research, should rest its discipline in ideas on a solid discipline in facts. Language should be thoroughly mastered both linguistically and as a medium for the adequate and artistic expression of thought. To attempt to train in ideas students who have received no previous discipline, not even the discipline of common accuracy, is to expect them to fly before they have learned to walk. It will probably be easy enough to start a reaction against the present methods of our philologists, but this movement of protest will prove worse than useless if it is simply to turn to the profit of the dilettante. The natural tendency of the philologists themselves when goaded beyond a certain point by their critics is to promote a few dilettantes to college positions as a sort of sop to the literary element. If the philologist has to choose between a humanist and a dilettante, he is likely to prefer the latter, moved perhaps by an obscure instinct of self-preservation, but even more by that secret alliance which we have already noted between his own nature and that of the dilettante. In fact, the danger just now is greater from the dilettante than from the philologist, provided we include the dilettanteism of the philologist himself. There has been a decrease of late in scientific dogmatism, that dogmatism of the nineteenth century which was often as profound and unconscious as that of mediaeval theology. The arrogance of the philologist is bound to diminish, and indeed is already diminishing, with that of the scientist. One can even now observe in the philologist who has "arrived" an increasing anxiety to assume a literary pose. His friends talk with bated breath of his literary sense. He not only convinces himself and his friends, but college presidents, that he is "literary." Indeed, if the abuse of the word literary continues at the present rate, one will soon have to abandon the word entirely to the dilettante and the philologist in his dilettante moods. It is only just to the philologist to admit that his way of giving courses in literature is often a rather convincing substitute for a genuinely humanistic treatment. As Sainte-Beuve phrases it, when seen from a distance, and from behind, and by moonlight, the literary philologist and the humanist might almost be mistaken for one another. The philologist profits by the common failure to distinguish between literature and literary history. And then, too, he often has that enthusiastic and appreciative temper which is not only easier to attain than the judicial attitude, but also more popular. He usually betrays himself, however, when he tries to handle general ideas and especially to relate these ideas to something higher than his own temperament.

The humanist who at present enters college teaching should not underestimate the difficulties he is likely to encounter. He will find a literature ancient and modern controlled by a philological syndicate, a history dehumanized by the abuse of scientific method, and a political economy that has never been humane.* Under these circumstances the humanist will have to undertake the task that Wordsworth so modestly proposed to himself, that of creating the taste by which he is to be enjoyed. He will be more or less out of touch with his colleagues; and, though he will attract some students of the more serious sort, will not necessarily win wide and sudden popularity among undergraduates. As a result of long practice, from the kindergarten up, the American undergraduate has often acquired a remarkable dexterity in dodging every kind of discipline. If he takes a course given in a humanistic spirit, he is likely to have exacted from him a good part of the philological discipline in facts, and an additional discipline in ideas with which the philologist is generally not overmuch concerned. It is not surprising that many students should prefer the kind of course given by the dilettante who is less preoccupied with the whole question of discipline, and so freer to devote himself to being clever and entertaining. A man of ideas once said in my presence that intellect will tell in the long run—even in a college faculty. In the meanwhile he himself resigned a college position and took up another occupation in the evident fear that otherwise he might suffer the fate of Dryden's Achitophel:—

> "Yet still he saw his fortune at a stay—
> Whole droves of blockheads choking up his way."

---

* From the outset the orthodox political economy has been humanitarian rather than humane. The end of man, as it views him, is not the attainment of wisdom but the production of wealth. It therefore tends to reduce everything to terms of quantity and power and, as an offset, resorts to various mixtures of altruistic sympathy and "enlightened self-interest." Everything of course depends on the individual teacher. Political economy taught by a Walter Bagehot would be more humane than Plato as taught by many of our American classicists.

Academic recognition is likely to come at present not to the man of ideas, but to the man who can present the most plausible mixture of philology and impressionism. It requires courage to prefer to what is so plainly the "way to promotion and pay" the difficult and unpopular task of thinking. . . .

With more liberal methods we may hope in time to get more American students, and of a stronger type, to go into the classics. I have known firstclass men in both the ancient and the modern field who have been literally driven away in disgust by the present requirements for the Ph. D. I have known others who have accepted these requirements, but in bitterness of spirit. The wail of the dilettante who lacks backbone to acquire the philological discipline we can afford to neglect. The case is more serious, however, when the student humanistically inclined is likewise repelled from a career of literary teaching by the barbed-wire entanglements with which our philologists have obstructed its entrance.

Herein lies the justification of the new degree, or at least of a radical revision of the requirements for the existing degree. The problem, of course, is not so much to devise some new form of academic machinery as to change the spirit which is responsible for the present superstition of the doctor's degree. This will be a necessary preliminary to the liberalizing of our study of either the ancient or modern languages. But though we must have the spirit first of all, we must not be neglectful of our methods. It already savors of the dilettante to have too fine a scorn for questions of method. Right methods without strong men and strong men without right methods are equally unavailing. Taken individually and apart from their methods our classical scholars are probably as able a body of men as will be found in any other department.

For these and other reasons, then, a new degree would seem to be required as an alternative, if not a substitute, for the present Ph. D.; a degree that would lay due stress on æsthetic appreciativeness and linguistic accuracy, but would insist above all on wide reading and the power to relate this reading so as to form the foundation for a disciplined judgment. There would then be some hope of our having humanists as well as philologists and dilettantes, and our literary instruction would be safeguarded from the dry rot of Alexandrianism.

14

"The Dark Ages," *PMLA* (1913)
Charles Hall Grandgent

Charles Hall Grandgent (1862–1939) was a Harvard University graduate who, after study in Europe, tutored in Romance languages at Harvard, directed modern language instruction in the Boston City Schools (1889–96), and returned to Harvard as Professor of Romance Languages (1896–1932). A noted Dante scholar, Grandgent inherited the legendary Dante course which had been taught at Harvard by Charles Eliot Norton. He authored four books on Dante between 1916 and 1924 and edited the *Divina Commedia*. Grandgent became president of the Modern Language Association in 1912.

The selection below, another MLA presidential address, illustrates the bitterly defiant estrangement from American life—including particularly contemporary art and literature—felt by many early scholars and their tendency to see democracy as inevitably leading to the debasement of cultural standards. Those who in 1988 complain that college students lack "cultural literacy" may be surprised at Grandgent's remarks about the "vast and growing ignorance" of college students in 1912.

There is a supreme type of self-complacency which is born of sheer ignorance, an ignorance so absolute as to be unaware of the existence of anything to learn. And this self-complacency . . . is not confined to school-children: it is shared by old and young. It may be called the dominating spirit of our time. One of its marks is a contempt for thoro knowledge and a profound distrust of anyone who is really well-informed. An expert opinion on any subject becomes valueless the moment we learn that it emanates from a "college professor." When a conspicuously competent person is suggested for public office, the most damning accusation that can be hurled at him is the epithet "academic." Few, indeed, can bear up under the suspicion of actually knowing something.

A very serious college paper publishes an article by an evidently earnest young man who maintains that scholarship is essentially narrow and selfish; the really generous student is he who works, not for the cultivation of his own mind, but for the glory of his college. As if a college could derive glory from anything but the fulfilment of its proper mission, the cultivation of the individual minds entrusted to it! The altruistic tone assumed by devotees of college amusements is peculiarly irritating. I am willing that children should make mud pies: it is their nature to. But when they begin to declare that they are making mud pies, not for their own delectation, but for the embellishment of their city, it is time they were sent on errands for their mother. Students are always ready to do anything but study. Study is hard and distasteful, because our boys and girls have never been used to mental concentration; any other activity, whether it be athletics or "social service," seems to them less painful, hence more profitable. You are all aware how dangerous it is to assume, on the part of our college classes, any definite knowledge of any subject. Last year I had occasion to question a good many students about our friend Charlemagne; and one after another unblushingly assigned him to the eighteenth century. A colleague in a "fresh water" college could find no one in his class who knew what event is celebrated on the fourth of July. In a course in French literature, taken mainly by Juniors, a request to compare a certain drama with *Othello* drew forth the admission that a considerable part of the class knew nothing of Shakspeare's play. "We had *Hamlet*," they cried, as if Shakspeare were a disease from which one attack made them immune. Of course it had never occurred to them that anyone could be so mad as to read a book not prescribed. You must have noticed how very difficult it has become for college students not only to write but to read their mother tongue. We give them books to study, and the boys, for the most part, obligingly plow thru them, for they are good fellows; but they are no wiser after than before. The text has conveyed nothing to them, because they do not know the meaning of common English words.

It is not to be supposed (let me say once more) that this vast and growing ignorance is peculiar to school and college. It pervades society. Even the teacher and the author are coming under its sway. Men of note are losing the power to speak or write their own language. This subject was tellingly discussed by our last year's president, and I need not dwell upon it.

The confusion of tongues, however, is not the only plague fostered by darkness. Ignorance, having no means of comparison, necessarily lacks a criterion, and is therefore an easy prey to specious fallacy. It runs after every novelty that for the moment appeals to its rudimentary imagination. At what previous age in the history of mankind has there been such a cult of the absurd as we see today? In art, literature, music, science, history, psychology, education, religion, politics, the charlatan is sure of a congregation, provided his antics be sufficiently startling and grotesque. . . .

In art, the Impressionists have long since been succeeded by the Post-Impressionists, the Futurists, and the Cubists. The Futurists, according to their own definition, "stand upon the extreme promontory of the centuries; and why should they look behind, when they have to break in mysterious portals of the Impossible." "To admire an old picture," they say, "is to pour our sensitiveness into a funeral urn, instead of casting it forward in violent gushes of creation and action." "We stand," they declare, "on the summit of the world, and cast our challenge to the stars."

"We must destroy in sculpture, as in every art, the traditional nobility of marble, and bronze also must go. The sculptor can and must employ twenty different substances, such as glass, wood, cardboard, cement, horsehair, leather, wool, mirrors, electric light, and concrete. In the straight lines of a match there is more truth and beauty than in all the muscular contortions of the Laocoön." One of the products of this school is thus described: "Today at the Salon d'Automne I have seen a Futurist sculpture group, and a most extraordinary achievement it is. It does not fulfil all the demands of the new art, for it is in the medium of plaster, and there were no signs of such adventitious adornments as horse-hair, mirrors, electric lights, and so on. I should judge that it is intended to represent a group of wrestlers, but I speak humbly and under correction; it may have been intended for a battle-field or a surgical operation. It is a medley of arms and legs, flowering, so to speak, from a single torso. No head was visible. It is the principle of the cinematograph applied to sculpture." "Futurism," says an English journal, "is nothing but a Latin Quarter escapade. But it is none the less a symptom of the age. . . . It is the cult of violence for its own sake. It finds a motor-car more beautiful than the Victory of Samothrace. . . . It is the art of an age which is turning to irrationalism in politics as in metaphysics." I remember examining, a few years ago, a pretentious Italian periodical devoted to Futurism. Its battle-cry was "Down with everything!" It would be satisfied with nothing short of the overthrow of all existing institutions and the creation of a brand-new society and art. Especially were museums and libraries to be consigned to utter destruction. The publisht specimens of the new art, which thus modestly offers itself as more than a substitute for all that has been, make one quite content to die before the Futurist future dawns. . . .

Does all this signify that we are more vicious, more depraved than our fathers? Are we witnessing a violent reaction against accepted canons of decency in life? I do not think so. It does not seem to me that the general moral conduct of the community is worse than it has been before. If art, letters, dress are more indecent, it simply means that we are more ignorant. By our neglect of the past we have cut ourselves off from standards of all kinds, and hence, like the new-born moth, are attracted by the first glare. . . .

There was a time when schools attempted, at least, to cultivate discrimination and to furnish the material on which selection can be founded; but in these days of "vocational training," when pupils are encouraged "to practise nothing but their handicraft," it is, in Dante's words, "impossible for them to have judgment." And it is inevitable that in their blindness they should follow false guides; for the loudest bellow is sure to issue from the windiest prophet, the biggest blaze from those luminaries that would rather be flashlights, and dazzle for one instant, than gleam as modest but permanent stars in the sky. "They that be wise," says a once popular book, "shall shine as the brightness of the firmament; and they that turn many to righteousness as the stars for ever and ever." But none of this for our Futurists, Post-Futurists, and Neo's of every description. They have all taken as their watchword the motto of the melancholy jockey in *The Arcadians*:

"A short life and a gay one!"

One is tempted to say that the motto of their disciples is that phrase of Tertullian's: "Credo quia absurdum." But that would not be quite just. They do not believe in folly (as Tertullian, for a quite different reason, did in wisdom) because it is absurd, but because they do not know how absurd it is, and because folly has a louder voice than common sense. Just as, in a crowded street on a rainy day, every wayfarer tries to lift his umbrella above all the others, so every preacher today is trying to raise his utterance to a higher pitch than all his competitors. Only by surpassing shrillness of exaggeration can we get a hearing. We all feel it—the politician on the stump, the clergyman in the pulpit, the professor in the class-room—even the president of a learned society delivering his presidential address: and we all yield more or less to the temptation. If we do not, we are consigned to back seats as "mere teachers," and get no more attention than an organ-grinder playing *Trovatore*.

By this time it may have occurred to some of you that the Dark Age I am discussing is not the period extending from the fifth to the eleventh century, but a much nearer one. I suggest, indeed, that we alter the *Century* definition to something like this: "The *dark ages*, an epoch in the world's history, beginning with or shortly after the French Revolution, markt by a general extension and cheapening of education resulting in a vast increase of self-confident ignorance. It was induced by the gradual triumph of democracy, and will last until the masses, now become arbiters of taste and science, shall have been raised to the level formerly occupied by the privileged classes."

It is doubtless true that the aggregate of knowledge, at the present day, is greater than ever before; but it is equally true that the large share-holders in this knowledge are no longer in control. Leadership has been assumed by the untrained host, which is troubled by no doubt concerning its competence and therefore feels no inclination to improve its judgment. The ignorance characteristic of our Dark Age is a supremely self-satisfied ignorance. Ours is, I think, the first period in human history to belie Aristotle's saying, "All men naturally desire to know." Never before were conditions so favorable to the easy diffusion of a false semblance of information. Cheap magazines, Sunday supplements, moving pictures have taken the place of books. Quickly scanned and quickly forgotten, they leave in the mind nothing but the illusion of knowledge. On the other hand, it must be admitted that the number of persons who have received some schooling is more considerable than in any previous century; but this admission must be accompanied by the corollary that the schooling is proportionately ineffective. The more widely education has been diffused, the thinner it has been spread. We have now reached a stage where it seems to be on the verge of reverting to the old system of apprenticeship to a trade. All this is natural and inevitable. It is scarcely conceivable that democracy should ever relinquish its hold. The civilized world is committed to the principle of majority rule, believing that the supremacy of the many results in the greatest good to the greatest number. The masses must come into their inheritance, even if that heritage, in their unskilled hands, bear for a long time but little fruit.

In the early stages of the leveling process, the tendency was to lift the plebs up toward the mental condition of the patricians. Little by little, however, the power of inertia has reverst the movement, and now equalization has come to mean the lowering of the brahmin to the dead level of the intellectual pariah. It is of this "downward revision" of education that I am complaining, not of the great democratic evolution of which it is an unfortunate by-product. We are confronted by a definite evil, which can and must be corrected; otherwise it would be useless to complain at all. How frequently do we hear that the high school diploma, and even the college degree, should be "within the reach of every American boy"! And the strongest tendency in our education today is to put it there. When this dream shall have been realized, the result will evidently be that the degree will be worth nothing to anybody. The Spaniards have a saying that all Basques are noble; so every American, it would seem, should be *ex officio* a Bachelor of Arts. I have often thought that the only way to satisfy the popular demand would be to confer the A. B. on every child at its birth. But we can never make a man a scholar by calling him one. If democracy is to be a success (as we all hope and believe), that end must be reached not by degrading education to the present taste of the lowest part of the demos, but by lifting the demos to a better understanding of the value of learning.

This all-important task has fallen of late into poor hands. The principal of a big high school was discussing with me, not long ago, the wholesale migration of the better class of pupils from public to private establishments. "Parents," he said, "are discovering that their children are getting next to nothing in the public school. Why is it? When I compare the men who taught me, and taught me well, with the present teachers, who can hardly be said to teach anybody anything, I am puzzled to account for the difference. The older men were really no better scholars than the new ones, and worked no harder. The only explanation I can offer is that the earlier generation knew nothing of pedagogy." What he rashly spoke, many masters are thinking. However, it seems to me that we must, in justice, make a distinction between pedagogy and pseudo-pedagogy. The former exists, altho the latter is so much more in evidence that the name "educator," for many intelligent people, has become a term of opprobrium. While the genuinely serious student of education is still groping, trying to find a spot on which to lay the foundations of a science, a host of pseudo-educators, too uninstructed to know any better, are loudly proclaiming themselves sole possessors of the whole secret of the art of teaching. An easy career has been opened to young men not overburdened with wit or learning. Having collected some information about school administration and the history of pedagogical speculation, a set of arbitrary formulas, some bits of dubious psychology, and, above all, an imposing technical vocabulary, they are accepted as prophets by an equally ignorant public, and given control of our schools. A specialist writes in *The Forum*: "For a decade or two we have taught theories rather than children, and the result is that the children have scarcely been educated."

Even worse than empty theorizing is the disposition to cater to the native indolence of the pupil and the foolish indulgence of the parent. Listen to the words of the new president of Amherst College, as reported by the press: "The boy chooses on some special line—the line of vocation, the line of 'snaps,' the line of a certain profession or the days that will let the student get out of town. What do you get? Any sort of training? None at all. . . . The old classical curriculum believed that if you take certain studies and work them through you'd get out of them the deepest things of human experience." Alas! what does the typical boy or the typical parent or the typical educator care for "the deepest things of human experience"? The phrase has an unpleasant suggestion of the difficult and the unpractical, and to call a study "unpractical" is to damn it to the "lowest hell." What we term "vocational training," being the most "practical" thing of all and offering no considerable difficulty to the pupil (much of it being, in fact, in the nature of play), is now first in favor. It is surely an excellent thing in its place—as a supplement to education or as an apprenticeship for those who must remain uneducated. I believe it is destined to render great service. But let us not make the mistake of calling it "education." It should prepare a boy to succeed in his business; probably it will, when it is better developed. But it affords no more education than is to be derived from the business itself. When we say that "life is a school," we are conscious that our phrase is a figure of speech: "vocational education" is another. Perhaps the worst feature of it is that "vocational" subjects are so apt to be chosen, not from vocation, not with any intention of preparing for a career, but merely for the purpose of avoiding real study.

Not long ago I listened to a shout of triumph from the head of a normal school. "At last," he cried, "we have got the colleges where we want them! They can no longer dictate to us; they must take what we see fit to give. If we say that four years of blacksmithing make a suitable high school curriculum, then they must accept four years of blacksmithing as a preparation for college." Here we have an absolute *reductio ad absurdum*. We can, of course, open our colleges to smiths, and turn them into smithies; but it is hardly necessary to point out that they will then cease to be colleges, and we shall be left with no higher education at all.

The confusion arising from a new conception of the functions of the state and the school, and from the necessity of providing some kind of training adapted to the needs of all, has given currency to certain fallacies, which it is the duty of the better informed members of society to meet and combat. First of all, let us ask ourselves what should be the purpose of education in a democracy. Should it be solely to fit men and women to perform efficiently their daily economic task? That is, of course, an important function, but it cannot be all. Otherwise progress would become impossible as far as schooling can make it so, and the life of man would hardly differ from that of a horse. If the only object of life is to stay alive, of what use is it to live at all? The ideal of economic efficiency is best realized by a machine. But the individuals we have to deal with are not machines: they are human beings of almost infinite capacities, destined to be citizens and parents. They must be capable of living the life of the spirit, of appreciating the good things in nature, in conduct, and in art; they must be able to cope intelligently with weighty problems of public policy; they must leave behind them descendants who shall be more, rather than less, competent than themselves. The higher we rise in the scale of development, the less conspicuous the purely economic aspect of the individual becomes.

"Let us cut loose from the past," is another favorite cry, "and devote ourselves to the practical issues of the day! The past is dead. We will turn our backs upon it, and give ourselves to the living present." How familiar these words have become in the public press and in college papers, and in assemblies of educators! Anything that bears the label of actuality attracts the throng, whether it be on the book-shelf or on the stage, in the public lecture-hall or in the academic class-room. College courses dealing with supposedly practical and contemporary things are as crowded as those which reveal the treasures of the past are deserted. Significant of this mood is the frequency with which we see on a theater program the notice: "Time—the Present." "Only the present is real," say the modernists. On the contrary, say I, nothing is more unreal, more elusive, more fictitious. The time that was present when I began this sentence is now gone by. The present is an illusion: it is a perpetually shifting mathematical line dividing the future, of which (humanly speaking) we know nothing, from the past; of which we know much. . . .

Let me quote a paragraph from a contributor to one of our leading journals: "Universities are beginning to see that theoretical, or absolute, truth—the sort upon which ideals are founded—is difficult to deduce from a narrow study of actual, contemporary life. Existence examined at close range means loss of perspective. . . . Not only do young men find it hard to project themselves back of the present, but equally hard to pursue any line of thought which has no practical bearings." Why is it that the study of the past seems irksome to the new generation? It is partly because such study requires concentration and judgment. But a more potent reason is to be found in a false view of life, due to a shallow interpretation of socialism—an idea that humanity is about to take a fresh start, unhampered by all the influences that have made it. Progress is possible only thru utilization of experience. A child with no parents or other elders to direct it would be an idiot. If each individual had not profited by the successes and failures of his predecessors, we should still be in a state of primeval protoplasm. The present generation calls itself practical. But think of the waste of effort that even partial ignorance of the past entails! We must compute not only the trials and losses that might have been avoided by knowledge of what others have done, but also the labor spent in duplication, in learning lessons and working out results long since accessible to the world.

Another prevalent fallacy, which has found favor even in high quarters, is the belief that for the training of the young one subject is just as good as another. This is surely, on the face of it, an amazing doctrine to promulgate: it runs counter to all tradition and, as far as I am aware, to all contemporary experience. One would think the burden of proof should rest on its confessors. Yet they have offered not a shred of evidence—nothing but bald assertion. And on the basis of this empty vociferation school programs and college admission requirements are overturned. Perhaps our age has furnisht no better example than this of its sheeplike sequacity. We, here present, are nearly all of us teachers, and as competent as anybody to testify in this case; and I venture to say there is not one among us who has not observed, in students who have pursued widely different studies, a corresponding difference in general aptitude. It does not stand to reason that algebra should develop the same faculties as free-hand drawing, or Greek the same as blacksmithing. Probably the greatest divergence in the educational value of studies is due to the varying degree to which they require concentration, judgment, observation, and imagination. Some occupations can be pursued with tolerable success while the mind is wandering; others, like arithmetic and algebra, demand close and constant attention. Some can be carried on by an almost mechanical process: others, like Greek and Latin, call for continual reasoning and the application of general principles to particular cases. Some exact little of the mind, but much of the eye. Some, restricted to practical realities, make no appeal to esthetic sense; others, such as literature native or foreign, tend to develop the imagination while awakening appreciation of the beautiful. This, I know, is old-fashioned doctrine; but until we have conclusive evidence to offset our own observation and that of all our ancestors, we shall do well to foster the studies most conducive to the habits we wish to cultivate.

The fallacy just defined is closely related to another, which it has been used to support: namely, the doctrine that all study must be made agreeable to the student. More and more the difficult subjects have been replaced by easier ones, and these have been made easier yet by the extraction of obstacles and the invention of painless methods. Grammarless modern languages, delatinized Latin, simplified mathematics omit the very features that make study valuable. Predigested foods of all sorts have almost deprived our youth of the power to use their own teeth. Amusement is looked for, rather than instruction. "Snap" courses have, indeed, been seriously defended on the ground that even tho they teach nothing tangible, they confer an indefinable something that is better than knowledge. I would not deny that contact with a superior mind may serve as an inspiration; it reveals unsuspected possibilities of culture, and moves the responsive lad to emulation. But if the responsive lad does not follow this impulse, if he wilfully neglects a recognized opportunity, he loses more than he gains. He has begun the acquisition of a vicious habit which will make it harder for him, the next time, to obey the call of duty. . . .

The great tragic poet Alfieri has described his experience at the Academy of Turin as "eight years of uneducation." "Uneducation," a natural fruit of our present pedagogical theories, is perhaps the principal cause of our intellectual darkness. Only when the educator shall have been educated, the air cleared of noxious fallacies, and a sound and virile conception of learning restored, will the reign of Humbug come to an end. Not until then will light begin to dawn on our Dark Ages.

Part III
MEMOIRS AND
PERSONAL ACCOUNTS

15

"The 'English' Classes of the University of California," *The Wave* (1896)

Frank Norris

Frank Norris (1870–1902) was a gifted young writer when he contributed this piece to *The Wave* in 1896, not the famous novelist he is today. He had been a student in the University of California from 1890 to 1894. The selection here, therefore, offers a rare look at professional criticism and pedagogy from the point of view of both the student and the writer. Norris's description of Professor Gayley's class may be compared with Charles Mills Gayley's own version of what his courses were about (see Chapter 6).

In the "announcement of courses" published annually by the faculty of the University of California the reader cannot fail to be impressed with the number and scope of the hours devoted by the students to recitations and lectures upon the subject of "literature." At the head of this department is Professor Gayley. . . . Be pleased for a moment to consider these "literary" courses. They comprise "themes" written by the student, the subject chosen by the instructor and the matter found in text books and encyclopedias. They further include lectures, delivered by associate professors, who, in their turn have taken their information from text books and "manuals" written by other professors in other colleges. The student is taught to "classify." "Classification" is the one thing desirable in the eyes of the professors of "literature" of the University of California. The young Sophomore, with his new, fresh mind, his active brain and vivid imagination, with ideas of his own, crude, perhaps, but first hand, not cribbed from text books. This type of young fellow, I say, is taught to "classify," is set to work counting the "metaphors" in a given passage. This is actually true—tabulating them, separating them from the "similes," comparing the results. He is told to study sentence structure. He classifies certain types of sentences in De Quincey and compares them with certain other types of sentences in Carlyle. He makes the wonderful discovery—on suggestion from the instructor—that De Quincey excelled in those metaphors and similes relating to rapidity of movement. Sensation!

In his Junior and Senior years he takes up the study of Milton, of Browning, of the drama of the seventeenth and eighteenth centuries, English comedy, of advanced rhetoric, and of aesthetics. "Aesthetics," think of that! Here, the "classification" goes on as before. He classifies "lyrics" and "ballads." He learns to read Chaucer as it was read in the fourteenth century, sounding the final *e*; he paraphrases Milton's sonnets, he makes out "skeletons" and "schemes" of certain prose passages. His enthusiasm is about dead now; he is ashamed of his original thoughts and of those ideas of his own that he entertained as a Freshman and Sophomore. He has learned to write "themes" and "papers" in the true academic style, which is to read some dozen text books and encyclopedia articles on the subject, and to make over the results in his own language. He has reduced the writing of "themes" to a system. He knows what the instructor wants, he writes accordingly, and is rewarded by first and second sections. "The "co-eds" take to the "classification" method even better than the young men. They thrive and fatten intellectually on the regime. They consider themselves literary. They write articles on the "Philosophy of Dante" for the college weekly, and after graduation they "read papers" to literary "circles" composed of post-graduate "co-eds," the professors' wives and daughters and a very few pale young men in spectacles and black cutaway coats. After the reading of the "paper" follows the "discussion," aided and abetted by cake and lemonade. This is literature! Isn't it admirable!

The young man, the whilom Sophomore, affected with original ideas, does rather different. As said, by the time he is a Junior or Senior, he has lost all interest in the "literary" courses. The "themes" must be written, however, and the best way is the easiest. This is how he ofttimes goes about it: He knows just where he can lay his hands upon some fifty to a hundred "themes" written by the members of the past classes, that have been carefully collected and preserved by enterprising students. It will go hard if he cannot in the pile find one upon the subject in hand. He does not necessarily copy it. He rewrites it in his own language. Do you blame him very much? Is his method so very different from that in which he is encouraged by his professor; viz. the cribbing—for it is cribbing—from text books? The "theme" which he rewrites has been cribbed in the first place.

The method of English instruction of the University of California often develops capital ingenuity in the student upon whom it is practiced. We know of one young man—a Senior— who found himself called upon to write four "themes," yet managed to make one—re-written four times—do for the four. This was the manner of it. The four "themes" called for were in the English, chemical, German and military courses respectively. The young fellow found a German treatise on the manufacture of gunpowder, translated it, made four copies, and by a little ingenuity passed it off in the four above named departments. Of course the thing is deplorable, yet how much of the blame is to be laid at the door of the English faculty?

The conclusion of the whole matter is that the literary courses of the University of California do not develop literary instincts among the students who attend them. The best way to study literature is to try to produce literature. It is original work that counts, not the everlasting compiling of facts, not the tabulating of metaphors, nor the rehashing of text books and encyclopedia articles.

They order this matter better at Harvard. The literary student at Cambridge has but little to do with lectures, almost nothing at all with text books. He is sent away from the lecture room and told to look about him and think a little. Each day he writes a theme, a page if necessary, a single line of a dozen words if he likes; anything, so it is original, something he has seen or thought, not read of, not picked up at second hand. He may choose any subject under the blue heavens from a pun to a philosophical reflection, only let it be his own. Once every two weeks he writes a longer theme, and during the last six weeks of the year, a still longer one, in six weekly installments. Not a single suggestion is offered as to subject. The result of this system is a keenness of interest that draws three hundred men to the course and that fills the benches at every session of the class. The class room work consists merely in the reading by the instructor of the best work done, together with his few critical comments upon it by the instructor in charge. The character of the themes produced under this system is of such high order that it is not rare to come across one of them in the pages of the first-class magazines of the day. There is no sufficient reason to suppose that the California collegians are intellectually inferior to those of the Eastern States. It is only a question of the means adopted to develop the material.

16

From *And Gladly Teach* (1935)
Bliss Perry

Perry's autobiography, *And Gladly Teach* (1935), is one of the most revealing
sources of information about the atmosphere of academic English studies in the era
of professionalization. On Perry, see note to Chapter 12.

Finding a Job

A college graduate, in the year 1881, was supposed to be headed for some
profession. To become an expert in natural history required years of training;
so did the ministry (for which, in any case, I felt little 'vocation'); and so did
medicine, though I thought very seriously of following that profession and
indeed went so far as to plan, with my classmate Amadon, to enter a medical
school in Philadelphia. But the stubborn fact was that I could not fairly ask
Father for any more help. . . . Was there anything that I could teach, without
further preparation?

Once, lying on the bluffs of Bald Mountain, I had ventured to confess to a
friend that if I could have what I really wanted, I should like sometime to
teach English literature! What a dream it seemed then! It was like a boy about
to take his first violin lesson, and saying that he would like to be a Kreisler.
But just before graduation I received two offers to teach English; one in Robert
College, Constantinople, and the other in the American College at Beirut,
Syria. I talked it over with Father, and decided in favor of Beirut, though it
meant a contract for two or three years. I looked up the steamer routes, and
was on the point of promising to go, when the incoming President of
Williams, Dr. Franklin Carter, made me a proposal which took me utterly by
surprise.

It appeared that Professor Raymond, who was leaving Williams for
Princeton, had recommended that I should be asked to take over his work.
(Perhaps I had been his only pupil who took *The Orator's Manual* seriously!)

Professor Pratt, of the chair of Rhetoric, was also leaving, and it seemed that Professor Griffin, who was to be transferred from Latin in order to succeed him, wished to be relieved of the freshman and sophomore work in Rhetoric. Would I take the position of Instructor in Elocution and English, on a one-year appointment with leave of absence for four months in the winter for special study? The salary was microscopic, but would be increased in case I were reappointed. . . .

The title 'Instructor' had not been used at Williams for years. All of the twelve teachers listed in the catalogue for 1880–'81 bore the rank of Professor; the theory being that instruction should be in the hands of experienced men. My appointment broke this tradition, and I became the pioneer of a long line of young fellows who had to learn their job by doing it. Perhaps it is not the worst way to learn, though one's pupils may suffer in the process.

Two events of the opening year are still vivid to me. One was the surrender of my soiled varsity baseball suit to the '84 man who was to take my place upon the team. . . . The other event was my first faculty meeting, in President Carter's library. Four or five new professors had been brought from other colleges; all the others were my former teachers, men with grey beards and black frock coats. Never, at any subsequent faculty meetings at Princeton and Harvard have I had anything like the sense of dignity which I felt then: I was really a member of the society of gentlemen and scholars. Idealists all! The top of the ladder reached even unto Heaven, and though I was perched insecurely on the very lowest round, I was already seeing visions and dreaming dreams. . . .

I remember but little about meeting my first classes. The freshmen had individual drill in declamation; for the sophomores, I think I used Bascom's *Rhetoric* and Earle's *Philology of the English Tongue*. Brother Arthur was in that first class; later I had Walter and Carroll and (in a graduate course at Princeton) Lewis. I was an intensely earnest instructor. Arthur still makes fun of my zeal in that period for the divisions of the Indo-European family of languages and for the profound distinction between metaphor and simile. In the matter of discipline there was never any trouble except once, and that was a plain case of disobedience. I may have been merciless, for I was still under twenty-one; but it was clear that either I or the other boy had to go, and I preferred to stay. On this whole matter of discipline, over which so many sensitive young teachers have agonized, I think my father's advice to me then was the word of final wisdom: 'Remember that your classroom is, for the time being, your own house. Treat the men as your personal guests, and you will have no trouble.' I must at times during the next fifty years have seemed an anxious and worried host, but the guests—and what thousands of them there have been!—were uniformly considerate.

I worked feverishly during that autumn term. I lived at home, but otherwise my position was solitary. As one of the faculty I was already infinitely removed—by the tradition of that day—from any real companionship among the boys with whom I had played the year before, and the new professors were much older men. I took no recreation except walks across the fields to the Smedley farm. Most of the daylight hours were spent in the old chapel, coaching declamations and orations. The evenings were devoted to the correction of essays, and to preparation for the morning classes; there was sometimes a little Browning or Walt Whitman or Montaigne before I went to bed. . . .

In the evenings I worked steadily at French and German, reading Chaucer through, and re-read Shakespeare and other Elizabethan dramatists. It was obvious that I could never teach the history of the English language thoroughly without a knowledge of Anglo-Saxon. No one in Williamstown knew a word of it, but I sent for March's Anglo-Saxon grammar and reader, and mastered them as well as I could. I went in one vacation to Dr. Sauveur's summer school at Burlington, Vermont, to improve my Anglo-Saxon under a tall, sandy-haired Texan named Primer, and also took a German course with H. C. G. von Jagemann, then of the University of Indiana. Later we were colleagues at Harvard. Von Jagemann told me, with the enthusiasm of a true philologist, that Anglo-Saxon would not be enough: I ought to study Gothic, and Old and Middle High German. He gave me a list of textbooks and I ordered them from Germany. Again there was no one in Williamstown to help me, but I had faith in Von Jagemann, and ploughed on by myself. I hoped sometime to get leave of absence for work in a German university. Beyond that goal, in those days, the imagination of a young fellow anxious for scholarly training could not go! It seems to me now that in my early twenties I had intellectual curiosity, energy, and patience, but whether these qualities were sufficient for the making of a true scholar, I could not tell. . . .

In 1885 I was called to the University of Indiana, then under a new and vigorous President, David Starr Jordan. I had never been west of the Hudson River, and had no desire to go to Indiana. The technique of using a call to a larger institution in order to boost one's salary at home had not been developed, and I said nothing to anyone about the call. In fact, I had forgotten the incident completely when many years later at a college dinner in San Francisco President Jordan, then of Leland Stanford, amused the audience by relating how he had once called three young fellows to the University of Indiana without knowing any of them personally. They had all declined. One was a Norwegian named Nansen, who had published something about fishes. Another was a recent graduate of Johns Hopkins named Wilson, whose book on Congressional Government struck Jordan as original and well written. The third (and, it must be admitted, a bad third in that company!) was the former instructor at Williams whom Jordan then proceeded to introduce. The young President had gambled in 1885, and lost; but the other young men had gambled too, and whether they won or lost by declining to go to Indiana, who can tell?

Eighteen-eighty-six was a red-letter year. It opened with the greatest happiness that could possibly come to me, my engagement to Annie L. Bliss, of New Haven, daughter of those old friends of Father and Mother after whom I had been named. We had known each other since childhood. She was now a student at Smith, but was planning, with her room-mate, to spend the winter of 1886–'87 in Berlin, studying literature and music. It became necessary to count upon a long engagement, for in the spring of 1886 I was promoted to a professorship, with a two years' leave of absence for graduate study. The college granted me part salary for this period, and as I had saved a little money and could borrow a little more, the travelling expenses could be met; but we decided to postpone our marriage until my return from Europe. Naturally I discovered plenty of reasons for preferring Berlin, for the coming winter, above all other German universities.

That one should go to Germany in order to study the language and literature of England seemed in the eighteen-eighties far more natural than it would today. For seventy years the more ambitious young scholars of America had gone to Germany for their training; slowly until 1850, but rapidly thereafter. It scarcely occurred to them that they could go anywhere else. At Oxford and Cambridge there was then no provision whatever—save a single course in Anglo-Saxon offered by Oxford—for the study of 'English.' The remarkable development of English scholarship in France, headed by such pioneers as Jusserand, Legouis, and Angellier, and continued brilliantly to the present day, had not yet begun. At Harvard, it is true, Professor Child, in 1886, was offering courses in Anglo-Saxon and Chaucer in alternate years, and Professor J. W. Bright was beginning to teach the history of the English language at Johns Hopkins. But the very few graduate courses offered in my field in American universities were chiefly modelled upon German methods and given by men who had received their own training abroad. That Germany possessed the sole secret of scholarship was no more doubted by us young fellows in the eighteen-eighties than it had been doubted by George Ticknor and Edward Everett when they sailed from Boston, bound for Göttingen, in 1814. When my classmate Starr Cutting and I sailed on the *Pennland*, New York to Antwerp, in July, 1886, we were very certain that we were no Ticknor and Everett, but at least we had something of their sense of the boundless intellectual horizons awaiting young Americans in Germany. . . .

Harvard: The Cockpit of Learning

My colleague F. N. Robinson and I have had many a laugh over the deplorable scene which made memorable my first attendance upon a meeting of the English Department. The gentle Dean Briggs was presiding, and the business of the afternoon was the approval of the courses proposed for the next half-year. If accepted by the Department, they were then submitted to the Committee on Instruction, who in turn presented them to the Faculty for final adoption. Professor X indicated his desire to offer again a course on 'The English Bible,' which he had already given with marked success. But Professor Y, whose nerves were often out of tune, made sudden and violent objection: declaring that Professor X was ignorant of Hebrew, and that it was a disgrace to the Department and to Harvard that a course in the Bible should be taught by a man who could not read the Old Testament in the original. Professor X naturally resented this attack upon his scholarship, particularly as Y was himself ignorant of the Hebrew tongue. I happened to be sitting between X and Y, and as their voices rose higher and higher, while their gesticulating fingers shot across my face and the sweet-natured Briggs writhed in humiliation for his Department, I saw the Cockpit of Learning at its worst. If 'rare Ben Jonson' had been presiding instead of Briggs, he might have enjoyed the quarrel for a season, but surely he would have ended by taking X and Y, one in either hand, and knocking their hot heads together.

Both X and Y are dead long ago, but that scene taught me something about the jealousies and animosities that may underlie the decorous surface of a department; and I am tempted to set down another instance of the emotional instability of justly famous teachers. Within a few months after I had begun work at Harvard, the French Ambassador, M. Jusserand, was to receive an honorary degree. It is customary in such ceremonials to appoint some professor to escort the candidate—walking with him in the Commencement procession, and taking him to his assigned seat upon the platform. President Eliot asked me if I would escort the Ambassador. I could not decently decline, although I have little love for the pomps of college Commencements, having seen too much of them all my life. Besides, to wait in Cambridge for Commencement Day meant a loss of three days of fishing! Nevertheless I walked with the friendly M. Jusserand, just as I walked in later years with Henry James and with my brother Lewis, when they in turn were candidates for honorary degrees. Not until autumn did I learn that my endeavour to be courteous had had dire consequences. Another professor, it appeared, had considered that the honor of escorting the Ambassador should have been his, and that President Eliot had passed him over with the deliberate intention of insulting him. For two years he refused to speak to Eliot. He wrote me a letter, however, explaining that he knew that I was innocent of having done him an intentional injury, and that the fault lay wholly with the President. I kept that letter as a curiosity, and should not mention it now except to illustrate the pitiful misunderstandings and rivalries which sometimes fester in the professorial heart. Yet when faced by the real troubles of life—as distinct from imaginary maladies—such men often act with silent and magnificent heroism. Ours is a queer profession.

Hitherto I had known little of departmental psychology. At Williams I had

had but one colleague in the field of English, and at Princeton only two or three; and in those colleges, after we had once settled upon a fair division of labors, each man went his own way. But now I began to perceive that the English problem at Harvard was not so simple. One had to reckon with the 'filio-pietistic' loyalty to the methods of dead masters: if Child had taught Milton or Bacon in a particular way, that was the way to teach those courses still. One had to reckon also with the prescriptive right to certain authors or fields, claimed by men already giving instruction in them. I remember my surprise when an exceptionally competent young professor wished to offer a new course in one corner of a great field, large enough for half-a-dozen specialists at once. But the cautious Department felt compelled to refuse the request: Professor Z was already lecturing upon that general period, and his feelings would be hurt if any portion of it were assigned to another man.

Obviously, a new member of this Department had to walk delicately. Here was a brilliant array of prima-donnas, each supreme in a chosen rôle: men like Briggs, Wendell, Copeland, Robinson, Baker, and the famous Kittredge, with younger scholars like Neilson and Greenough coming on. But it was difficult for a stranger to discover any common denominator of their activities. What was the underlying philosophy of the Department, its ideal aim, its relation with liberal studies as a whole? I had no intimate friends in the Department, and there was no one to explain its state of mind, if indeed it had one. Fundamental questions were avoided in our meetings; the precious time was consumed in the discussion of wearisome administrative details. The separate parts of the English machine seemed to be in competent hands, but how were the parts related? One was tempted to think, with the old lady who listened to one of Emerson's discourses, that 'it had no connection save in God.' Years afterward, when I had grown accustomed to our irresponsible individualism, I remember that a colleague in English said to me gloomily: 'We *have* no real Department, and never have had.' But we were then six hundred miles from Cambridge, salmon fishing, and he had had had no luck that day.

The steel core of the English work at Harvard, then as now, was in the solid linguistic and historical courses covering the period from the earliest Anglo-Saxon writers to the decline of the Elizabethan drama. These courses were essential for candidates for honors in English and for the higher degrees. My own graduate work in Germany had been largely in this field, but I had ceased to teach Anglo-Saxon and Chaucer after going to Princeton, and during the dozen years before coming to Harvard I had fallen quite out of step with the philologists. I had, and still have, deep respect for the science of linguistics, but the very best I could say for myself in 1907 was the remark of the futile Mr. Brooke in *Middlemarch*: 'I went into that a good deal at one time." An out-of-date philologist is worse than none.

But I could be trusted, Dean Briggs thought, with 'English 7^b,' a large lecture course covering the period between the death of Swift and the publication of the *Lyrical Ballads*, for in the eighteenth century I had long felt at home. Then Schofield, desirous of new courses for his Department of Comparative Literature, proposed that I should offer something on 'Types of Fiction' in the eighteenth and nineteenth centuries, the material to be drawn partly from Continental and partly from English novelists. The idea was to follow the currents of Realism, Sentimentalism, Romanticism, etc., as they swept from one European country to another. We had to study Russian fiction in translations, but a portion of the assigned reading might be done in French, Italian, or German, at the preference of the student.

It was in these two courses, 'English 7ᵇ' and 'Comparative Literature 12,' that I began my half-time work in February, 1907, after returning from the holiday in Italy. In the next year, 1907–'08, I find that I gave a course in Tennyson, to be given alternately with one on Carlyle; and, for graduate students only, a Comparative Literature course on 'Political Satire since the Renaissance.' In 1908–'09 I was offering a new course on 'Lyric Poetry,' and wondering whether my colleagues in the Department would sanction a course on Emerson. Finally they did, with the remark that in their judgment Emerson was the only American author worthy of having a course devoted exclusively to him. Perhaps they were afraid that I might offer a course on Walt Whitman! As far as I am aware, this was the first Emerson course to be given in any American college; and when my friend Dr. George A. Gordon heard of it, he remarked grimly that he had himself been graduated from Emerson's own college, and had heard the seer mentioned at Harvard precisely three times. . . .

It should be remembered that by 1910 the old 'free elective' system once championed by President Eliot had passed into a kind of twilight of the gods. We were struggling with the new theories of 'concentration and distribution' of studies, with a faculty adviser for each student—although the student was not really obliged to follow the advice. He could still 'shop around' a good deal, as in a huge department store. The achievements of President Lowell in establishing the 'general examination,' the tutorial system and the 'reading period'—to say nothing of the Houses with their libraries and resident Masters and Tutors—were still in the future. For all but a small minority of ambitious undergraduates, incoherence in the choice of courses and the mechanical accumulation of course-credits were still the order of the day.

A full-time professor was then supposed to give two and a half courses of three hours each, although in the large lecture courses the third hour was usually delegated to the assistants for conferences, quizzes, or written tests. Many professors increased this schedule by repeating certain of their courses at Radcliffe, either through pure altruism or with the aim of eking out the still slender professorial salary. President Eliot had explained to me that a Harvard teacher was under no obligation to offer courses at Radcliffe, and I never did so. There were always more Harvard applicants for work in English than we could handle effectively. We had three general groups of courses: those restricted to undergraduates; a 'middle group' where supposedly qualified undergraduates sat side by side with graduates; and an 'upper group' for graduates only. Also, we offered 'research courses'—'English 20'—to individual candidates for the Ph.D., intended to guide the student in the investigation of material for his thesis.

My own work fell in all of these groups. 'English 28,' for instance, was a survey course in literature, for freshmen, given by several different professors, each taking a certain period. 'English 41,' which I was asked to take over after Wendell gave it up, was another survey course open to any undergraduates who had never elected 'English 28.' To tell the truth, I preferred at that time to be assigned to another course, but was too proud to ask for it. Yet '41' proved to be the most widely elected of any of my courses. I hope that it was never considered a 'snap,' but the numbers rose to six hundred until finally I admitted only three hundred—which happened to be the capacity of Sever II—and kept a waiting list of applicants. The success of these large lecture courses for undergraduates—a reasonable skill on the part of the lecturer being taken for granted—lies almost wholly in the selection of proper assignments for reading and in the devotion of the assistants in conducting the 'third hour' conferences. I took my turn in these conferences, naturally, for a lecture system without them, however successful in France or Germany, does not work for American boys.

The middle group courses faced a peculiar difficulty. The teacher had to present his material in such a way as to meet the needs of two different types of men: properly qualified undergraduates who were candidates for the A.B., and graduates who were bent upon securing an A.M. or Ph.D. degree. The professor had to be the judge of the qualifications of undergraduates, and a boy's rank in other subjects was not always an indication of his ability to grasp Emerson or Carlyle or Lyric Poetry. Unless one happened to know the graduate student personally, it was equally difficult to assess his qualifications in advance. Usually about one quarter of a middle group course, comprising altogether perhaps one hundred or one hundred and fifty men, would be graduates of other institutions; for there were relatively few graduate students from Harvard. Those institutions represented every variety of training and of no training. My own courses open to graduates were what were then known in the Department as 'luxury' courses—which meant, not that they were special delicacies, but that they did not belong in the list of those solid linguistic courses essential for the Ph.D. The theory was that if a graduate student spent most of his time, let us say, on Gothic, Anglo-Saxon, and Middle English, a course in Carlyle or Tennyson or Emerson would give him some measure of variety for his programme and do him no harm, though it was not likely to help him directly in his oral examination for the Ph.D., which rarely touched, in those days, upon nineteenth-century literature.

We were still in bondage to the mechanical 'course-system' of credits which is disappearing today. But during my term of service, an A.M. could be secured by four 'B's' in any approved list of courses; and a 'B' under Robinson or Kittredge needed more steady daily work than the average graduate student would give to a course on Lyric Poetry or Types of Fiction where the majority of the class were undergraduates. I always read the graduate blue-books and other papers myself, instead of leaving them to the assistants, and devised various methods of putting extra work on the advanced men, but in the lectures I had to keep in mind the capacities of the undergraduate majority.

My purely graduate courses, such as Political Satire and the English Critical Essay, were easier to manage. Sometimes I limited them to a Seminar of a dozen men, for the discussion of texts, with but little lecturing; in other years there might be forty or fifty students, with lectures for their general guidance, but with the stress laid upon the thesis prepared by each man. In the 'English 20' courses to direct the research of Ph.D. candidates, I met each man by himself in my study in the Widener Library, usually once in two or three weeks. These conferences often took many hours, but it was, I trust, real teaching, whereas in lecturing one cannot always know whether he is teaching or not. I happen to be one of the men who enjoy the excitement of lecturing in big courses. Although I worry about the lecture beforehand and afterward, I find that the mental and physical stimulus of holding the close attention of a large audience is a thrilling experience. If one puts the very best he has into it, he is limp when the lecture is over, and needs an hour's rest—though he cannot always get it—before proceeding to another classroom. But I think I have often worked as hard with the mind of a single graduate student in my study as I ever did with the six hundred men in 'English 41.'

The case of these graduate students was often pitiable. Most of them were poor in purse—though perhaps a true scholar ought to be poor. Cambridge is an expensive city, and the Unversity has thus far been unable to provide adequate quarters for graduate students in the Arts, or anything like the opportunities for social intercourse now offered to undergraduates who can afford to live in the Houses. Many of the graduates of the smaller Southern and Western colleges had married early, and had been saving a few hundred dollars in the hope of securing an A.M. or Ph.D. from Harvard, and thereby bettering their chances of professional promotion. They appeared in Cambridge without knowing the precise requirements for securing these degrees, since the printed statements were somewhat ambiguous to the stranger. Their programmes for study were perforce hastily approved by the authorities, for hundreds of cases had to be passed upon within a couple of days. Misfits evident at once could be corrected, and the authorities were kindly, but often months went by before the new graduate student recognized his predicament. Sometimes it appeared that his college training had been grossly deficient, though his marks had been high enough. He was supposed, for instance, to be able to use French and German as tools in his graduate work, but no one had really examined him in those subjects, and often he could not use them at all. The pace set in his linguistic courses was a stiff one, and soon he felt a stitch in his side. Then he jumped to the conclusion that his real obstacle in this race was 'philology,' and he began to worry and then to curse and then to seek out some professor who would listen to his troubles.

Perhaps I did not have more than my fair share of these interviews, but I had a great many. I was not identified with any of the philological courses, and the graduate students who had what they thought was a literary turn of mind sought me out for advice. They had no idea that I had ever gone through a rigid philological discipline myself, and I think that G. L. K. would have been amused to hear me defend the emphasis which the Department and Division were laying upon that side of the necessary training of a teacher. To the sentimentalists who believed, in Stuart Sherman's phrase, that attention to linguistics was 'killing the poet in them,' I pointed out that if a poet could be killed by a year or two of hard work on the early stages of Germanic or Romance languages, the quicker he died the better. To the modernists who wished to confine their work to the eighteenth and nineteenth centuries I replied that the main thing was to learn to paddle one's own scholarly canoe, and that if some of the most skilful canoe-men at Harvard chose to exercise and teach their craft upon the rough upper reaches of the river instead of upon the broader and smoother currents lower down, it was the duty and privilege of a pupil to learn from the master on those waters where the master loved to teach. After the pupil had once learned what the linguistic specialists had to impart, he would be free to paddle his own canoe on any waters he preferred!

Thus did a very rusty and at best inept philologist, who was himself giving 'modern' courses, preach patience and docility and loyalty to the Powers that Were. But at heart I felt that the requirements for the Ph.D. in our Division were—not too severe, for they should be severe—but too inelastic and unchangeable, recognizing too little the value of equally important disciplines in parallel fields. I remember that we once refused to give a candidate any credit for a year spent in the graduate study of Catullus at the University of Munich. He wished to substitute this for the Harvard course in Gothic, and I thought that for a teacher of literature there was more virtue in Catullus than in the language of the excellent Bishop Ulfilas. Very recently, it is true, the programme for the Ph.D. in our Division has been modified. With no loss in severity, it allows for more flexibility of choice in the fields to be covered. . . .

Another thing that puzzled me at Harvard was the persistent faith, among undergraduates and many teachers, in the value of courses in Compositon. This tradition went back to the days when John Quincy Adams held the Boylston Professorship of Rhetoric and Oratory, a chair subsequently filled by 'Ned' Channing, Child, and A. S. Hill. Surely these men, followed by such expert teachers of composition as Briggs, Wendell, Copeland, and the rest, could not have labored in vain! Although it was known that Child and Wendell, toward the end, had grown sceptical of the value of 'themes,' there was a comfortable creed that the graduates of Harvard wrote better than the graduates of other colleges. I kept to myself the dreadful secret that in ten years of reading manuscript for the *Atlantic* I had never observed that Harvard men wrote any better than Yale men or Bowdoin men or men like Howells and Aldrich and John Burroughs who had never gone to college at all! It seemed to me that writing was a highly personal craft, to be perfected only after long practice, and that it made little difference where or how the practitioner learned the rudiments of his trade. Many years afterward, I admired Professor Grandgent's courage in declaring his fear that Harvard students 'write rather poorly, and speak worse.'* Having been myself in youth an enthusiastic teacher of English composition, and in middle age infected somewhat with Wendell's scepticism as to its unique worth as a college study, I may be allowed to unburden myself of some truisms:

(1) The mechanics of English compositon can be taught. They are taught well in hundreds of schools, and may if necessary be imparted to such college students as have failed to receive proper instruction. Beyond this field of mechanical correctness lies the domain of literary art, and art in writing is mainly a matter of self-discipline, although the practitioner may be helped by expert criticism. (2) We expect too much, however, from the teachers of English in American colleges. They have had to shoulder a great part of that burden of accurate training in the mother tongue which was formerly carried by means of daily drill in translating Greek and Latin. Year after year in the Harvard Graduate School, I used to notice that the best writers were the Canadians who had kept up their classics. No boy well trained in Latin or Greek compositon ever found difficulty in expressing himself clearly in English. It was hoped that drill in the modern languages would ultimately supply the discipline once given by the classics, but thus far the results are disappointing. (3) Undergraduates with literary ambitions should have the opportunity for writing verse, prose, drama, fiction—any literary form they prefer—under competent instruction. This individual instruction is, however, very costly, both in time and money, and it should be limited to students of special promise. Even from these youths one should not expect immediate triumphs. One cannot make bricks without straw or a work of art without materials, and very few undergraduates have read enough, experienced enough, pondered enough, to have even the raw material for a literary masterpiece.

---

* S. E. Morison, *Development of Harvard University, 1869–1929*, p. 104.

17

"Professor Kittredge and the Teaching of English," *The Nation* (1913)

Stuart P. Sherman

Stuart Pratt Sherman (1881–1926) was born and raised in Iowa, attended Williams College (A.B., 1903), and did graduate work at Harvard. There he became the leading younger member of the New Humanist group led by Irving Babbitt and Paul Elmer More, and reacted against the model of the scholar represented by the great Shakespearian and medievalist, George Lyman Kittredge. After one year at Northwestern, he taught in the English Department at the University of Illinois from 1908 till his resignation in 1924 to devote full time to journalism as literary editor of the *New York Herald Tribune*. Through his journalistic pieces in the *Nation* and other periodicals, Sherman earned a reputation as a fierce moralistic opponent of new literary movements (an opposition he later qualified) and the arch adversary of their defender, H. L. Mencken. Sherman's books include *Matthew Arnold: How to Know Him* and numerous essay-collections.

In the present selection, Sherman depicts Kittredge as the epitome of the positivistically-inclined research scholar, who bears responsibility for the "sterilizing divorce between philology and general ideas."

The distinguished scholar whose scientific curiosity burns its way through no man knows what thorny tangles of contemporary research, and who, according to common report, in his heroic vigils nightly outwatches the Bear, very possibly sat down some summer evening to the congratulatory volume marking his twenty-fifth anniversary at Harvard, and between curfew and cockcrow digested it all, formulated his opinion on the point of each of the forty-five contributions, and slept the sleep of the just. We others, who are but "men of mould," may well content ourselves on this occasion with merely a cursory glance at the stones of this monument of honour and pass on to a consideration of its general significance. Briefly, then, let it be said that in bulk and quality it is comparable with perhaps three or four numbers of the Publications of the Modern Language Association, and that the individual articles, though for the most part of no concern to the non-professional reader, will be perused with interest by those who have reached divergent conclusions upon such points as the date of Hegetor, swan maidens, Celtic cauldrons of plenty, the priority of the A or B versions of the prologue to the *Legend of Good Women*, mediæval lives of Judas Iscariot, Vegetius in English, or Caiaphas as a Palm Sunday prophet. Let it be added that the forty-five contributors are but chosen representatives from Professor Kittredge's great following, that perhaps scores of others are chagrined that their names do not appear in the table of contents, that uncounted young Doctors of Philosophy would gladly have come bringing similar gifts with them, who, should they fall in their spring, would be pleased with the simple Grevillian epitaph—"He was a pupil of Kittredge's." Let it be noted, finally, that the entire cost of issuing the volume has been handsomely contributed by the publishers, and that the proceeds of the sale are to constitute a special book fund for the Harvard Library, to be expended under the direction of the Master.

Had it been only what some famous wit has called "a mere damned professor" lapsing quietly into the retiring age, had it been any but he, one would have been inclined to murmur, *sunt hic etiam sua praemia laudi**—a tolerably adequate testimonial, as academic distinctions go, to a quarter of a century spent in the self-effacing life of a scholar. But Professor Kittredge's has not been precisely a self-effacing life, he is not so far as we know about to retire, and we cannot imagine him "quietly lapsing" into anything. He has written learned books and articles on subjects ranging from *Arthur and Gorlagon* to *The Old Farmer and his Almanack*, but one wonders whether his reputation would have been perceptibly less today if he had not written a line. He has not dulled his palm by the entertainment of newspaper reporters, nor popularized his science for the magazines, nor been a delegate to a national political convention, nor even, we believe, been presented to the Kaiser. He has kept his name austerely within professional circles. Yet he has had his way in his profession. If a ballot were taken, among those qualified to vote, on the most eminent and influential professor of English in America, who would head the list if it were not he? He has exercised, indeed, a kind of overlordship upon English instruction in this country. But whether by virtue of his official position, or his erudition, or the merit of his ideas, or by his organizing power and the singularly dynamic force of his personality, the big congratulatory volume does not indicate—is as inarticulate as a cairn on a battlefield. The occasion demands a tablet and an inscription, and perhaps the unveiling of a portrait.

I

First of all, let us declare that Professor Kittredge belongs to that generation of great college teachers which well-informed observers tell us is rapidly giving

* these are certainly his deserved praises. [ed.]

place to a later undergrowth of special investigators. There are, to be sure, a few small colleges left in the land, which, without much regard for "productive scholarship," still bestow their pudding and praise upon the man who can master his classroom, stab the laggards broad awake, and by the venerable inquisitorial methods discover and develop the young men of parts. But generally nowadays the word is passed round among the rising generation of instructors that the way to get on in the academic walk is not to waste time on one's pupils, but to publish—it matters not what. Whatever indirect responsibility Professor Kittredge may share in the propagation of this notion, it is undeniable that his own example has not sanctioned it. When the "efficiency" experts began last spring their abortive inquiries into the time spent by members of the instructional staff in preparation for each lecture, Professor Kittredge said, as it is reported, "I shall refuse to answer; it is my trade secret." A thoroughly characteristic *mot*, and it helped reveal the Philistine futility of the investigation. The special flavour of it lay in one's certainty that the questionnaire would, as a matter of fact, be dropped by him summarily and with perfect impunity into the waste basket, and in the universal recognition that as a teacher, pure and simple, Professor Kittredge is, as they say in Cambridge, "one of the glories of the University." We are thinking now particularly of that famous course in Shakespeare which for many years has been one of the good reasons for going to Harvard.

There is a persistent tradition that Professor Kittredge formed what we may call his undergraduate manner in his preliminary pedagogic experiments long ago at the Phillips Exeter Academy. It is a manner primarily adapted to young, resistant, "tough-minded" persons, and it is perhaps not unconsciously reminiscent of Dr. Boyer of immortal memory and of that older schoolmaster at whose hands John Dryden received, as he gratefully testified, the only thrashing that he ever deserved. Exponents of the new style of teaching salute their assembled pupils in the French fashion with a courteous "Gentlemen," deliver an essay spiced with epigrams, or twitter extemporaneously through the hour, bow, and disappear. Or—of another type—enter the lecture room, weary, dreary from their private lucubrations, explain that they are but fellow workers with their pupils in the same vineyard, pull out a sheaf of ill-digested notes, and drone away till the welcome bell. The new style is based not merely on the assumption that the student is "interested in his own intellectual welfare," but also on the far wider assumption that he is interested in his teacher's intricate "special problem." In dealing with undergraduates, Professor Kittredge is an educational realist. He assumes nothing but the general ignorance, indolence, and inattentiveness of undisciplined youth. He sees congregated before him, in that curious mixture fostered by the Harvard system, boys of eighteen and men with hair as white as his own, hard students and loafers from the "Gold Coast," keen-eyed freshmen from the Cambridge and Boston Latin Schools and untrained bachelors from the soft Southern colleges, stiff-necked elderly schoolmasters who wish to "brush up a bit," and opinionated, unlicked cub professors on leave from the exuberant West. He does not cast a farewell glance about the room and dive into a manuscript. He envisages the situation. Before instruction proper can begin this unequal conglomeration of alertness and dullness, humility and conceit, must be subjugated, must be terrorized, must be welded by common apprehension into one homogeneous whole.

Perhaps the technique of terror is a "trade secret," too, but it is also a rich legend recited by every group of men that have studied English at Harvard. After the lapse of a good many years we can call up with perfect distinctness some of the Black Fridays when there was great slaughter of the Innocents. A pretty abrupt hush follows his rapid footsteps up the aisle, deepens as he seats himself sidewise, and menaces us thunderously from behind the formidable blue glasses, becomes painfully intense as he rises to stride to and fro the length of the platform in a kind of tiger tread, and the blackboard pointer, overstrained by his nervous fingers, breaks with an electrifying snap. We are about to enjoy a bad quarter of an hour. "Mr. A! How does a play begin?" "With dialogue," hazards Mr. A. "Mr. B! How does a play begin?" "With the introduction of the characters," stammers Mr. B anxiously. "Mr. C! How does a play begin?" Mr. C, who is from the Gold Coast, quietly mumbles, "I don't know." The hunt is afoot. The next dozen men go down amid derisive snickers—no one dares to laugh aloud—like clay pipes before a crack marksman. Panic spreads. Half of us refuse to answer to our names. The other half, in desperate agitation between an attempt to conjure up any sort of reply and a passionate desire to sink through the floor, shudderingly wait for the next victim, till the pursuer, at last weary of the sport, cries out, "A play begins *in mediis rebus!*" Then we turn to the text. "'We would not die in that man's company that fears his fellowship to die with us.' Mr. X! Explain 'that fears his fellowship to die with us.'" Mr. X proffers something very elaborate and very confused. "Somebody explain that explanation!"—this with the true Johnsonian shout. "Mr. Y!" Mr. Y moistens his lips, starts, hems, hesitates, fumbles for words. "Come! Come! Mr. Y. Time flies! Hell threats! Heaven invites!" Mr. Y shuns salvation and hangs silent in Limbo. Mr. Z ventures on a surly pleasantry and is greeted with an invitation to "come over and swap jests with me at 2:30 this afternoon." We all envy Mr. Z as we should envy a man invited to take supper in a lion's den. Like many other of the great experiences of life, it was a rigorous ordeal while one was undergoing it, but it was pleasant to look back upon years afterwards, and, like Purgatory, it was very salutary.

The instruction proper had, also, as we recall it, a powerful purgatorial quality. What has subsequently seemed to us to be Professor Kittredge's guiding spirit is happily embodied in one of the "golden sayings," to use his own phrase, of Josh Billings: "It ain't the things we don't know that makes such fools of us, but a whole lot of things that we know that ain't *so.*" This, despite the vernacular dress, is the spirit of science, and for at least once in a lifetime it was an entirely wholesome spirit to encounter amid the bogs and fens of Shakespearian "interpretation." "War to the death," was the cry in that course, "on gushing Mrs. Jamesons, moralizing clergymen, and fantastic Teutonic metaphysicians." "There are many ways of studying Shakespeare," he told us, "but the object of this course is to ascertain what Shakespeare said and what he meant when he said it." The session ordinarily began with five or ten minutes during which we called out questions on difficult points in the previous day's reading. These he answered instantly, always without consulting the book, and succinctly or copiously as the case required. For the next ten or fifteen minutes he subjected us in our turn to a grilling examination on whatever we had prepared for the day. For the rest of the hour he commented with racy phrase and startling illustration, and left the room at the last minute, talking all the way down the aisle and halfway down the stairs.

II

For graduate students there was another manner. Jupiter Tonans gave way to benignant Jove, a being of equal or greater fascination, but with its terrors laid by, alert, omniscient as it seemed, a hawk-eyed critic still, but of princely amenity, tireless helpfulness, and the cordialest interest in one's personal destiny. This is the Kittredge of the disciples—the candidates for the doctorate—who hand down his *obiter dicta* from year to year, and speak of his chance commendation of some former pupil or pupil's work as one speaks of the conferring of an Order of Merit.

There was nothing lethargic in the atmosphere of those meetings. When the analysis and destruction of a great piece of German interpretation was completed one felt such a glow of satisfaction as must have thrilled the blood of a red-handed Saxon churl when he had assisted good King Alfred in flaying off a Dane skin and nailing it up on a church door. Nor, under that leadership, did one's interest flag when occasion failed for noble rage and cannibalistic enterprise. Fired by that unrelenting ardour, one fixed one's attention with as intense a concern upon a disputed comma in the Canterbury tale as one could have felt for the most momentous crisis in the affairs of a nation. One could sit for week after week copying down under that dynamic dictation an endless ballad bibliography that one never used, nor ever hoped to use, and yet maintain through it all the spellbound gravity of one hearkening to a seraphic discussion of fate and foreknowledge absolute.

Best of all were the ever-memorable individual conferences, when the candidate, now going heavily with his dissertation, visited the arbiter of his fate by special appointment at some hour not far from midnight, and came upon him, in the midst of his study, seated at the centre of a great half moon of tomes and treatises, and enveloped and clouded, like a god, in infinite smoke. You began the interview with a half-hour of wizardry, during which, while you helped thicken the smoke, he told you of the smoking customs of barbarians or poured out odd stories of witchcraft and alchemy in New England. Then you explained your difficulties and he cleared them up, or you told him what you were hunting for, and he pulled out of some recess or other a box full of references bearing exactly upon the point, and filed away months or years before, when he was working upon the same topic. You returned to your labours with a persuasion that there was no topic which had not, on one occasion or another, engaged his attention. You returned with a feeling, also, that your academic fortune was insured. For it may be said of Professor Kittredge, as it was said of the old Germanic chiefs, who never forgot their friends nor forgave their enemies, he has been a good "Ring-Giver."

III

We have spoken with some fullness of the more personal side of Professor Kittredge's teaching, because it is only by dwelling upon his dæmonic energy, his relentlessly positive temper, and his passion for domination that we can make wholly credible, even to ourselves, the nature and extent of the influence that he has exercised upon the teaching and the study of English at Harvard and throughout the country. For it must be frankly admitted that he has wielded his authority against a good deal of bitter opposition, and that many who have been constrained to submit to it have been rather subjugated than pacified.

There is a current story that a certain student, hankering vaguely in his uncorrected youth for the divine elation and finding himself out of the way of experiencing it, admitted to Professor Kittredge that he was not interested in "mere facts." "I am interested," was the withering response, "in nothing but facts." Doubtless the word "facts" had a wider meaning in the retort than in the provocation, and perhaps the whole incident is apocryphal. It is none the less suggestive. It hints at a type of pitcher, not empty nor entirely worthless, that is not readily filled at that well. It is a curious matter that though for years we have heard witnesses testifying various indebtedness to their guide, philosopher, and friend, we do not recall that anyone has acknowledged indebtedness to him for a "love of good literature." We are inclined to doubt whether he considers it any part of his function to impart to his students a love of literature. We are certain that they receive little encouragement from him to form opinions upon the æsthetic or other merits of the pieces with which they are engaged. Possibly an early abhorrence of elegant lecturers and uninformed enthusiasms has hardened with time into an unconcealed, somewhat contemptuous antipathy for "literary fellows," concerned with the ideas and emotions which constitute the spirit of letters. "What did you learn in those graduate seminars that was permanently useful to you?" the writer once inquired of a favourite pupil, who was teaching modern English literature. "To verify my references," was the reply, "and to transcribe quoted passages with punctilious accuracy." That was, of course, a jest. What the speaker meant was that he had carried away the technique and the ideal of scientific research. That, as we take it, is what Professor Kittredge has principally desired to impart to graduate students.

Now, it is impossible to make the study of literature a rigorously scientific pursuit without terribly impoverishing it. You cannot give it the standing of a science unless you deliberately choose to ignore those scientifically imponderable elements of thought and feeling which essentially and permanently distinguish the field of humane letters from the field of science. In the approach to these elements the scientific spirit is, as everyone would admit, an indispensable lamp to the feet, but in dealing with them one must use a headlight filled with another oil. The moment that you touch upon them, you have passed the boundaries of the unvarnished verifiable fact. You are in the Debatable Land; you are in the moral world. Philosophy and religion lie before you, and ethics and æsthetics—which is not a science outside of Germany—encompass you around. You must proceed with tradition, authority, and a seasoned judgment to guide you, yet walking mainly by the "inner light." You are shoulder to shoulder with the thrice accursed "literary fellows" in the demesne of the man of letters. You are in imminent peril of becoming a literary dilettante, and there is one chance in a thousand that you may become a great critic or literary historian.

Professor Kittredge has taken few chances at making great literary historians or critics. Hating the literary dilettante with a perfect hatred, he has probably never paused to consider whether the odds are not equally heavy against the production of a great philologist, nor whether, for the service to which he is called, the literary dilettante is not on the whole about as useful a kind of humbug or mediocrity as the linguistic dilettante. Pausing, we may suspect, to meditate neither of these important questions, he has squarely turned his back upon the Debatable Land and has led his followers by forced marches into the opposite quarter of the English field, where he has taught them the elements of textual criticism and linguistic science, interested them in the editing of unpublished manuscripts and the collection of folklore, and made them all zealous bibliographers and compilers of card indexes. In short, he has been a potent force in bringing about the present sterilizing divorce of philology from general ideas. If his school has not been very prolific in important books, it should be remembered that one of its maxims is, "Anyone can write a book; the difficult thing is to write an article." This appears to be a veiled way of saying that the digestion of facts, however, weighty, sinks into insignificance in comparison with the discovery of facts, however trifling.

The great field for the discovery of facts, memorable chiefly because they have been forgotten, has long been the Middle Ages, and Professor Kittredge is a mediævalist. To a mind in which the master impulse is a wide-ranging curiosity this tract of literature is endlessly fascinating, by virtue of just those qualities which, to a mind with ulterior purposes like Matthew Arnold's, for example, make it seem almost negligible—its prolixity, its formlessness, its naïve superstitions, its lack of high seriousness, its insolidity of substance.

We are not so foolish as to object that an eminent mediævalist has followed his bent. Our objection is only that he has, in no very indirect way, prevented other men from pursuing their bents. There should certainly be room and following at Harvard for a distinguished scholar in the mediæval period. But there should also be room and following for men qualified to deal in a really distinguished fashion with the vital ideas and movements of English literature since the Renaissance. We will not speak for the present year of grace—conditions vary somewhat from year to year. But within, say, the last fifteen years, there have been long intervals when, barring the drama, there was almost no instruction in English offered at Harvard that an intelligent graduate student could take seriously in the period from the Sixteenth to the Nineteenth Century. There were popular "snap" lecture courses for miscellaneous good-natured auditors; but for the student who had got beyond that, neither guidance nor encouragement. When, in conformity with the printed invitation, the candidate for the higher degree unfolded to the Department his plans and desires for work in modern literature, a majestic figure waved him to a more removed ground. There was nothing on paper to indicate objection to his enterprise, but after a few weeks he began to perceive that the modern period was not, so to speak, in good odour with those in authority. There was the system which incorporated the leading ideas of the Chairman of the Divison of Modern Languages, and which prepared one for research in the Middle Ages. The core of the course was prescribed and the rind very strongly intimated—Germanic Philology, Romance Philology, Historical Grammar, Old Norse, Anglo-Saxon Grammar, Beowulf, Cynewulf, Old Irish perhaps, Ballads and Metrical Romances, Chaucer, Shakespeare, another course in the Drama also desirable. It was notorious that in the grand ordeal of the far-dreaded final examination serious inquisiton into your scholarship would, in nine cases out of ten, end with the Fourteenth Century.

Without drawing too closely the links between cause and effect, we may say that the conditions prevailing at Harvard at the period which we have been describing have affected more or less seriously the teaching of English throughout the country. Departments in the older institutions with established and more humane traditions of their own have, of course, been less subject to the influence, and at least one great department has gained in prestige in proportion as it has reacted against it. It is in the small colleges and in the younger universities with rapidly growing faculties that the new generation of English teachers have been planted and have had their way. And it is when you see the newly fledged philologist at work, teaching compositon (an art which he has never practised) and Eighteenth Century prose (a sea which for him has never been charted), it is then that you begin to recognize that something is out of joint in the state of Denmark. It is when you have observed half a dozen aspiring instructors publishing in the learned journals first-hand comments on mediæval syntax, etymology, and beast fable, and uttering in their classrooms third- and fourth-hand comments on Milton, Dryden, and Tennyson—it is then that you understand the vogue of the teachers who "vitalize" literature by the use of the magic lantern. It is when you have attended the annual advertising picnic of the "scientific investigators" and have compared the quality of the papers and discussions at a convention of the Modern Language Association with those of the historical and philosophical societies—it is then that you wonder why it is that, wherever English scholarship is taken seriously, from the Great Lakes to the Gulf of Mexico and from the James River to the Golden Gate, all America mediævalizes. It is when you have lived for some years in an English department, and have watched your colleagues settling into the role of routine teachers, losing their zest for discovery or taking it as a recreation like golf, abandoning the hunt for subjects and letting the dust gather on their card catalogues—it is then that you feel what Professor Grandgent, in his Anniversary contribution, has described as "the necessity of self-deception regarding the futility of human endeavour." You feel in this "fellowship of scholars" an almost tragical lack of common interests and ideas. You feel as one wandering in an intellectual Sahara in a silence unbroken save by an investigating sparrow chirping from time to time over a kernel of musty wheat in the shroud of Ptolemy the Great.

18

From *Autobiography with Letters* (1939)

William Lyon Phelps

William Lyon Phelps (1865–1943) was a minister's son and New Haven resident
who took both his B. A. (1887) and Ph.D. (1891) at Yale University, with an
A. M. from Harvard University (also 1891) as well. After teaching at Harvard for
one year, he joined the Yale English Department in 1892, where he remained till
retirement in 1933. In 1895, against departmental faculty opposition, he initiated
one of the first college courses ever given in contemporary fiction. A popular
public lecturer and a spellbinding undergraduate teacher at a time when
professional attitudes were such that "popularity with students was a serious
handicap" to promotion, Phelps, along with Irving Babbitt and Stuart P.
Sherman, was probably the most famous English professor in America from the
turn of the century through the 1930s.

Primarily a popularizer in his writings, Phelps was author of some twenty-six
books, including *The Beginnings of the English Romantic Movement, Essays on
Modern Novelists*, and *Autobiography with Letters*, from which the present selection
is taken. Phelps's autobiography suggests what it was like to be a "generalist" man
of letters in the highly professionalized atmosphere of the early deparments.

I had entered college intending eventually to become a lawyer; I read some law
in leisure moments, and occasionally visited city courtrooms. I had visions of
myself winning great cases in crowded courtrooms, and then entering politics,
and becoming a United States Senator; for a boy of eighteen, I was deeply read
in American political history. There was no moment in my college course
when with a theatrical gesture I 'renounced the law,' but becoming more and
more interested in literature, I was, in spite of my ambitions, slowly, at first
imperceptibly, but finally, drawn entirely away from legal studies or ambitions.

Most of our classrooms were dull and the teaching purely mechanical; a
curse hung over the Faculty, a blight on the art of teaching. Many professors
were merely hearers of prepared recitations; they never showed any living
interest, either in the studies or in the students. I remember we had Homer

three hours a week during the entire year. The instructor never changed the monotonous routine, never made a remark, but simply called on individuals to recite or to scan, said 'That will do,' put down a mark; so that in the last recitation in June, after a whole college year of this intolerable classroom drudgery, I was surprised to hear him say, and again without any emphasis, 'The poems of Homer are the greatest that have ever proceeded from the mind of man, class is dismissed,' and we went out into the sunshine. Two Freshmen instructors shone by contrast; a young teacher of Latin named Ambrose Tighe, who left Yale in a few years, and had a fine career as a lawyer and member of the legislature in Minnesota. He tried to teach us Roman history as well as Latin grammar; he talked about Horace as though Horace were a man about town, and he himself looked and acted like a man of the world. I remember his saying that he would like to teach us Lucretius, but that he did not know enough; 'for,' said he, 'in comparison with Lucretius, the entire works of Horace and Virgil sink into insignificance.' The older members of the Faculty looked upon Mr. Tighe with suspicion. He made Latin interesting; and they got rid of him. . . .

Life at Harvard

On my second day at Harvard I called on the professors under whom I was to study; and first of all on Professor Francis J. Child, known to the students as 'Stubby' Child. He hated to be interrupted in his home in Kirkland Street, but he was kind and considerate. At that time it was considered both by the Faculty and students in the Harvard Graduate School, that everyone who took advance studies in English must spend nearly all his time on philology. Thus I found the students were all studying Anglo-Saxon, the history of the English language, Historical English Grammar, Old Norse, Gothic, and what not; furthermore, the Doctor's theses were on linguistic subjects. I asked some of these men if they really preferred to write on such themes. 'No, of course not; but you can't write a doctor's thesis in literature.' I replied that my thesis would have nothing whatever to do with philology. They regarded me with a mixture of incredulity, wonder, and envy.

Now when I called on Professor Child, he began to make out a programme for me consisting of the unpalatable subjects mentioned above. I told him I had had one year of Anglo-Saxon at Yale, and that would have to last me all my life. But he said I must have these other linguistic studies. I told him I had the highest respect for those studies and for the professors who taught them; but that they did not interest me. I wished to confine myself to English literature. He was so astounded at this and perhaps thought I was not taking graduate work seriously or was lazy or dilettantish or something, that he became rather severe; and my career at Harvard very, very nearly came to an end on the second day. I finally said, 'Professor Child, I have come to Harvard to study literature under you and your colleagues; if you refuse to allow me to take the studies I came here for, I shall take the first train back to New Haven.' Suddenly his whole manner changed. 'You go ahead and take anything you like. It is refreshing to find a graduate student who knows what he wants.'

Accordingly the first year I took Shakespeare with Professor Child; History and Principles of English Versification, with Dean L.B.R. Briggs (God bless his heart!); Elizabethan Drama, with Mr. George Pierce Baker, who nearly forty years later was to be my colleague at Yale and Head of the Department of Drama; and a course in research in eighteenth century literature, where I reported my results every week or so to Professor Barrett Wendell. In the following year I took Chaucer under Professor Kittredge; Elizabethan literature (outside drama) under Professor Wendell; and English literature of the seventeenth century, under Dean Briggs. . . .

As an undergraduate at Yale, there were hardly any courses in English literature; and even in the Yale Graduate School, there were not sufficient courses in English, so that I took philosophy, history, and economics as well. But now, at Harvard, I had only the studies I wanted. My eyes grew better all the time, and although I lived like a hermit, had hardly any exercise and no recreation, I was happy.

Once more, as has so often happened in my life, realization was better than anticipation. I went to Harvard as an experiment, thinking it would be good for me, but not expecting to enjoy it. It was like a new lease of life. I felt like Andrea del Sarto at the court of François Premier. There was a keen intellectual atmosphere created not only by the members of the English Department, but by a Department of Philosophy which I suppose was the most brilliant that has ever existed—William James, Josiah Royce, George Santayana, George Herbert Palmer, Hugo Münsterberg; I knew these men and heard them give public lectures. On Sunday afternoons I went occasionally to the house of Professor Nathaniel Shaler, who was a brilliant talker on anything and everything; Charles Eliot Norton was in his prime, and his *obiter dicta* in his famous course in Fine Arts were reported all around the place. There was a vitality indescribable. Bliss was it in that dawn to be alive. . . .

The Harvard professor with whom I came most closely in contact was Barrett Wendell; we became intimate friends; he was very kind to me, and I shall always think of him with grateful affection. In many ways he was the most peculiar man on the Harvard Faculty and President Eliot waited a good many years before promoting him to a full professorship. It speaks well for Harvard—it is indeed meant by me to be the highest possible compliment to Harvard, both to the authorities and to the undergraduates—that in the nineties Harvard was the only university in America that could or would have kept Wendell. There have been some universities (not Yale and not Harvard) where the oddities, indiscretions, and other characteristics of professors as revealed in the classroom have been a source of revenue to students whose love of money has been more acute than their sense of honour. These students, ignoring the fact that things said in the classroom are not for publication, have furnished to the papers sensational statements made or supposed to be made by their teachers; and as college professors are generally 'news,' these indiscretions form what the newspapers call a 'story.' To the everlasting credit of Harvard undergraduates, I never knew of a single one of Wendell's remarks or acts being supplied by them for public consumption. They had much good-natured fun with him in the articles and in the pictures of the *Harvard Lampoon*, but that was all in the family; and if there had been any talk of letting Wendell go, these students would have been the first to rise in his defence. . . .

Wendell's peculiarities seemed at first like affectations; yet I have never known any teacher of English composition who showed more common sense. For many years he carried the all but intolerable burden of reading and correcting themes, day after day. His room was filled with these compositions; they were all over the table and on the chairs, and when he lay down on the sofa, to get a little rest, he used a bunch of themes for a pillow. However picturesque and bizarre his own manner and way of expression, he never tolerated affectation in the compositions of his students. Ruthlessly he combed out of them every bit of 'fine writing,' every trace of insincerity, and taught them how to express themselves clearly and with economy of words. His book *English Composition* is the best treatise on the art of writing I have ever seen, and certainly the only one I read through from first page to last with undiminished interest.

In the early Spring, obsessed by the work I was doing on my Doctor's thesis and by the fear that I should not finish it in time, I became afflicted with insomnia. This became so severe and so long-continued that finally I went back to my parents' house in New Haven to rest. But what people need who suffer from sleeplessness is not rest but diversion; and there was no diversion. I suffered so much that I really do not care to write about it. But it was a remark made by Professor Beers of Yale that did me more good than any physician or any medicine. I went to him and said that I had hoped to have my thesis completed by the first of May, which was the time for submitting it, but that I feared I should have to give up my degree that year, as I was in such poor health. He merely remarked, 'You have already done enough work on your thesis to deserve your degree, and you will get it anyway. Hand in your incomplete work at the proper time, and you will receive your degree at Commencement. You can polish it and if necessary add to it next year.' I do not think that he ever knew what he did for me; for I might have had a complete and prolonged breakdown.

But his statement took a tremendous load off my mind. I returned to Harvard immediately, and although I felt that I wrote that thesis not in ink but in blood, I finished it some time before the date, and did not have to ask any favours. During those weeks of depression, before temporarily giving up and going to New Haven for rest, and while at New Haven, although in no danger of suicide, I constantly longed to die. If any robber then had pointed a pistol at me in the night, I should have regarded him as my best friend. I am always sympathetic with sufferers from 'nerves' or from melancholia or depression, for I know the particular part of hell they are in. And I feel when any young person commits suicide that if someone could only have been with him or if he could only have got through that month of misery, he might have had before him forty or fifty years of happiness. . . .

Although I shall always be grateful to Harvard for giving me an appointment as Instructor, and although my year of teaching was advantageous to me in every way, nothing would have induced me to consider a reappointment. I did not believe in the Harvard system of compulsory English compositions or in the enormous labour required of the instructors. The only subject required of Harvard undergraduates was the writing of compositions; this was required of every Freshman, every Sophomore, and at least for part of the year, of every Junior. The result was that a large number of men on the Faculty spent nearly all their time and energy in reading and correcting these themes; it seemed to me that this work was not University work at all, and that any primary schoolma'am would probably have been more efficient in the correcting job. That a man should graduate from Harvard with honours, spend two years in advanced study in the Graduate School, then a year of research in Europe—only to correct spelling, grammar, paragraphing, etc., seemed to me a hideous waste of time and energy. Furthermore, although many of these Freshmen and Sophomores wrote abominably when forced to sit in a room and compose a theme on an assigned subject, whenever they wrote a letter asking excuse on account of sickness, their style was correct and respectable. I knew of no work anywhere that so well illustrated the law of diminishing returns as this forced English composition.

I believed then and I believe now, that *elective courses* in advanced composition for men who wished to cultivate the art of writing and loved it, were exceedingly valuable; there were such courses at Harvard offered to picked men by Professor Briggs and Professor Wendell which were most profitable. After I had taught at Yale a few years, I sent up to Professor Wendell a collection of themes written by my Yale Sophomores, in connexion with their studies in English literature; these men had never received any college training in English compositon; but I felt sure that technically their themes would be as good as those written by Harvard Sophomores, though the latter were thoroughly trained in technical compositon. Mr. Wendell read them and wrote me that they were in every way equal to the work of Harvard Sophomores.

The only men on the Harvard English Faculty who were excused from reading themes were Professor Child and Professor Kittredge; and these men, with Wendell, did not believe in the required system. The most bitter expressions came from the venerable Professor Child, usually regarded as the foremost English scholar in America. For many years he had been forced to read hundreds and hundreds of undergraduate compulsory compositons; he said the system was bad for both students and teachers. He regretted the enormous amount of time and energy he had thus wasted. One day I met him in the Yard, and he asked me what I was doing; I replied, 'Reading themes.' He looked at me affectionately and said, 'Don't spoil your youth.'

During the entire academic year at Harvard, I read more than eight hundred themes every week; I read all day and a good part of the night. Once I was sick for two days, and a substitute read for me, because even one day's lapse made it impossible to keep up. . . .

Teaching at Yale

I began regular work as a full-time Instructor in English at Yale in the Autumn of 1892. The College was nearly two hundred years old, but this was the first time that English literature had ever been taught to Freshmen. I was given one-third of the class from September to Christmas, another third from Christmas to Easter, and the last section from Easter to June; so that I was to meet intimately in small divisions, three hours a week, all the members of the incoming class of 1896. I was twenty-seven years old and looked eighteen. When I came to the door of the lecture-room and found it locked, one or two Freshmen waiting there, naturally taking me for a classmate, said 'Oh, the Prof hasn't got here yet.' When I took a key from my pocket and unlocked the door, they looked at me in amazement.

I taught the Freshmen As You Like It, Macbeth, and King Henry IV, Part I. I enjoyed the work unspeakably; and at the end of the Autumn term, when the first alphabetical third of the class found that they were to have no more English until Sophomore year, they sent to me a delegation headed by John Berdan (now Professor of English at Yale) asking me if I would continue to teach a volunteer class in the evening. I agreed to this—though it was an unprecedented thing at Yale. Accordingly for the next three months, I met a large group of Freshmen one evening a week and taught them English poetry of the nineteenth century.

At the end of Freshman year, I was directed to continue the teaching of English to this same class of 1896 in their Sophomore year. It was for Sophomores an elective study, but all except three men took it. I had one-half of the class until February and the second half for the rest of the year. Our friendly and intimate relations were still further strengthened. Then, when they became Juniors, I began to offer elective courses in addition to my work with the lower classes; many took these courses, so that I really taught them for four years. When they graduated in June 1896, they presented me with a large silver cup.

I suppose there has never been a member of the Yale Faculty who knew intimately every member of a large class as I knew these men; and although they are now over sixty, my friendship with them has only been strengthened by time. As it happened, this class, the first I taught at Yale in regular daily work, contributed more men to the Yale Faculty than any other class in Yale's history; so that a considerable number of my first pupils became my colleagues.

The intense affection between these undergraduates and their young teacher was refreshingly exceptional because of the traditional teaching at Yale. To me my methods seemed simply natural and unaffected; to some of my older colleagues on the Faculty they seemed revolutionary, deliberately sensational. . . .

The reason my teaching in 1892 seemed to my older colleagues revolutionary was that Yale was a place where traditions counted enormously. In the traditional teaching at Yale, formality was the rule. Nearly all the members of the Faculty wore dark clothes, frock coats, high collars; in the classroom their manners had an icy formality; humour was usually absent, except occasional irony at the expense of a dull student. It was quite possible to attend a class three hours a week for a year, and not have even the remotest conception of the personality of the man behind the desk. The teachers seemed to believe this was the only method by which discipline could be enforced and maintained.

There was a blight, a curse on the teaching, unfortunate both for teachers and pupils. Instructors who were thirty years old had the classroom manner of old men; I remember how astounded I was at discovering that one whom we all believed to be venerable was thirty-eight. These men certainly gave no indication of enjoying teaching; and of course the students found no joy in learning.

I will give two illustrations. There was one of our professors who was like the rest in merely hearing recitations and marking them; he never made comments and never betrayed emotion. One day I happened to meet a lady who was his contemporary, who had known him well when he was an undergraduate. She told me that he was the life of every party, outdoors or in; that whenever there was a picnic or an excursion anywhere, if they could get him, success was assured; that he was the finest and wittiest and most delightful conversationalist she had ever known. I told her she must be thinking of someone else; but no, this was the man. It was incredible. Officially he was one person and on other occasions he was another.

The most extraordinary case however, and yet different from the majority only in degree, was that of a professor whom it was my misfortune to have in Freshman, Sophomore, and Junior year. He never gave the slightest indication of having any human emotion, like sympathy, humour, consideration. He was a remorseless machine in the classroom, holding us down by iron discipline; it was impossible for me or any other student to penetrate the barrier between this man and the class he taught; and there was a steadily disagreeable attitude on his part that made us hate him. If he had died during my undergraduate years, I should have rejoiced greatly. Not only was this man icily contemptuous in the classroom, he made himself obnoxious to the students by interfering with many of their extra-curricular activities; so that for at least thirty years successive generations of undergraduates regarded him with hatred.

It was not until some years after my graduation, and after I had become a member of the Faculty, that I discovered he was generous, kind, considerate. He was also full of fun, delighting in jokes and ridiculous puns. The special papers that he used to write for a club were full of original wit.

Now this man was Jekyll and Hyde. Unofficially he was absolutely lovable; officially he was detestable.

He was a martyr to his theory of discipline. He ought to have been admired and loved by all those generations of youth; and how they would have loved him if he had given them a chance, and how he would have appreciated their affection and their esteem! Instead of that, this tenderhearted man had the tragedy of knowing that year after year he was hated and despised.

I mention these things because they help to explain why my teaching seemed revolutionary and sensational; I simply made up my mind that I should be exactly the same man in the classroom as out of it; there would be no detectable difference. I would assume that the undergraduates and I were equally interested in the subject, and that we were studying it together. Thus I was not sensational; I was natural.

But as in the old days of rhetorical oratory, when any exceptional individual spoke from the platform in a natural, easy, conversational manner, it seemed astounding; when an actor on the stage, dispensing with conventional mannerisms, spoke and acted with unaffected naturalness, the result was amazing; so my natural manner in the classroom produced an effect that must be called startling. The response from the students indicated it.

Informality in college teaching is common enough now; but in the nineties at Yale, it was almost unheard of.

Informality does not necessarily mean any loss of dignity; it may mean simply that one throws away all pretense. I began to teach with absolute naturalness; later in my public addresses, in my sermons in church, in my dinner speeches, in my orations at funerals, I have never changed. Whether I am talking to two persons or to two thousand, my manner is exactly the same. As a great deal is said about the technique of public speaking, I will say that this is all the technique I know. But whenever I address a strange audience, there is always that same opening shock. I can feel it; it is not unpleasant. I never begin with conventional platitudes and generalities; no matter how large the audience may be, I always feel as if I were talking to each one separately. 'This only is the witchcraft I have used.' . . .

There is no doubt that in those days (1880–1900) popularity with the students was a serious handicap; if promotion to professorships had been in the power of the President and Corporation, as it was in most other American universities, it would have been otherwise; but the Permanent Professors on the Faculty had the power of election; thus it was in some ways like being admitted to a very select club. It was easier to be elected if one were an 'available' candidate; that is, if one had not attracted undue attention; but extreme popularity made the ruling powers feel that the candidate must have stooped to conquer. Professor Sumner used to say it was often easier for a man from another college to receive an appointment than for a man on the ground; 'the latter's faults we know, and all we know of the distant man is that he has faults, but as we do not know what they are, we forget their certain existence.'

I had already as an undergraduate witnessed what I have always regarded as disasters for Yale. Mr. Ambrose Tighe, who taught us Latin in our Freshman and Sophomore years made his classroom so interesting that he incurred the displeasure of the higher powers, and was released. Frank Tarbell, our Instructor in Greek and Logic, was released just when his influence was becoming really profound. Tarbell later was very happy at Chicago, with his colleagues in the classics and in archaeology, and with his intimate friends Robert Herrick, William Vaughn Moody, Robert Lovett, and John Manly, of the English Department.

Now, after I had taught at Yale for seven or eight months, I was warned by several professors that my stay would be short; some were friendly, and merely told me to look out; others were quite the reverse, and gave me distinctly to understand that I could never look for promotion. Every time I received an offer elsewhere, I was earnestly advised to take it. I do not believe any member of the Faculty ever received so many invitations to leave Yale that came *from the inside*. One of my superiors told me that if I went on, I should be like Ambrose Tighe (my hero) whom he mentioned with contempt, and would share his fate.

After four years as Instructor, however, I was promoted to an Assistant Professorship, but only after a fierce battle in the Faculty, which was not settled until Commencement Day! Three years later an endowment for a Professorship in English Literature was given to Yale, and it had to be filled; a younger colleague of mine, and one who had had much shorter service was appointed. (I am glad that my friendship with him was never injured by this; we were dear and intimate friends till his untimely death.) But when this appointment came up to the President and Corporation, they, feeling it to be unfair to me, ratified it and at the same time unanimously elected me as well, and sent the two names back to the Faculty. The Faculty rejected me, and the letter I got from President Dwight that evening was one of the severest disappointments of my life. He said that his own disappointment was very great; and I knew that he had pleaded with the Faculty during a long session urging that I be appointed along with my colleague. And he added in his letter to me that what distressed him most was that he believed that now I could never become a Professor at Yale. This letter I received at night and my suffering was so intense from the shock of it that I was actually in physical agony. Nor did I get a good night's sleep for many weeks. . . .

The reading of exam papers was the only part of my academic work that I disliked; it was drudgery. Until I was sixty, however, I read every paper myself, over five hundred twice a year. . . .

One day in the Spring of 1895 I called on Professor Beers and told him that I should like to give a course on Modern Novels, confining the subject-matter entirely to contemporary works. Rather to my surprise and greatly to my pleasure, he gave his immediate assent to this, saying there was no reason why the literature of 1895 could not be made as suitable a subject for college study as the literature of 1295.

Thus was inaugurated what I believe was the first course in any university in the world confined wholly to contemporary fiction. I called the course *Modern Novels*. It was open to Seniors and Juniors, and was elected by two hundred and fifty men.

It was a good time to begin the serious academic study of contemporary prose fiction, for the preceding year 1894 was remarkable for the appearance of new novels many of which belong to literature: *Trilby, Lord Ormont and His Aminta, Esther Waters, The Ebb Tide, The Jungle Book, Life's Little Ironies, Jude the Obscure* (serially), *Pudd'nhead Wilson, Pembroke, The Prisoner of Zenda, The Dolly Dialogues, Under the Red Robe*; and Conrad's first novel *Almayer's Folly* was in press. Hall Caine's *The Manxman* and Mrs. Humphry Ward's *Marcella* also appeared in this same year. Although they both attracted immense attention from the public and intellectual respect from the critics, both novelists were unimportant and ephemeral, and for exactly opposite reasons.

When I gave the first lecture in the Autumn, I hoped the course would attract no attention outside of academic halls; for in those days, newspaper notoriety was often fatal to a university career. It is hard to say just how this publicity began, for I gave out no interviews, nor did I mention the subject anywhere; but a notice in the New Haven newspapers was quickly followed by a whole column in the *New York Times*, and it seemed as if every newspaper in the country followed suit. The usual headline was "They Study Novels," and a page was devoted to the revolutionary theme. Editorials usually appeared in the same issue. The vast majority of newspaper comment was favourable; but there were some editorial writers who looked with disapproval on the course, the separate novels studied, and the young instructor. . . .

Although the undergraduates apparently enjoyed both the course and the writing of a weekly critical theme, which I made obligatory, and although the newspaper comment was on the whole highly favourable, the majority of the older professors gave me distinctly to understand that unless I dropped the course at the end of its first year, I should myself be dropped from the Faculty. President Timothy Dwight, always the best friend I had among my superiors, sent for me, and advised me not to continue the course another year. I told him that I fully believed in the value of the course, but that I had no illusions as to my place in the university. 'You are the President—you are my chief and it is only a pleasure to obey you.' I knew that he had only my welfare in mind. Then the Dean of the college, Henry P. Wright, sent for me and made the following remark: 'If your course had been a failure there would have been no objection to its continuance.'

I had no desire to pose as a martyr and I hoped that the silent omission of the course for the following year would not be observed; but unfortunately it was. Learning that emissaries from the New York papers were on their way to New Haven to interview me, I left town and for a week only my wife knew where I was. On my return, the teapot-tempest had somewhat subsided, and to all the newspaper men I stated that I had voluntarily given up the course for one year. This was at least technically true; for the President had told me that I had a perfect right to continue it if I wished, only he advised me as a friend to conform to the judgement of my superiors.

Two years later I gave a course in American literature, in which I included all the American novels I had discussed in the previous course; and five years later I gave a course, the first of its kind, I believe, in any university, which was confined to contemporary dramatists.

My term as Instructor expired with the Novel course; and the Professors, perhaps relenting, perhaps pleased with my determination to avoid publicity connected with the withdrawal of that course, promoted me to an Assistant Professorship for five years. I learned this fact on Commencement Day. So that I began my work as Instructor at Yale with the Freshmen of the Class of 1896, and on the day this class was graduated, I ceased to be an 'Instructor' and became an Assistant Professor. At the expiration of my term in 1901, I was promoted to a full professorship, and a few months later, was made Lampson Professor of English literature, which position I held until my retirement, when I became Professor Emeritus.

William Lampson was a Yale graduate of the class of 1860, who lived at Leroy, N.Y. He left in his will money for three professorships, one in Greek, one in Latin, one in English, the balance of his estate to pay for the erection of a Yale building for lectures and recitations. This was an admirable bequest, as it provided for the foundation of three professorships and released money for current expenses. Thus for thirty-five years my salary came from the estate of a man whom I had never seen. I did what I could to make his name known, and kept a large portrait of him in my college office. I have always felt grateful to him and wished that I could have known him personally. His estate provided for an annual salary for every one of the three professorships of four thousand dollars a year. This was in 1901 the maximum salary for a full professor at Yale.

I was told on a cold morning of February that the professors were to meet that afternoon and recommend me for a professorship. I had to lecture at Madison, New Jersey, that evening. I came back over the ferry at New York near midnight; the river was filled with huge blocks of ice. I reached New Haven at half-past two in the morning. My wife greeted me with the glorious news of my promotion and had a supper ready of oysters and champagne. I wrote in my diary, 'I am very happy. My future is settled.' A number of professors called on me the next day, and said that whatever opposition there had been to me in the past was entirely dead, and that the Faculty were wholly appreciative. This gave me unspeakable delight.

Although their discussions were secret, several of them told me of one amusing incident that was too good to keep. A dignified and elderly Professor of Latin said in the meeting, 'Well, I am going to vote for Mr. Phelps, but there is just one thing about him I don't like. I wish he had a little more dignity. Everyone calls him Billy.' There was a moment's pause which was suddenly broken by the decisive and harsh voice of Professor William Graham Sumner, 'They call me Billy, too!' Everyone roared with laughter, and that remark made my calling and election sure. Professor Sumner was regarded as the most distinguished man on the Faculty; the students and his colleagues were somewhat in awe of him; yet by the undergraduates and alumni he was always spoken of as 'Billy' Sumner. . . .

19

From *Great American Universities* (1910)
Edwin Emery Slosson

Edwin Emery Slosson (1865–1929) was a chemistry professor and scientific popularizer whose book, *Great American Universities* (1910), is the most comprehensive survey of the condition of American higher education before the First World War. The passage from Slosson's book excerpted here reflects the growing awareness of the problem of apathetic students in this period, when universities were starting to take the form of massive, bureaucratic institutions with large, anonymous student bodies.

Comparisons and Conclusions

It would be well if the teachers did not know quite so much, if they knew how to tell what they did know better. It is a principle of hydraulics that the flow of water depends on the character of the outlet and the head, and not at all on the amount of water in the tank. In many cases it has seemed to me that the instructor has come into the room without the slightest idea of how he is to present his subject. He rambles on in a more or less interesting and instructive manner, but without any apparent regard to the effect on his audience or the economy of their attention. The methods of instruction are much the same as those used in the universities of the thirteenth century. . . .

I have heard of a professor of English in one of our universities who evidently felt that his department was under the same disadvantage as mathematics. Finding that his scientific colleagues were getting appropriations of astonishing liberality for illustrative apparatus, he put in his annual report a request for $5000 for an aviary. When the president asked him to explain, he said that it was impossible for him to teach poetry properly unless he had an aviary connected with his classroom. "Then," he said, "when the class is reading Shelley's 'Skylark,' I reach my long-handled net into the cage, catch a lark, and hold it up to them. And when we are studying 'The Rime of the

Ancient Mariner,' my assistant will be stationed in the gallery with a crossbow to shoot a real, live albatross on the platform, thus giving the students opportunities for observation that doubtless Coleridge himself never had."

The literary faculty has borrowed and misapplied so many of the methods of scientific research and instruction that it is impossible to say that we may not come to this yet. At any rate, the project shows a commendable enterprise and appreciation of the desirability of stimulating the interest of the students by bringing them into closer contact with reality.

If the lectures could be made more inspiring and stimulating, they could be made fewer and shorter. A flash of lightning makes a more lasting impression than a 16-c.p. incandescent running all night. But the students have not sufficient resistance to stand shocks of lightning for eighteen hours a week, nor could the instructor keep up the necessary voltage. The really eloquent and inspiring speakers in the universities, are not numerous enough to go around, and they are often poor drillmasters and inefficient administrative officers. Their gift could be utilized to the best advantage by having them address large classes once or twice a week and in several different institutions during the year. Then the ordinary and stationary instructors could devote themselves to working with the students at close quarters. That is, should not there be recognized in university work the distinction of function which, in some form or other, has always been made in the ecclesiastical work, the distinction between prophet and priest, revivalist and pastor?

As it is, the professors give too many lectures and the students listen to too many. Or pretend to; really they do not listen, however attentive and orderly they may be. The bell rings and a troop of tired-looking boys, followed perhaps by a larger number of meek-eyed girls, file into the classroom, sit down, remove the expressions from their faces, open their notebooks on the broad chair arms, and receive. It is about as inspiring an audience as a roomfull of phonographs holding up their brass trumpets. They reproduce the lecture in recitations like the phonograph, mechanically and faithfully, but with the tempo and timbre so changed that the speaker would like to disown his remarks if he could. The instructor tries to provoke them into a semblance of life by extravagant and absurd statements, by insults, by dazzling paradoxes, by extraneous jokes. No use; they just take it down. If he says that "William the Norman conquered England in 1066," or "William the German conquered England in 1920," it is all the same to them. They take it down. The secret is that they have, without knowing anything about physiological psychology, devised an automatic cut-off which goes into operation as they open their notebooks and short-circuits the train of thought from the ear directly to the hand, without its having to pass through the pineal gland or wherever the soul may be at the time residing and holding court.

One of the unfortunate results of the lecture system is that the professors get so used to talking that they cannot stop. Faculty, departmental, and council meetings are apt to be unduly extended, and in the end the wisdom of the whole body is not equal to the sum of its parts. On account of their ineffectiveness as a branch of administrative machinery, the tendency is to curtail their power and throw more responsibility upon the president, who is, like the Speaker of the House of Representatives, forced to become an autocrat. So far as my experience and observation go, the deliberative bodies of universities, small and large, have substantially the same method of procedure, and I suggest that if the following rules were framed and hung on the wall of the faculty room, it would save time now wasted in discussing the proper order:—

ORDER OF BUSINESS AT FACULTY MEETINGS

1. Present motion.
2. Pass it.
3. Discuss it.
4. Reconsider it.
5. Amend it.
6. Amend the amendment.
7. Discuss it.
8. Move to lay on the table.
9. Discuss it.
10. Refer to a committee with power to act.
11. Discuss it.
12. Adjourn.
13. Discuss it.

20

From *On Journey* (1937)

Vida Dutton Scudder

Vida Dutton Scudder (1861–1954) was born in India, the daughter of a congregationalist minister, grew up in Boston and was a member of the first graduating class of the Boston Girls' Latin School. After taking her B. A. from Smith College in 1884, Scudder became one of the first women to be admitted to graduate study at Oxford University, where she attended the lectures of John Ruskin. Returning to Smith for her M. A. (1889), Scudder was appointed to the English faculty at Wellesley College in 1887, where she remained until her retirement in 1928. She was related to both the publishing magnates Horace Scudder and E. P. Dutton.

An ardent Christian socialist at a time when it was dangerous even to sympathize with labor unions, Scudder worked in the Settlement Movement in New York's Lower East Side and spoke at rallies in support of strikes. For the latter activity, in 1912, Wellesley came under pressure to fire her, which it successfully resisted. In the 1890s, Scudder initiated a then unprecedented course entitled "Social Ideals in English Letters," the lectures for which were published in 1898 under that title. She was also the author of *The Life of the Spirit of the Modern English Poets* (1895) and an autobiography, *On Journey* (1937), from which the present selection is taken. Of interest for the sense it gives of the experience of one of the first successful women professors, the selection illustrates the curious mixture of sentimental spirituality and social radicalism underlying Scudder's view of literature and teaching.

Fortunate is he who, in times of sorrow, possesses an exacting purpose; I meant to become a good teacher, and I knew already that the task was no easy one. Teaching a task? An art, rather, and one in which I was a stumbling neophyte, keenly aware of blunders and failures. In my second year, Clara's proposed course fell into my hands, and I zealously explored the nineteenth-century field. Teaching "nineteenth century" was a very different matter then; for teachers and taught were alike within the period. The Romantics we saw in a certain perspective, but even the early Victorians spoke to us in our own language; they were mirrors of a culture still extant. It has been curious to note the changing angles from which a literary period is viewed as decades pass. Contemporary courses have their place, but experience, especially since the World War, has clinched my conviction that they should be kept at a minimum till some knowledge of their background is assured. There is, I know, something to be said on the other side, apart from the constant wish of youth to run away from its inheritance; the issue is hotly debated. I am not writing for the "Journal of Education," and I did enjoy teaching books of the hour. It was fun, for instance, to teach G. B. S. hot-and-hot from the griddle.

So far as pedagogical method went, I started with only one maxim, for even in that helpful class at Oxford, the tutor had done all the talking; a method fifty per cent easier than leading discussions, though I suppose I must not label it, as I am tempted to do, unless in advanced university work, the refuge of the lazy. My one maxim came from the father of my Clara, a well-known educator in his day: "Never ask a question which can be answered by Yes or No." I held to that rule like grim death, and it served me excellently. Had I held recitations the method might not always have worked; but my students never "recited," they "discussed." In these days of Institutes and summer schools, the technique of effective discussion, whether in Round Table or Panel, is much to the fore, and I smile as I recollect how many puzzles I anticipated, in the difficult and dubiously conclusive art of group thinking.

What should be the proportion of discussion to lecture in a class, say, of twenty-five students,—the normal size of one of our "sections" at Wellesley? About two to one, I decided, and stuck to that ratio fairly well; though when, as in the last class I taught, I confronted eighty-eight students, discussion went perforce by the board. . . . How far may young minds be allowed to run wild in their recreations? How preserve their sense of freedom to explore, while steering them toward a right conclusion? Shall a teacher cite authority when honest youth proclaims itself bored by "The Merchant of Venice"? How far shall one's own sympathies play a part in instruction? Suppress them, and you are dull; give them play, and you imperil the direct impact of the book on the student.

So down the years I experimented with unfailing zest in educational phases of ancient quarrels. And "'Now I will make avaunt,' said Sir Lancelot." I know I had the knack often of throwing a flashlight on what the student saw hazily and darkly. I used to come from a class concerned, say, with "The Ancient Mariner" or "The Ring and the Book" tremendously excited; and so were my students. The prelude to teaching was awful, however; I walked, between bells, through jostling crowds of girls, down the long corridors to my classroom, hands clenched till the nails scratched the palms; I feared to be overcome with nausea. (A noted preacher told me that he was similarly affected before each sermon.) This was not due to shyness; I have already said that I was never shy when teaching; it must have been due to sheer terror of fulfilling my task unworthily. . . . I had a special way of meeting my difficulties, and once in presence of the class, the air cleared. Anyone who does not find the process of teaching as alarming as it is exhilarating would better abandon the profession.

The greatest puzzle confronting the teacher is that of adaptation to varying types of minds, differing in temperament, and in maturity. Some girls have minds old enough to make one believe in reincarnation, others are infantile. The teacher who disregards these differences to indulge in direct self-expression seems to me lazy; yet I sometimes wonder if his is not after all the wiser way. All down the long years I tried to be merely the clear pane of glass through which the student could peer at landscapes new to him. Yet however one seeks to avoid the personal equation, it creeps in, and I suppose the high lights in my teaching fell on what I loved best. Shelley's "Prometheus Unbound," for instance; I edited it in 1892, and minute royalties assure me that the edition is still in use in an English university. Wordsworth's "Prelude" was always a central light. "Sartor Resartus" is potent with youth as ever, my successor tells me. Year by year I watched that book leading pilgrim spirits through the abysses of "The Everlasting No" and the arid lands of "The Centre of Indifference" to the fair if austere uplands of "The Everlasting Yea." Many other works became to me like my own voice speaking: Blake's winged lines, Newman's "Apologia." Here let me mention one more useful rule; never under whatever stress did I repeat a lecture, never did I fail to reread each year each book I taught. This habit cut me off more or less from the books of the hour. But I shuddered at the example of a German professor, early cited to me: "My lecture room, once crowded with students, is empty; yet these are the same lectures," mourned the dear old man. . . . The day came when, despite my perennial joy, dating back to my ninth year I think, in "The Pickwick Papers," I found myself unable to read the book over, one October more. When that happened, I gave up the course which included it.

As time went on, I taught a large variety of courses, and perhaps this is the best place in which to talk about them, even though I anticipate. The modern field was for some time assumed to be mine, but before long instincts and tastes drove me irresistibly backward. Soon, moreover, the work in the modern poets for which I had been brought to Wellesley, passed out of my hands into those of a woman who was herself what I was not, a poet of rare delicacy: Sophie Jewett. I confess that I mourned for that course; but there was compensation in a seminar, now on Shelley, now on Wordsworth or Browning, which I carried for many years. I enjoyed the scope offered by Victorian prose, with the opportunity for varying emphases. Also, I greatly enjoyed my colleagues. "The Department" of those days is tenderly remembered by many old Wellesley students as an unusual group. Sophie Jewett, Margaret Sherwood, and I were the nucleus, working under the genial, witty, and resolute leadership of Katharine Lee Bates. Scrupulously she left us free in handling our courses, even when, as must by and by be told, anguish and perplexity were involved for her; but in general department planning, her mind held firm control. When, rather late in the day, democratic rotation of department heads was introduced in the College, I for one found the shared responsibility somewhat of a nuisance; I fear I am a fascist, in the field of academic administration. The old group was sadly broken when Sophie Jewett died in 1909. But it was a happiness when students of our own training, after graduate work at Yale or elsewhere, joined our staff. . . . We elders are no longer teaching; but "The Department" survives, and the old tradition lasts; conscientious scholarship concerned with the quickening of life, rather than with the accumulation of knowledge.

Specialization was less rigid then than now. Scattered courses fell to my lot. Once or twice, an eighteenth-century course; nobody in the last century wanted to teach that period, for which candidates clamor today. Once at least, in 1892, I gave, *con amore*, a course on Spenser. Lectures on the Early Romantic Movement refreshed me; also a masterpiece course with no prerequisites, where we did exactly what we pleased. But I was assigned to a more serious task,—a Survey Course for advanced seniors. This went on for many years. It spanned the centuries from Beowulf to Kipling, one of many desperate attempts in the desperate experiment of education, to preserve continuity and proportion, while escaping hopeless shallowness. I used to say that we "rode a wallop" like Malory's knights, through English civilization; today I might use a better figure, and liken that course to an automobile trip, where one keeps exclaiming: "How interesting a country this might be, if one had time to look at it." I confess, however, to a weakness for generalizations and a "Kulturgeschichte" effect, and I ran that course with a firm hand, avoiding at least by careful text assignments the cheap device of letting students read about books instead of in them. As late as 1914, I wrote a textbook, "History of English Literature." I meant to adapt it to High Schools, but I fear I didn't, and it never took with the school public.

As time passed, I was caring more and more for intensive work; before the end of my forty years, I was teaching mainly small seminars. Yet I like both large classes and small, and have worked hard at their distinctive problems. Technical study was not neglected. Close analysis of style and structure summoned; concentrated attention in both verse and prose to undertones and overtones, the mysteries of individual cadence. I reveled in minutiae, even if I could not cope in this respect with the Chinese. There were always examinations in the offing; I am a firm believer in examinations. As a rule, in the undergraduate courses, we stuck to masterpieces, yet now and then came a bit of research, though "contact" was rather my key-word. Research, I am persuaded, should never be attempted till the great masterpieces have become part of the blood and bone; a principle which if adopted would deal a deathblow I fear to many a dissertation in America.

Despite my love of detail, my methods moved steadily toward that broad treatment which was, I suppose, the distinctive feature of my later teaching: such treatment as related a living book to the matrix in which it was formed, the organic social life of its period. I slipped away from desire to teach the nineteenth century. Friends are justified, I suspect, who tell me laughing that my real home is either in the Middle Ages or in the Utopian future; I know that in both the nineteenth and the twentieth century, I have often felt homesick enough. There were two courses in which any special aptitudes I may have as an interpreter found free play; in both I was something of a pioneer, so I shall talk about them a little.

Very pleased I was to be permitted, in 1904–5, to offer work in Arthurian romance, centered in Sir Thomas Malory's "Morte d'Arthur." Such a course is common now but I think it was seldom given anywhere at that time. I was no scholar in the wide and developing Arthurian field. But I did think in all modesty that with Malory as a center I could open to young students exceptional understanding of the Middle Ages, and I did not despair of preparing the way for scholars. Nor was my hope disappointed. In surveying my long academic years, few things gratify me more than that Laura Hibbard (Mrs. Roger Loomis), fine medieval scholar that she is, received her first impulse to Arthurian studies in my classroom. She is my successor in teaching the subject at Wellesley, with equipment such as I never had and a status such as I could never hope for, and the course is now on a permanent foundation.

Arthurian romance spans the Middle Ages, from the twelfth century to the fifteenth, even if one does not go back with Laura Loomis's husband and scholar-comrade, into the dark backward and abysm of Celtic myth. When first I offered my course, I was living my mental life, as shall be told, chiefly in the fourteenth century, with hankerings after the thirteenth; Malory led me back to the twelfth through his sources, and onward to the edge of the Renaissance through his tone and quality. While I can not claim competence in knowledge of any century, I do feel a certain power to enter into unison with the rhythm of the great formative forces in varied periods of European culture; and this course, for which I read exhaustively, gave me greater gifts than it did my students. It is my contention that Malory, compiler though he were, was also a creative artist, with a genius for synthesis enabling him to present with extraordinary dramatic passion and power the loyalties that made the Middle Ages by their intensity and wrecked it by their conflict. All my insight and initiative went into my study of him; and I finally published in 1912, "An Interpretation of Sir Thomas Malory," summarizing my course. It has gratified me to learn of more than one American college where that book is valued. Teachers especially have found it helpful.

The other course I founded faced toward the future, as the Arthurian course toward the past. It bore the title: "Social Ideals in English Letters." I first offered it in spite of administrative disapproval and departmental indifference, in the later Nineties, as a one-hour lecture course. Though mentioned in the College Calendar, it was not at first even included in the department list; yet in the second year, '97–'98, it attracted over fifty students, a large number for those days. Then came a long absence, of which I must presently write; but on return to Wellesley I revived that course, albeit with scant encouragement. For years I alternated it with "Arthurian Romance," offering it first for sophomores, then for seniors, and finally as a seminar open only to advanced students. I was never allowed, perhaps for good reason, to include it in our carefully organized majors; but in spite of handicaps it was often largely elected, and more alumnae thank me for it than for any other course I ever taught; they tell me that its worth to them grows with the years.

I judge that course to be the most original and significant contribution that I had to make to the teaching of English Literature. It was the permanent link between my social concern and my love of letters; I think most people left my classroom both more alive to the future and more sensitively conscious of the past than they went in. I said that the course faced the future; but we often began with "Piers Plowman." I am a queer sort of radical, for I am sure that intelligence about the future demands perspective.

> "Past and Future are the wings
> On whose support, harmoniously conjoined,
> Moves the great Spirit of human Knowledge."

The Soviet government in its early phases apparently did not agree with Wordsworth and me; it showed a tendency to throw the human past casually on the scrap heap. A similar attitude is familiar among American youth. Lately a Ph.D. candidate was referred to me, to talk over her plans. She wished to direct her "research" to the social aspects of English letters. Splendid, said I, here was a field with rich waiting harvests; and where would she like to reap? She had thought, was the answer, to study the proletarian novel from 1930 on. I persuaded her to push back her date a little. O Research, what crimes are committed in thy name!

We of course could only skim over the field, with a sort of aeroplane effect. We began with Langland. Social criticism, social delineation, social prophecy,—all were grist to our mill; and English literature is rich in all three. It is, to be sure, more concerned in some periods than in others with phenomena of mass consciousness; we passed, for instance, with surprising swiftness over the High Renaissance, with its intensified individualism. But phenomena of the collective life determined by economic conditons are always implicit as a shaping force, they are the background even when the foreground is occupied by private reactions. One need be no Marxist to recognize this, though as Marx helps us increasingly in our understanding of life and its movements, I hope and expect that such courses as I feebly sought to initiate are likely to multiply. We began, as I said, with Langland; but we went on, gaily and quickly, to Sir Thomas More. (That great and true saint was not yet canonized; had he been, I should have been tempted to point out the humor of the exaltation of a communist to the altars of the Church which most solemnly and officially defends the institution of private property.) . . . We continued, through the Renaissance to the sad check on all interest in the future, and the consequent superb vogue of social satire in the age of Swift (one of the most stimulating authors to teach), on to the revival of the prophetic note in Blake, to the great Romantic and revolutionary break-up of static conceptions, and so to the effort of the great Victorians, discarding illusion, to see life steadily and see it whole. Finally, against the background of triumphant industrialization and mechanization of life, we reached the quickening of restlessness and Utopian speculation at the end of last century, and the students were at long last, as the course drew to an end, encouraged to cultivate a bit of Utopian speculation for themselves. I have always believed with Blake that the imagination is the greatest creative force; but one must associate long with "the daughters of memory," before one is worthy or able to receive the message of "the daughters of inspiration."

It is my contention that a course of this nature has a legitimate place in a department of English literature. I have taught courses of many types: those focused in a period; those dealing with a literary form—drama, essay, lyric, novel; biographical courses, masterpiece courses, courses treating of a single author; not to speak of sundry cross-varieties. In addition to these diverse approaches, I plead for approach from a point of view. Nature in the English Poets; Side Lights from Letters on English History (I just made that up; I should dearly like to teach it); Religious Aspects of English Literature (I have given such a course, but not at Wellesley). Or, Social Ideals. Such would often be liaison courses, perhaps independent, perhaps under interdepartmental control; links between literature, and history, philosophy, or as in my case, sociology and economics. I am wondering if the recently instituted "Roving Professorships" at Harvard may not perhaps be planned to meet the need I have in mind.

I was asked once to give my course in the department of sociology, but I declined, for the substance of it was literature in the strictest sense. We used much outlying illustrative material, from both history and economics, and I accepted students qualified by work on either of these lines; but all the prescribed texts came under my definition of literature. Incidentally, the variety of provenience of the students proved unique and refreshing, in its influence on class discussions. I consider the scarcity of such courses regrettable, if we desire to overcome the inveterate student impulse to lock their knowledge away in watertight cupboards, and if we seek on the contrary to impart to them some slight sense of life as a living and developing whole. Literature—and I would add, art of all kinds, sculpture, painting, architecture, calligraphy, is the expression of such racial culture as has proved worthy to survive; that is why it is our best help toward discerning the realities under the shams in civilization.

In teaching such a course, one has to be peculiarly on one's guard against a personal slant of opinion. I was skating on the thinnest ice on which my pedagogic feet ever ventured. But I know that the ice never broke. I instinctively recoiled from propaganda in the classroom; I could never approve of a dear radical colleague, who used to drag the Communist Manifesto into her lectures on astronomy, nor of a professor in a neighboring college who introduced a questionnaire on Sex into his course on medieval history. My own view of social trends inevitably affected my organization of the work; but selected books spoke for themselves, and I taught the conservatives with special gusto. Burke, for instance, is amazingly valuable pedagogic "material." (May he pardon me the word, in Elysium!) I got into trouble, as I shall presently have to narrate; but my conscience is clear.

The course was certainly a success, as far as the students went; and my book based on it, "Social Ideals in English Letters," published in 1898, sold for years better than almost any of my books. It is matter of mortification and regret to me that since my retirement, the course has been dropped at Wellesley. They say nobody else can do it; but that is nonsense.

21

From *The Making of a Feminist:*
Early Journals and Letters of
M. Carey Thomas (1871–83)
M. Carey Thomas

Martha Carey Thomas (1857–1935) is best known for her distinguished tenure at the head of Bryn Mawr College: the school's first dean in 1884, she was its president from 1894 to 1922. She was also one of the first women ever to take a Ph.D., which she received in philology after studying at several German universities. Her father, a Quaker physician in Baltimore, sat on the boards of Johns Hopkins University and Haverford College. Educational figures such as Cornell University President Andrew D. White were among the family friends, and it was at White's encouragement that Thomas attended Cornell as an undergraduate. Even with these important connections, however, Thomas encountered stiff resistance when she began seeking a professional career. After graduation from Cornell, she began to study classical philology at Hopkins as its first woman graduate student, but left in anger and frustration after a year. At Hopkins, she had been allowed tutoring, but had not been permitted to attend seminars. A story—possibly apocryphal—has it that she was admitted to seminars on condition she sit behind a screen. In later life, Thomas took part in the suffrage movement, and endowed a women's center at Hopkins that is still active.

We excerpt her diary and letters covering the years 1871–83, partly for their exceptionally vivid picture of student experience in the early days of professionalization. More importantly, however, the selection is eloquent testimony to the virtually complete male domination of the early profession. Thomas's own response to this masculinism was to outdo the professionals on their own turf in a vocabulary of disinterested science. Yet some letters (e.g., June 26, 1880) express her sense that the scientific discourse of philology was limited precisely by its inability to articulate her membership in an "enslaved race." Interestingly, she associates the hope of such articulation with literature.

1871

February 26, 1871

An English man Joseph Beck was here to dinner the other day and he don't believe in the Education of Women. Neither does Cousin Frank King and my such a disgusson as they had. Mother of course was for. They said that they didn't see any good of a womans learning Latin or Greek it didn't make them any more entertaining to their *husbands*. A woman had plenty of other things to do sewing, cooking taking care of children dressing and flirting. "What noble elevating things for a whole life time to be occupied with." In fact they talked as if the whole end and aim of a woman's life was to get *married* and when she attained that *greatest state of earthly bliss* it was her duty to amuse her husband and to learn nothing; never to exercise the powers of her mind so that he might have the *exquisite* pleasure of knowing more than his wife. Of course they talked the usual cant of woman being too *high* too *exalted* to do anything but sit up in perfect ignorance with folded hands and let men worship at her shrine, meaning in other words like all the rest of such high faluting stuff that woman ought to be *mere dolls* for men to be amused with, to kiss, fondle, pet and love maybe, but as for associating with them on terms of equality they wouldn't think of such a thing. Now I don't mean to say these two men believed this but these were the principles they upheld. I got perfectly enraged. How *unjust*—how narrow-minded—how *utterly uncomprehensible* to deny that women ought to be educated and worse than all to deny that they have equal powers of mind. If I ever live to grow up my *one* aim and consentrated purpose *shall* be and is to show that a woman *can learn can reason can compete* with men in the grand fields of literature and science and conjecture that opens before the 19 century; that a woman can be a woman and a *true* one, with out having all her time engrossed by dress and society—that the woman who has fought all the battles of olden time over again whilest reading the spirited pages of Homer, Vergil, Heroditus, who has sympathised in the longings after something beyond mere daily exhistance found in the works of Socrates, Plato and Eschelus, who has reasoned out all the great laws which govern the universce with Newton, Cirago, Galleleo, who has mourned with Dante, reasoned and speculated with Shiller, Goethe and Jean Paul, been carried away by Carlyle and "mildly enchanted by Emerson" who has idealised with Milton and emerged with strengthened intellect from the intricate labyrinth of Geometry, Trigonometry and Calculous is not any less like what God really intended a woman to be than the trifling ballroom butterfly the ignorant doll baby which *they* admire. . . .

1875

[Journal]

July 16, 1875

Well, it is *done*: on the 13, 14, 15 of last June I passed the entrance examinations at Cornell University for the Admission into the Classical Course. This last summer it seemed impossible. But the whole of this year with a steady, unalterable determination that surprised myself even—I have been working for it. Father was terribly opposed and last Christmas when Miss Slocum was at our house, said he never while he lived would give his consent. Many and dreadful are the talks we have had upon this subject, but Mother, my own splendid mother, helped me in this as she always has in everything and sympathized with me. Again and again last winter did the old difficulty of deciding between "duty to ourselves and others" come up—for it was not a religious duty of course to go to Cornell and sometimes it seemed as it ought to be given up. I know all the Grove people thought so—but I *could* not. Then too the difficulty of preparing without knowing how they examined and of getting teachers, but, above all, Father's feeling so about it. For I love him dearly and cannot bear to disappoint him. How it was done I do not know but if it had not been for Mother I am sure he would not have consented. But about three weeks before, he gave up and I began to prepare for the examinations.

I never did such terrible studying every moment for those three weeks. . . . However, it is over with—Professor Peck said I passed a splendid examination in Latin, ditto Professor Oliver in Algebra and Geometry. . . . Almost all the professors complimented Father and Mother upon my passing so well. Mr. Howland when he saw me said he was proud that a *Howland* graduate, etc., etc. The strain was terrible because I could not have endured failure. And it was an inexpressible satisfaction to pass well. Father and Mother were up there and explored the university while I was getting examined. Mother was delighted with it and I think Father was pleased. The last night he said to me, "Well Minnie, I'm proud of thee, but this university is an awful place to swallow thee up."

If I can help it he and Mother shall never regret having yielded to me in this thing. . . .

1877

[Journal]

September 23, 1877

Yesterday I made application to the Johns Hopkins Univerity to study for a second degree. Mr. Gilman was very polite and it will come before the

Trustees in a month and I (oh I hope there is some chance for ladies!) am in great anxiety. . . .

I am glad I went [to Cornell], I learned far more than was possible at home. I broke away from old rules and mingled with different classes of people; but there was no real earnest intellectual companionship, not much earnest heartfelt study. When so much could be offered so little was given. I suppose I expected too much; the other girls seemed satisfied. . . .

There is much that is very hard for a *lady* in a mixed university and I should not subject any girl to it unless she were determined to have it. The educational problem is a terrible one—girls' colleges are inferior and it seems impossible to get the most illustrious men to fill their chairs, and on the other hand it is a fiery ordeal to educate a lady by coeducation—it is impossible to make one, who has not felt it, understand the living on a volcano or on a house top . . . yet it is the only way and learning *is worth it.* This summer at Anna's when I heard Mr. Cadbury and Mr. Gummere* talk of Harvard it filled me with envy and yet Mr. Gummere himself told me that he found no earnest companionship there. I do wonder if Mr. Gummere will accomplish anything—the majority of people I feel sure will not but I do think that there is a chance for him. We had one very nice talk this summer—a continuation of one two years ago and he is full of enthusiasm for all my favorite things—poetry, literature, my literature books are his favorites and altogether we are very congenial on literary and other logical subjects. I hope he will persevere and go to Germany and I wish I were a man for that; because *Germany* is shut to ladies along with the J.H.U. and a few other of the very most glorious things in the world; yet I would not be a man. . . .

[Letter to Anna Shipley]

October 31, 1877

. . . The Executive Committee of the J.H.U. passed a vote last week—the motion proposed by the very gentleman who opposes women most fiercely, "to admit Miss Thomas to study for a second degree." The Board [will] act upon it next week but of course it is virtually decided. Oh, Anna, I am so delighted and yet it makes me a little sober too when I think what it means. I had a long talk with Gildersleeve,* the Greek Professor in his *sanctum sanctorum* and he said that they meant that a degree of the Johns Hopkins University should count with the German ones, that he had two students who had graduated at

---

* Francis B. Gummere (1855–1919), eminent teacher and Anglo-Saxon scholar, briefly a suitor of M. Carey Thomas, became an instructor at Harvard and later Haverford. [ed.]

* Basil L. Gildersleeve (1831–1924), eminent professor of classical philology at Johns Hopkins, founder of the *American Journal of Philology*. [ed.]

college, studied three years, one of them in Germany, and who will have been two years under him when they try to take their second degree next summer; so, he said, from that I might see the amount of work he expected; he said I *might* be able to take it in three years. . . . Well, thee sees a little what a terrible undertaking it is; especially the German. I feel a mild curiosity as to how I shall succeed in *mastering* the German language by Christmas. So the die is cast; if I enter upon this I give up medicine forever and become a scholar. . . .

[Journal]

November [?], 1877
   They admitted me to the J.H.U. and I am now studying three mornings in the week from 9 to 3 with Bessie. . . . I am very much discouraged now that I have entered upon a three years' course of work, I feel the recoil and I feel how absolutely impossible is my knowledge of Greek and it does seem hopeless and then after all—there seems to be something degrading in the minute study classical notes require. What difference can it make if a second *a* is used once or twice in a certain writer? I cannot bend my mind to it and yet I *must*. I must now be a good scholar or nothing. . . .

1878
[Journal]

May 8, 1878
   Another distracting letter from Miss Ladd. Mr. Gilman's contemptible, mean treatment. He told her he could not say whether she would receive, after her examinations [at Johns Hopkins] a degree or a certificate. Wretch, he *knows* the motion stands "Resolved that Miss Thomas be received as a candidate for a second degree" and of course her case is the same. . . .
   I think I am now determined to get the degree in spite of them. It will always be useful to me, Ph.D. is not to be despised, if I write, and especially if I teach, or if I take any distinguished educational position. . . . I will take the degree in their teeth if I only have FAIR PLAY. . . .

[Letter to the Board of Trustees of the Johns Hopkins University]

October 7, 1878
Gentlemen,
   A year ago by your kindness I was admitted into the Johns Hopkins University as a candidate for a second degree. I naturally supposed that this would permit me to share in the unusual opportunities afforded to post graduate students under the able instruction of Professor Gildersleeve.

But the condition "without class attendance" has been understood to exclude my attendance upon the Greek Seminarium and the advanced instruction which is given to the other students of the University. I have thus found myself dependent upon such assistance as Professor Gildersleeve could give at the expense of his own time, which, notwithstanding his great personal kindness, I hesitated to encroach upon.

My object in entering the University was not so much to obtain a degree as to profit by the inestimable assistance Professor Gildersleeve gives to his pupils.

A trial of a year during which I received no help other than advice in reference to my course of reading and the privilege of passing an examination, has convinced me that under the present regulations, the assistance referred to cannot be obtained.

I make this explanation to you in order that my withdrawal may not be prejudicial to any other applicant, and because, so far as I have been informed, the only official recognition of my relation to the University exists upon your Minutes.

Respectfully,

M.C. Thomas

[Letter to her Father]

Leipzig, November 10, 1879

. . . Our lectures are proceeding regularly—Curtius is minutely analyzing the Alexandrian Grammarian, Braune, tracing the Anglo Saxons, Goths, Vandals and Scandanavians in their wanderings over Europe. Zärncke is in the fableland of the Nibelungleid, Wülcker,* stupid Wülcker whom we cut today, is over the Anglo Saxon homilies and Hermann—the philosopher—little son of a great father (the great Grecia-Godfried Hermann) is tearing Bunsen and Hegel into little shreds. . . . I can hardly understand a word as he speaks all in a breath without comma or period and then suddenly gasps, ducks his head down and wipes his forehead with a red bandana handkerchief. Miss Channing said to me today, "I would have given everything to be invited by Curtius." . . . * Really there is so much liberality here. Prof. Ebers said he thought women should have degrees given them. Mrs. Ebers said two years ago a woman studied here in man's dress and associating freely with the students and professors escaped detection. Just as she was coming up for her degree she declared herself, feeling in honor bound. She was married and studied to be able to support herself and her husband. . . .

---

* Richard Wülcker (1845–1910), professor of English at Leipzig and founder of the journal *Anglia*. [ed.]

* Ernst Curtius (1814–1896), archaeologist and historian who directed the excavation of Olympia, the first large-scale excavation of Greece. [ed.]

Curtius said he gets the most ridiculous letters from America—one for example from a woman, "Honored Prof. Curtius, should I come to Leipzig, *what have you to offer me?*" and another from a grocery store clerk who had become entranced with Caesar and asked if Curtius would advise him to take up classical studies. Curtius wrote advising him to continue weighing out sugar. . . .

1880

[Letter to her Mother]

Leipzig, February 7, 1880
  . . . I wish I knew what it would be best to take as my second subject. I shall make English literature my chief—the one on which I want to try to do independent work, but I suppose for example I wished ever to try for a chair in Taylor College? I shall certainly be better qualified than any other woman in the Society* and it may sound conceited, but I have not the slightest fear of my being able to teach girls of that age. I know I have a personal influence that will enable me to inspire them to care about what I do. This is after all the secret of successful teaching. I am sure I have this power and these lectures in Germany have given me the method.

  I have been thinking very seriously especially since thy letter about the money you owe. Study, as thee knows, and influence are the two things I care about—these I can best obtain by being a professor in some women's college. Yet if I only knew definitely it would, of course influence my method of study and enable me to be a much better professor. The only two I should be at all willing to teach in would be Smith or Taylor. Of course in Taylor College I should be less separated from you and there is more hope in working out one's thoughts in a new institution. Then I do care for raising the tone and education of women and it presents a field. If I did not wish a chair in Taylor College I should undoubtedly take English literature and I am sure with my studies here and perhaps in England, I could get a professorship in Vassar, Smith or perhaps Cornell ultimately. Look at Miss Nunn without even a degree. Now of course Frank Gummere having received the appointment in English literature I must take some other subject unless I wish to cut myself off from Taylor forever.

  What I should prefer would be the department of general literature—working of the national literatures upon each other and the mixture of cultures—the way old Greek myths, through the Latin, were reflected in the French, German, Italian, English and Spanish literatures—the influence of form of

* The Society of Friends. Taylor College was the then preliminary name for Bryn Mawr. [ed.]

literature. I have a very fair start for this study. Frank Gummere of course treats English literature from its Germanic side. He knows no French, Italian nor Spanish and only a college graduate's Greek. I can read Greek and Latin easily, Gothic, High German, Middle High German, and of course modern German, French and soon shall Italian. Then I should study Spanish and Provençal and New Greek and be equipped. Thee sees what a field this opens for the most wide study and investigation. I might specialize this by in addition to general lectures, giving special interpretations of Italian and Provençal. I am sure I could do good work in this and work that I hope would eventually win me a reputation. . . .

[Letter to Richard Cadbury]

Leipzig, June 26, 1880

. . . Do you know civilization is gradually dispensing with man in his masculine prerogative of protector? The lady Miss Gwinn and I were to travel with received a telegram and we have travelled alone everywhere—not the slightest difficulty. There is an underground railway system of pensions extending from city to city. They are the paradise of old maids and thither we betake ourselves. One can study human nature in them—also numbers of solitary men drift into them, though why I can't imagine. . . .

Your letter put me into a bad humor—as perhaps you see. You know of course that the only thing I really care to do is what you are doing—try. But I dare not throw away the chance of knowledge—of images, and new furniture for my imagination which I can get here now and never afterward. It is a delight to dip more and more into literature and see the *Weltgeist* rising before one—but—tragic perplexity—I have to push him back into his bottle and cork him up, nay throw him into the sea for the next three years. A degree and a German lecturer and the German student are—so much philology, so much grammar, so much dictionary and oh so little spirit—the latter is of course all I care for; but how can one individual change the preordained order? You don't belong to an enslaved race—I am hampered by a desire if I fail in the highest, to at least try and prevent other girls from having even the struggle I have had. If I were a man I suppose I would try for it and in case of failure smoke away the rest of my life in "domesticity." Though even from a man's standpoint that seems hard to imagine—one doesn't know how late in Venice or on the Roman hills the god might descend and touch one's lips. . . .

[Letter to her Mother]

Leipzig, June 27, 1880

. . . I went to see Prof. Wülcker yesterday. . . . He said it depended entirely upon the examiner whether one required philology or a wide literary knowledge.

He then talked about degree subjects and showed me three that had just been accepted: One "The Life of Massinger," only Wülcker said that if one took a modern English subject like that, unless you proved your Anglo Saxon knowledge in examination, "a misfortune might happen" (the German expression for "flunk," "fluck"). . . .

1881

[Letter to her Mother]

Leipzig, July 6, 1881
. . . We stated our business, told him that we had studied in Leipzig for the past year and expected to study there two more years, told [Müller*] what we had read and asked him if we were on the right track. He said yes, but told us that in Göttingen the dissertation was the chief thing, that it was required to be something absolutely new and no literary subject or remarks were desired, that often he sent back theses that would have been accepted elsewhere. I said Wülcker had suggested tracing back the *qnellen*, the sources, of Beaumont and Fletcher's plays into Shakespeare and Ben Jonson. This he repudiated. I then mentioned a subject I had asked Wülcker about and which he had approved of: separating the two parts of Caedmon in regard to their word and rhyme-rise and following the subject matter—the creation—back into Greek, Latin, French, etc. and down into Milton. Both Ebert and Wülcker said this would be capital, and it was something I should have cared to do. But Müller would have none of it. On the entreaties of his wife he suggested two subjects (a thing he said he never did for his own students, but "as by being women we were to miss the incalculable privilege of hearing him"—he consented). . . .
. . . I was utterly disgusted with those Göttingen profs. I agree with thee—I want a literary training and yet I do think a degree most needful and it seems fully possible to take it. I am sure I can—it is only the waste of time in studying rather off my principal interest. It is a comfort to know definitely and I feel better. . . .

[Letter to her Uncle]

June 1, 1882
. . . when I went to Göttingen . . . each of the forty-two profs had to be asked his opinion upon the woman question and if two or three disagreed my fate would be decided in the negative. The head of the Philology interested himself very much for me, wrote my petition himself, made me send him my degree, a sample of my thesis, all my Leipzig certificates and did his best to put it

* Müller: Professor of English at Göttingen. [ed.]

through. He failed, but wrote me the nicest letter saying that he hoped my successful scholarly work would meet with the deserved recognition at some other university, etc. You will understand what a disappointment this was because I should have preferred a Göttingen degree. . . .

I suppose Mother told thee that Engl. Philology had led me into German and now I find that the Old French will be a great advantage. The three are so connected. What they call "the new philologie" and the "young Grammarian" movement seems to be carrying all before it. It certainly simplifies everything; it is like evolution in science but Mamie begins to put her fingers in her ears when I start to ride this hobby of mine. Nevertheless it is worth riding. I have been very much struck by the very thing thee mentioned in thy letter—the great difference between knowing a subject and being able to impart one's knowledge. Among all the lecturers we heard at Leipzig only two had the latter gift. Indeed I have ceased to think that scholarship as such is one of the world's best things because almost every prof. we heard *knew* everything in his own special line, had edited texts, written original studies upon important and unimportant subjects, and yet so many lacked "literary sense" and unbiased thinking and real *ability*. Realizing this, as I did during the last year, was a shock. . . .

1882

[Letter to her Mother]

Zürich, November 25, 1882
. . . in a week I was well enough to go up for my written examination of six hours on *German Philology.* That also was accomplished most satisfactorily. This was a week ago and then I began to get very much excited. I knew from the manner of the professors that they thought I ran the chance of taking a good degree—they begged me to be calm in the oral examination and told me that so many students became unnecessarily confused from mere terror. As thee may think, this made me more frightened than ever. . . . The oral examination consists of a three hours examination before the philosophical faculty of the University and after the candidate has left the room a vote is taken which must be unanimous and the result is communicated by the Dekan. This semester two men have failed. . . .

As soon as I got into the room I felt perfectly calm and was able to answer with perfect distinctness. I made almost no mistake and knew everything they asked. All the laws of the development of Gothic out of Indo Germanic were never clearer to me than at the moment of the examination. The clock struck 6 (I had entered at 3) and the Dekan asked me to retire. I did so and found the *pedell* [proctor] and his wife waiting outside to console me during the time of the deliberation of the faculty. They said they were sure I would get a "cum laude." I felt as if I might possibly get a "magna cum laude." You can imagine what those five minutes of waiting were. I never never felt such a sensation of choking anxiety. The message came to enter. I did so and stood at the foot of the table—the Dekan rose and said he had the pleasure of welcoming me as a Dr. of Philosophy of the University and of informing me that the faculty had bestowed upon me the highest honor in its power to give—"SUMMA cum laude." He then handed me my documents and shook hands.

Mother, is it not too splendid to be true? I never dreamed of taking the highest possible degree—a degree which no woman has ever taken in Philol. before and which is hardly ever given. Often twenty-five or forty years will go by without its being given because they are so very strict here at Zürich. I can hardly believe it now. The *pedell* and his wife could not comprehend it—they said it was unheard of. But still it is true. . . .

Dr. Culbertson was almost as pleased as I was—if that were possible. You know that taking a degree here is very different from a degree at our colleges where whole classes go up. Here no one takes a degee except the few picked men who intend to be professors either in the Univ. or in the higher gymnasia. A number of women have taken medical degrees but I believe only one has ever taken a "Dr. of Phil." Now think what it is to get the highest degree among these few. There, I have crowed out all my delight and will try to write like a reasonable being. One more conceited remark I must make—that is, it is very unusual for a student to take a degree under five years or at the least four, and thee sees I have only studied three, beginning from the very beginning too, as my Classical studies were of no assistance in the New Philology. . . .

22

From *Up Stream: An American Chronicle* (1922)

Ludwig Lewisohn

Ludwig Lewisohn (1882–1955) was born in Berlin and emigrated with his family
to the United States in 1890. He was educated at the College of Charleston,
South Carolina (B.A., M.A. 1901) and Columbia University (M.A. 1903).
Lewisohn left Columbia after he was turned down for a fellowship to the Ph.D.
program, convinced he had been rejected because he was a Jew. A pacifist during
World War I and later a Zionist, Lewisohn taught German at the University of
Wisconsin (1910–11) and Ohio State University (1911–20). He left teaching to
become drama editor of *The Nation* and in 1932 published *Expression in America*, a
manifesto expressing the Freudian cultural radicalism of many of his generation.
He was appointed professor of Comparative Literature at Brandeis University in
1948.

    The present selection, from Lewisohn's intellectual autobiography, *Up Stream*
(1922), deals with his rejection for the Columbia fellowship and the generally
anti-Semitic atmosphere of American colleges and universities at the time.

. . . The faculty elected my friend G. I went, with a heavy heart, to
interview Professor Brewer,* not to push my claims to anything, but because I
was at my wits' end. I dreaded another year of tutoring and of living
wretchedly from hand to mouth, without proper clothes, without books.
Brewer leaned back in his chair, pipe in hand, with a cool and kindly smile.
"It seemed to us," he stuttered, "that the university hadn't had its full influence
on you." He suggested their disappointment in me and, by the subtlest of
stresses, their sorrow over this disappointment. I said that I had been struggling
for a livelihood and that, nevertheless, my examinations had uniformly
received high grades and my papers, quite as uniformly, the public approval of
Brent and himself. He avoided a direct answer by explaining that the
department had recommended me for a scholarship for the following year. The

---

* Lewisohn evidently changed the names here. [ed.]

truth is, I think, that Brewer, excessively mediocre as he was, had a very keen tribal instinct of the self-protective sort and felt in me—what I was hardly yet consciously—the implacable foe of the New England dominance over our national life. I wasn't unaware of his hostility, but I had no way of provoking a franker explanation.

I forgot my troubles in three beautiful months at home—three months seemed so long then—or, rather, I crowded these troubles from my field of consciousness. I wouldn't even permit the fact that I wasn't elected ,to a scholarship to depress me. Brewer wrote a letter of regret and encouragement that was very kindly in tone. The pleasant implication of that letter was, of course, a spiritual falsehood of the crassest. He knew then precisely what he knew and finally told me ten months later. But his kind has a dread of the bleak weather of the world of truth, and approaches it gingerly, gradually, with a mincing gait. He, poor man, was probably unconscious of all that. In him, as in all like him, the corruption of the mental life is such that the boundaries between the true and the false are wholly obliterated.

In the passionate crises of the second year I often walked as in a dream. And I was encouraged by the fact that the department arranged a loan for my tuition. In truth, I was deeply touched by so unusual a kindness and I feel sure that the suggestion came from Brent. If so, Brewer again did me a fatal injury by not preventing that kindness. For he had then, I must emphasize, the knowledge he communicated to me later—the knowledge that held the grim upshot of my university career.

Spring came and with it the scramble for jobs among the second year men. My friends were called in to conferences with Brewer; I was not. They discussed vacancies, chances here and there. It wasn't the chagrin that hurt so; it wasn't any fear for myself. After all I was only twenty-two and I was careless of material things. I thought of my father and my mother in the cruel sunshine of Queenshaven. Their hope and dream and consolation were at stake. I could see them, not only by day, but in the evening, beside their solitary lamps, looking up from their quiet books, thinking of me and of the future. . . . I remembered how my father had believed in certain implications of American democracy. I remembered . . . I was but a lad, after all. I couldn't face Brewer's cool and careless smile. I wrote him a letter—a letter which, in its very earnestness and passionate veracity must have struck like a discord upon the careful arrangements of his safe and proper nature. For in it I spoke of grave things gravely, not jestingly, as one should to be a New England gentleman: I spoke of need and aspiration and justice. His answer lies before me now and I copy that astonishingly smooth and chilly document verbatim: "It is very sensible of you to look so carefully into your plans at this juncture, because I do not at all believe in the wisdom of your scheme. A recent experience has shown me how terribly hard it is for a man of Jewish birth to get a good position. I had always suspected that it was a matter worth considering, but I had not known how wide-spread and strong it was. While we shall be glad to do anything we can for you, therefore, I cannot help feeling that the chances are going to be greatly against you."

I sat in my boarding-house room playing with this letter. I seemed to have no feeling at all for the moment. By the light of a sunbeam that fell in I saw that the picture of my parents on the mantelpiece was very dusty. I got up and wiped the dust off carefully. Gradually an eerie, lost feeling came over me. I took my hat and walked out and up Amsterdam Avenue, farther and farther to High Bridge and stood on the bridge and watched the swift, tiny tandems on the Speedway below and the skiffs gliding up and down the Harlem River. A numbness held my soul and mutely I watched life, like a dream pageant, float by me. . . . I ate nothing till evening when I went into a bakery and, catching sight of myself in a mirror, noted with dull objectivity my dark hair, my melancholy eyes, my unmistakably Semitic nose. . . . An outcast. . . . A sentence arose in my mind which I have remembered and used ever since. So long as there is discrimination, there is exile. And for the first time in my life my heart turned with grief and remorse to the thought of my brethren in exile all over the world. . . .

The subconscious self has a tough instinct of self-preservation. It thrusts from the field of vision, as Freud has shown, the painful and the hostile things of life. Thus I had forgotten, except at moments of searching reflection, the social fate of my father and mother, my failure to be elected to the fraternity at college, and other subtler hints and warnings. I had believed the assertion and made it myself that equality of opportunity was implicit in the very spiritual foundations of the Republic. This is what I wanted to believe, what I needed to believe in order to go about the business of my life at all. I had listened with a correct American scorn to stories of how some distant kinsman in Germany, many years ago, had had to receive Christian baptism in order to enter the consular service of his country. At one blow now all these delusions were swept away and the facts stood out in the sharp light of my dismay. Discrimination there was everywhere. But a definite and public discrimination is, at least, an enemy in the open. In pre-war Germany for instance, no Jew could be prevented from entering the academic profession. Unless he was very brilliant and productive his promotion was less rapid than that of his Gentile colleagues. He knew that and reckoned with it. He knew, too, for instance, that he could not become senior professor of German at Berlin (only associate professor like the late R. M. Meyer), nor Kulturminister, but he could become a full professor of Latin or philosophy, and, of course, of all the sciences. I am not defending these restrictions and I think the argument for them—that the German state was based upon an ethnic homogeneity which corresponds to a spiritual oneness—quite specious. I am contrasting these conditions with our own. We boast our equality and freedom and call it Americanism and speak of other countries with disdain. And so one is unwarned, encouraged and flung into the street. With exquisite courtesy, I admit. And the consciousness of that personal courtesy soothes the minds of our Gentile friends. . . . It will be replied that there are a number of Jewish scholars in American colleges and universities. There are. The older men got in because nativistic anti-Semitism was not nearly as strong twenty-five years ago as it is to-day. Faint remnants of the ideals of the early Republic still lingered in American life. But in regard to the younger men I dare to assert that in each case they were appointed through personal friendship, family or financial prestige or some other abnormal relenting of the iron prejudice which is the rule. But that prejudice has not, to my knowledge, relented in a single instance in regard to the teaching of English. So that our guardianship of the native tongue is far fiercer than it is in an, after all, racially homogeneous state like Germany. Presidents, deans and departmental heads deny this fact or gloss it over in public. Among themselves it is admitted as a matter of course.

I have not touched the deeper and finer issues, though I have written in vain if they are not clear. My purest energy and passion, my best human aspiration had been dedicated from my earliest years to a given end. It was far more than a question of bread and butter, though it was that too. I didn't know how to go on living a reasonable and reasonably harmonious inner life. I could take no refuge in the spirit and traditions of my own people. I knew little of them. My psychical life was Aryan through and through. Slowly, in the course of years. I have discovered traits in me which I sometimes call Jewish. But that interpretation is open to grave doubt. I can, in reality, find no difference between my own inner life of thought and impulse and that of my very close friends whether American or German. So that the picture of a young man disappointed because he can't get the kind of a job he wants, doesn't exhaust, barely indeed touches the dilemma. I didn't know what to do with my life or with myself.

In this matter of freedom and equality and democratic justice, then, I found in my Anglo-American world precisely that same strange dualism of conscience which I had discovered there in the life of sex. The Brewers in the academic world do truly believe that our society is free and democratic. When they proclaim that belief at public banquets a genuine emotion fills their hearts. Just as a genuine emotion filled the hearts of my Southern friends (who used Mulatto harlots) when in the interest of purity and the home they refused to sanction the enactment of any divorce law in their native state.

I do not wish to speak bitterly or flippantly. I am approaching the analysis of thoughts and events beside which my personal fate is less than nothing. And I need but think of my Queenshaven youth or of some passage of Milton or Arnold, or of those tried friendships that are so large a part of the unalterable good of life, or of the bright hair and gray English eyes of my own wife to know that I can never speak as an enemy of the Anglo-Saxon race. But unless that race abandons its duality of conscience, unless it learns to honor and practice a stricter spiritual veracity, it will either destroy civilization through disasters yet unheard of or sink into a memory and into the shadow of a name.

Bibliographical Note

For a theoretical interpretation of the history of professionalism, the most incisive and sophisticated study is Magali Sarfatti Larson, *The Rise of Professionalism: A Sociological Analysis* (Berkeley: University of California Press, 1977). More generally, the work of Pierre Bourdieu contains several powerful analyses of modern universities in their relations to culture and power. See especially Bourdieu and Jean–Claude Passeron, *The Inheritors: French Students and Their Relations to Culture*, trans. Richard Nice (Chicago: University of Chicago Press, 1979); Bourdieu and Passeron, *Reproduction in Education, Society, and Culture*, trans. Richard Nice (London: Sage Publications, 1977); Bourdieu, *Homo Academicus* (Paris: Editions de Minuit, 1984), and *Distinction*, trans. Richard Nice (Cambridge, MA: Harvard University Press, 1984).

The most general history of professionalism in this country is Burton J. Bledstein, *The Culture of Professionalism: The Middle Class and the Development of Higher Education in America* (New York: W. W. Norton, 1976). Similar in approach, but focusing on a specific profession, is Thomas L. Haskell, *The Emergence of Professional Social Science: The American Social Science Association and the Nineteenth Century Crisis of Authority* (Urbana: University of Illinois Press, 1977). See also Bruce Kuklick, *The Rise of American Philosophy: Cambridge, Massachusetts, 1860–1930* (New Haven: Yale University Press, 1977), though Kuklick emphasizes intellectual rather than professional history. Samuel Weber presents a trenchant critique of academic professionalism in *Institution and Interpretation* (Minneapolis: University of Minnesota Press, 1987), especially the Introduction and chapters 1, 2, 3, 4, and 9. The effects of the academicization of literary criticism are considered by the essays in *Criticism in the University*, Gerald Graff and Reginald Gibbons, ed. (Evanston, IL: Northwestern University Press, 1985).

Some of the arguments we make in the Introduction to *The Origins of Literary Studies in America* about the nature and future of the academic literary profession have been developed more fully in the two essays by Warner mentioned in the Prefatory Note and in the following essays by Graff: "The

University and the Prevention of Culture," in *Criticism in the University*, pp. 62–82; "Taking Cover in Coverage," *Profession 86* (1986), pp. 41–45; "What Should We Be Teaching—When There's No 'We'?" *Yale Journal of Criticism*, 1, no. 2 (Spring, 1988), pp. 189–211; "Conflicts Over the Curriculum Are Here to Stay; They Should Be Made Educationally Productive," *Chronicle of Higher Education*, XXXIV, no. 23 (February 17, 1988), p. A48; "Teach the Debate Over What Books Are In or Out," *Christian Science Monitor* (April 22, 1988), pp. B6–7. We have been particularly influenced by the model of critical hermeneutics put forward by John Brenkman in *Culture and Domination* (Ithaca, NY: Cornell University Press, 1987).

For modern versions of anti-professionalism, analogous to those represented in Part 2 of this anthology, see Russell Jacoby, *The Last Intellectuals: American Culture in the Age of Academe* (New York: Basic Books, 1987); see also Walter Jackson Bate, "The Crisis in English Studies," *Harvard Magazine* (September–October, 1982), pp. 46–53. A sharp critique of such anti-professional writers, particularly Bate, has been made by Stanley Fish in "Profession Despise Thyself: Fear and Self-Loathing in Literary Studies," *Critical Inquiry*, 10, no. 2 (December, 1983), pp. 349–64; "Anti-Professionalism," *New Literary History*, XVIII, no. 1 (Autumn, 1985), pp. 89–108. Bate responds to Fish in the December 1983 *Critical Inquiry*, pp. 365–70 (see also the response by Edward Said in the same issue, pp. 371–73). Samuel Weber challenges Fish's position in *Institution and Interpretation*, chapter 3.

Among general histories of modern American higher education, the most comprehensive and analytical is Laurence R. Veysey, *The Emergence of the American University* (Chicago: University of Chicago Press, 1965). An important historical study of the college curriculum is Veysey's essay, "Stability and Experiment in the American Undergraduate Curriculum," in Carl Kaysen, ed., *Content and Context: Essays on College Education*, Report to the Carnegie Commission on Higher Education (New York: McGraw-Hill, 1973), pp. 1–62. Also standard are Frederick Rudolph's *American College and University: A History* (New York: Random House, 1962), and Rudolph's *Curriculum: a History of the American Course of Study Since 1636* (San Francisco: Jossey-Bass Publishers, 1977). See also David O. Levine, *The American College and the Culture of Aspiration, 1915–1940* (Ithaca, NY: Cornell University Press, 1986), and the essays collected in *The Organization of Knowledge in Modern America, 1860–1920*, Alexander Oleson and John Voss, ed. (Baltimore: The Johns Hopkins University Press, 1979), especially John Higham, "The Matrix of Specialization." Also valuable (and unfairly maligned in the 1960s) is Clark Kerr's *The Uses of the University* (Cambridge, MA: Harvard University Press, 1963; revised, 1972).

For general history of higher education for women, see Barbara Miller Solomon, *In the Company of Educated Women: A History of Women and Higher*

Education in America (New Haven: Yale University Press, 1985). On women in the professions, see Penina Migdal Glazer, *Unequal Colleagues: The Entrance of Women into the Professions, 1890–1940* (New Brunswick, NJ: Rutgers University Press, 1987). A revealing study of academic anti-semitism at one institution is Dan A. Oren, *Joining the Club: A History of Jews and Yale* (New Haven: Yale University Press, 1985).

The earliest attempt at a retrospective on the rise of academic language and literature study is James Wilson Bright's Presidential Address of 1902, "Concerning the Unwritten History of the Modern Language Association of America," *PMLA*, 18, appendix I (1903), pp. xli–lxii. The series of statements by department representatives collected in *English in American Universities*, William Morton Payne, ed. (Boston: D. C. Heath, 1895) has already been mentioned above (see p. 50) as an invaluable source of views on the early history of literary studies by the scholars and teachers who were shaping it. A caustic early retrospective is the essay by Fred Lewis Pattee, "The Old Professor of English: An Autopsy," in *Tradition and Jazz* (New York: Century, 1925).

Among the personal memoirs that are particularly illuminating and readable are Brander Matthews (of Columbia), *These Many Years: Recollections of a New Yorker* (New York: Charles Scribner's Sons, 1919); Henry Seidel Canby (Yale), *Alma Mater: The Gothic Age of the American College* (New York: Farrar and Rinehart, 1936); Robert Morss Lovett (University of Chicago), *All Our Years* (New York: Viking Press, 1948); Fred Lewis Pattee, *Penn State Yankee* (State College, PA: Pennsylvania State University Press, 1953); John Erskine (Columbia) *The Memory of Certain Persons* (Philadelphia: J. B. Lippincott, 1947), and *My Life as a Teacher* (Philadelphia: J. B. Lippincott, 1948).

The best recent short history of "English" is William Riley Parker's pathbreaking essay, "Where Do English Departments Come From?" first published in *College English*, 28, no. 5 (February, 1967), pp. 339–51. Also of value is Parker's historical sketch of the Modern Language Association on its seventieth anniversary, "The MLA 1883–1953," *PMLA*, LXVIII, no. 4, Part 2 (September, 1953), pp. 3–39. Other brief historical reassessments include Richard Ohmann, *English in America: A Radical View of the Profession* (New York: Oxford University Press, 1976), pp. 234–54, and "Writing and Reading, Work and Leisure," in *Politics of Letters* (Middletown, CT: Wesleyan University Press, 1987), pp. 26–41; Wallace W. Douglas, "Accidental Institution: On the Origins of Modern Language Study," in *Criticism in the University* (pp. 35–61).

Until very recently, book-length histories of English have concentrated on British rather than American developments, or on the teaching of composition rather than of literature. Histories of the rise of English in British Universities begin with Stephen Potter's irreverent *The Muse in Chains: A Study in Education* (London: Jonathan Cape, 1937), followed by E. M. W. Tillyard's ripsoste, *The Muse Unchained: An Intimate Account of the Revolution in English Studies at Cambridge* (London: Bowes and Bowes, 1958), and D. J. Palmer, *The Rise of English Studies: An Account of the Study of English Language and Literature from its Origins to the Making of the Oxford English School* (New York: Oxford University Press, 1965); most recent and illuminating is Chris Baldick's Marxist study, *The Social Mission of English Criticism 1848–1932* (Oxford and New York: Oxford University Press, 1983). For the background of philology in the nineteenth century, see Holger Pederson, *The Discovery of Language: Linguistic Science in the Nineteenth Century*, trans. John W. Spargo (Bloomington: Indiana University Press, 1962).

On American developments, an informative general account is Arthur N. Applebee's *Tradition and Reform in the Teaching of English: a History* (Urbana, IL: National Council of Teachers of English, 1974). Also valuable on the history of composition and rhetoric teaching are James A. Berlin, *Writing Instruction in Nineteenth Century American Colleges* (Carbondale: Southern Illinois University Press, 1984), and *Rhetoric and Reality: Writing Instruction in American Colleges, 1900–1985* (Carbondale: Southern Illinois University Press, 1987), and Myron C. Tuman, *A Preface to Literacy: An Inquiry into Pedagogy, Practice, and Progress* (Tuscaloosa: University of Alabama Press, 1987).

Closer to a history of literary study in America is Jo McMurtry, *English Language, English Literature: The Creation of an Academic Discipline* (Hamden, CT: Archon Books, 1985), with a chapter on the career of Francis James Child, as well as on Henry Morley, David Masson, and W. W. Skeat. Useful information appears in the essays in the Modern Language Association's Centennial Issue of *PMLA*, 99, no. 3 (May, 1984), especially Phyllis Franklin's "English Studies: the World of Scholarship in 1883" (pp. 356–70), which traces the careers of George Perkins Marsh, Francis A. March, and Child.

The first book-length history to concentrate on the origins of literary study in America is Gerald Graff's *Professing Literature: An Institutional History* (Chicago: University of Chicago Press, 1987). Betty Jean Craige tells the story with special reference to the dominance and decline of Cartesian dualism in *Reconnection: Dualism to Holism in Literary Study* (Athens: University of Georgia Press, 1988).

Perhaps because of its newcomer status, American literature study seems to have begun to attract historical attention before the other standard literary fields. See Howard Mumford Jones, *The Theory of American Literature* (Ithaca, NY: Cornell University Press, 1948; reprinted, with a new concluding chapter, 1965); Richard Ruland, *The Rediscovery of American Literature: Premises of Critical Taste, 1900–1940* (Cambridge, MA: Harvard University Press, 1967); Russell Reising, *The Unusable Past: Theory and the Study of American Literature* (London: Methuen, 1986); and Kermit Vanderbilt's comprehensive *American Literature and the Academy: The Roots, Growth, and Maturity of a Profession*

(Philadelphia: University of Pennsylvania Press, 1987). Histories of the constitution of other literary fields are likely to occupy scholars in the coming years.

Histories of departments often provide unique insights into the profession's history. By far the most informative we have encountered is *The Department of English at Indiana University Bloomington 1868–1970*, Donald J. Gray, ed. (Bloomington: Indiana University publications, not dated). Other departmental histories of potential interest to scholars are Charles Hall Grandgent, "The Modern Languages," in Samuel Eliot Morison, ed., *The Development of Harvard University* (Cambridge, MA: Harvard University Press, 1930), pp. 65–105; Lionel Trilling, "The Van Amringe and Keppel Eras," and Justus Buchler, "Reconstruction in the Liberal Arts," both in *A History of Columbia College on Morningside* (New York: Columbia University Press, 1954), pp. 14–47 and 48–135, respectively; Douglas MacMillan, *English at Chapel Hill: 1795–1969* (Chapel Hill: Department of English, University of North Carolina, not dated).